Progressive Sight Singing

Progressive Sight Singing

Carol Krueger
University of South Carolina

New York   Oxford
OXFORD UNIVERSITY PRESS
2007

Oxford University Press, Inc., publishes works that further Oxford University's
objective of excellence in research, scholarship, and education.

Oxford   New York
Auckland   Cape Town   Dar es Salaam   Hong Kong   Karachi
Kuala Lumpur   Madrid   Melbourne   Mexico City   Nairobi
New Delhi   Shanghai   Taipei   Toronto

With offices in
Argentina   Austria   Brazil   Chile   Czech Republic   France   Greece
Guatemala   Hungary   Italy   Japan   Poland   Portugal   Singapore
South Korea   Switzerland   Thailand   Turkey   Ukraine   Vietnam

Published by Oxford University Press, Inc.
198 Madison Avenue, New York, New York 10016
http://www.oup.com

Oxford is a registered trademark of Oxford University Press

Library of Congress Cataloging-in-Publication Data

Krueger, Carol J.
    Progressive sight singing / Carol Krueger.
        p. cm.
    ISBN-13: 978-0-19-517847-0 (pbk.: alk. paper)

    1. Sight-singing. I. Title.

MT870.K87 2006
783'.0423--dc22

                                                                    2005050882

Printing number: 9 8 7 6 5 4 3 2

Printed in the United States of America
on acid-free paper

 Contents

Part I Rhythmic Reading

Part II   Melodic Reading

Appendices

 Preface to the Instructor

Progressive Sight Singing is designed to help beginning students develop rhythmic and melodic reading skills in aural skills classes. Whether students are novices and need basic instruction or have considerable background in music but need remediation to fill in gaps, they will find in this text the information they need to read with accuracy and fluency. Through carefully paced instruction and exercises, the text introduces concepts in a sequential manner and limits explanations to the essentials, thereby increasing the likelihood of students' success in attaining requisite aural skills.

The material in this text is a synthesis of my formal education and my experiences teaching musicianship skills to students of various levels and orientations: singers and instrumentalists; music education, performance, composition, and conducting majors; and middle and high school choral and theory students. The skill level of the majority of the students I encountered was surprisingly weak. Those who had prior knowledge and skills were missing crucial elements and were not truly independent musicians. To address these needs, I developed materials based on learning theory concepts that would facilitate the development of independent, literate musicians. The text has been successfully class tested at a number of institutions nationwide.

Organization

The book is divided into two sections: Part I presents rhythmic exercises only, and Part II presents melodic exercises. The two sections, which each contain 18 chapters, are designed to be used concurrently over a two-semester course sequence. The separate presentation of rhythm and melody allows each to be studied at a pace that suits the abilities and backgrounds of a particular class or course schedule.

Chapters follow this sequence: Building Aural/Oral Skills, Symbolic Association, Patterns, and Exercises. These sections reflect the literacy process incorporated in the book, a process based on the pedagogy of learning sound before sight before theory. This process is briefly outlined in the Music Literacy Process that follows the prefaces.

Building Aural/Oral Skills

Each skill or concept is introduced through the ear and voice by imitating patterns, the basic unit of meaning in music. Part II also contains vocal-pitch exercises (intervals, scales, chords, and so on) designed to develop the ability to hear the tones as scale degrees in relation to the tonic pitch and tonic chord tones (Reference Tones).

Symbolic Association

Sounds learned by rote in the first section are translated into musical symbols. Chapters in Part II also contain staff-familiarization exercises to aid in connecting the ear to the eye.

Patterns

Tonal and rhythm patterns prepare the ear and eye for reading the "new" element or skill. Melodic patterns are included when a "new" rhythm element is integrated into a tonal element.

Exercises

Concepts and skills are presented through graded, newly composed exercises as well as excerpts from folk and classical literature.

Features

A structure that reinforces skill-building

Only one new element is added per chapter. The element first appears in its simplest form, then previously learned elements are gradually integrated, providing constant reinforcement of learned skills.

Flexibility that allows instructors to use whichever tonal and rhythm reading systems they prefer

Instructors may use the Gordon, Takadimi, McHose-Tibbs, or Kodály rhythm syllables or a neutral syllable like "da" for reading rhythms. An overview of the basic rhythm systems can be found in Appendix A. The moveable *do* system of solfège syllables, scale-degree numbers and note names, or a neutral syllable such as "doo" may be used for tonal reading. Scale degree numbers and do-based and la-based solfège syllables are included in the chapters that focus on minor keys. A description of basic tonal systems can be found in Appendix B. Any tonal or rhythm system can be used successfully if that system is used consistently and incorporates the music literacy pedagogy presented in this book.

Ample and varied exercises

Many of the rhythm exercises are eight measures in length; consequently, multiple exercises with the same meter signature can be performed simultaneously. The rhythm exercises can also be performed as canons or retrograde canons. To further enhance independence, the text includes ensemble exercises and two-part exercises for one person.

Melodic exercises use multiple key signatures. Although reading in one key may be quicker at first, using a variety of key signatures from the beginning yields the most fluent reading skill. A number of melodic canons are included in each chapter to aid in the development of part-singing skills.

Each chapter includes ample exercises for classroom study and individual practice outside of class.

Patterns and exercises can be used as dictation exercises

There is a strong positive correlation between sight singing and dictation; improvement in one area will positively affect the other. Using a variety of instruments, with the different timbres this offers, can aid further in the development of dictation skills. Appendix C provides a dictation method that will assist students until their musical memory skills have been developed; the ultimate goal is to develop students' proficiency to such a level that the system is no longer needed.

Accompanying CD and additional student helps

To facilitate independent study and drill outside the classroom, the tonal and rhythm patterns for chapters 1–6 are available on the accompanying CD, prepared by John Moody. Detailed strategies for approaching the exercises in the text can be found in the book's front matter under "Strategies for Successful Sight Singing."

Instructor's Manual

An Instructor's Manual is available to adopting instructors. In it, you will find pedagogical pointers on the literacy process, supplemental reading exercises, and solutions to selected written exercises. I would also encourage you to share any creative or critical reactions with me so that the goal of this text might be fully realized.

Acknowledgments

A completed work of this type depends greatly upon the assistance and encouragement given by many. My deepest thanks and appreciation go to the following reviewers of the manuscript for their insightful critical assessments and most helpful suggestions: Robert Bean, Indiana University–Purdue University, Fort Wayne; Matthew Bribitzer-Stull, University of Minnesota–Twin Cities; James Burmeister, University of Wisconsin, Milwaukee; William Marvin, Eastman School of Music; Cynthia McGregor, Northwestern University; Paul W. Metz, Colorado State University; Neil Minturn, University of Missouri; Gary Potter, Indiana University; Stacie Rossow, Florida Atlantic University; and Scott Smith, Ohio University.

I also wish to acknowledge the following teachers, who used the book as a text in its formative stages and gave me encouragement and invaluable feedback: James Ewing, University of Miami; Stacie Rossow, Florida Atlantic University; Anna Ryan, Emporia State University; William Powell, Auburn University; and Karen Taylor and Christine Freeman, Indiana University–Purdue University, Fort Wayne. Further, I extend my gratitude to John Moody, Spartanburg High School, Spartanburg, South Carolina, for providing many suggestions and recording the rhythm and tonal patterns.

In addition, I am deeply thankful for the students in my sight singing classes and choirs who, over the years, have all contributed to the experiences that formed the basis of this book. They provided a setting in which many of the principles and strategies contained in this book could be tested and made suggestions for improving the manuscript.

I owe an immense debt of gratitude to Jan Beatty of Oxford University Press for her initial interest in the book and for her patient and encouraging guidance throughout the writing process. The production staff at Oxford University Press, in particular production editor John Carey and copyeditor Debra Nichols, contributed greatly to the clarity, organization, and appearance of the book. Finally—and most importantly—a special thanks to my husband, Jim, and daughter and son-in-law, Hillary and Kris Ridgley, for their unwavering support and patience, without which this book could not have been written.

 Preface to the Student

The ultimate goal of an aural skills curriculum is to produce a musician who can look at a musical score and hear it in his or her mind without playing or singing it out loud. This phenomenon is often referred to as "inner hearing," "aural imagery," or "audiation." Conversely, a musician should be able to hear music and envision it as it would appear on the printed page. In short, we should be able to "hear with our eyes and see with our ears." Singing melodies "at sight" (notes into sound) and writing dictation (sound into notes) are crucial to developing internal musical perception. These skills are also a means for measuring one's progress toward achieving the ultimate goal. This text will provide you with the training to develop your reading ability.

Reading melodies and writing dictation with accuracy and fluency are skills that demand practice and concentration. The amount of practice time required to achieve proficiency varies from one student to another. Short, daily practice sessions are far more beneficial than occasional marathon sessions. Ample material is provided in each chapter for the determined student to achieve accurate and fluent reading. Learning strategies that will aid in developing your reading skills are found in the book's front matter. The retention of these skills is dependent upon their immediate and continued use in practical application. It is essential that you apply your reading and aural skills during the early stages of learning solo (voice or instrument) and ensemble (chorus, band, or orchestra) literature.

The use of tonal and rhythm syllables is highly recommended as they provide a link between the aural and visual domains. Any tonal or rhythm system can be used successfully if that system is utilized consistently and incorporates the music literacy pedagogy presented in this book. An overview of the basic rhythm and tonal systems can be found in Appendices A and B, respectively. Your instructor will select the appropriate tonal and rhythm systems for you and your classmates.

The book is divided into two sections that should be used concurrently: Part I presents rhythmic exercises, while Part II presents melodic exercises. The separate presentation of rhythm and melody allows each to be studied at a pace that suits your abilities and background. Each chapter is organized to reflect the literacy process incorporated in the book. The process is based on learning sound before sight before theory and is briefly outlined in the Music Literacy Process that follows this preface. Study the process and notice how it relates to the chapter headings below.

Building Aural/Oral Skills: Each skill or concept is introduced through the ear and voice by imitating patterns, the basic unit of meaning in music. Part II also contains vocal-pitch exercises (intervals, scales, chords, and so on) designed to develop the ability to hear the tones as scale degrees in relation to the tonic pitch and tonic chord tones (Reference Tones).

Symbolic Association: Sounds learned by rote in the first section are translated into music symbols. Chapters in Part II: Melodic Reading also contain staff-familiarization exercises to aid in connecting the ear to the eye.

<u>Patterns</u>: Tonal and rhythm patterns prepare the ear and eye for reading the "new" element or skill. Melodic patterns are included when a "new" rhythm element is integrated into a tonal element. To facilitate independent study and drill outside of the classroom, the tonal and rhythm patterns for chapters 1–6 are available on the accompanying CD.

<u>Exercises</u>: Concepts and skills are presented through graded, newly composed exercises and excerpts from folk and classical literature. Each chapter contains ample material for classroom study and individual practice outside of class.

Using the CD

Listen to each pattern while following along in the text; echo the pattern while singing or chanting on appropriate syllables designated by your instructor. After sufficient practice, listen to each pattern without reading from the text and then echo the pattern using syllables.

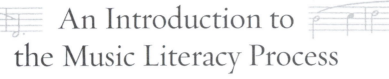

An Introduction to the Music Literacy Process

Musical skills are learned in much the same order as language skills; first we hear and perform, then we read and write. The ear must be trained through hearing and imitating patterns (Phase 1: aural/oral skill development) prior to training the eye (Phase 2: symbolic association). The pattern is the basic unit of meaning in music, not individual pitches or durations. In other words, patterns are to music what words are to language. Tonal and rhythm patterns should be learned separately at first and then integrated into melodic patterns (Phase 3).

Phase 1—Reading Readiness or Preparation (Aural/Oral): Process Centers on Rote Learning (Imitation)

The use of tonal and rhythm syllables is highly recommended as they give names to the sounds (see Appendices A and B for rhythm and tonal systems). To maintain the association of tonal syllables and rhythm syllables with musical sound, tonal syllables should be sung and rhythm syllables should be chanted. All patterns should be learned by rote using the following two-step process.

A: Naming Sounds

Tonal Procedure	Rhythm Procedure
Listen while your instructor sings a tonal pattern with tonal syllables, then echo the pattern with tonal syllables while using hand signs.	Listen while your instructor chants a rhythm pattern with rhythm syllables; echo the pattern with rhythm syllables while silently tapping the beat or conducting.

Patterns should be reviewed regularly. Words like *scale*, *chord*, *perfect fourth*, and other terms should also be associated with their sounds.

B: Identification of Pattern Syllables

Tonal Procedure	Rhythm Procedure
1. Listen while your instructor sings a tonal pattern using a neutral syllable, then echo the pattern with tonal syllables while using hand signs (sound to name).	Listen while your instructor chants a rhythm pattern using a neutral syllable, then echo the pattern with rhythm syllables while silently tapping the beat or conducting (sound to name).
2. Using a tonal ladder or only hand signs,[1] your instructor will indicate a typical tonal pattern; now sing the pattern using tonal syllables (name to sound).	

[1] See Appendix B for hand signs and tonal ladder.

Phase 2—Symbolic Association: Visual Representation of Pitch and Rhythm

During this phase, you will be shown a symbolic representation of the tonal and rhythm patterns learned during the "reading readiness" phase. The patterns sung or chanted previously by rote should now be sung following written notation. During the initial stages of reading, silently tap the beat, conduct, or use hand signs with one hand and, if necessary, track with the other hand. Focus on reading groups of notes (patterns) rather than a series of individual notes. The farther ahead one reads, the better one's reading skills will be. Flash cards will facilitate this process if each card is shown briefly and then hidden. Do not write the syllables by the notes or you will learn to read only syllables and not notation. In addition to reading, you should also compose and take dictation using these tonal and rhythm patterns. A shorthand method for dictation is found in Appendix C.

Phase 3—Integrating Tonal and Rhythm Patterns

In Phase 3, the goal is to simultaneously be aware of tonality and meter and to read with comprehension. Using the following multistep process will greatly aid in the development of accurate melodic reading.

Melodic Reading

A. Reading Readiness

  1. Listen as your instructor sings melodic patterns with tonal syllables and then echo with tonal syllables using hand signs, tapping the beat, or conducting.

  2. Frequently practice singing known vocal-pitch exercises (scales, intervals, etc.) on tonal syllables by rote while integrating a variety of known rhythm patterns. Silently tap the beat, maintaining the down/up kinesthetic feeling of the beat while integrating the hand signs minus the vertical pitch levels. Example: Sing the extended major scale integrating a dotted quarter–eighth pattern by rote.

     Example:

  3. Read the rhythm and integrate known vocal-pitch exercises by rote. Example: Read the following rhythm exercise and integrate the additive pentachord scale (do, re; do, re, mi; do, re, mi, fa, mi, re, do; do, re, mi, fa, so, fa, mi, re, do) by rote.

     Example:

  4. Read tonal exercises and integrate known rhythm patterns by rote. Example: Read the following tonal exercise and integrate a quarter note–two repeated eighth note pattern. Repeat the pitches on the eighth notes.

B. Reading

   1. Using tonal syllables, hand signs, and/or silently tapping the beat, read melodic patterns.

   2. Read melodic exercises utilizing tonal syllables, hand signs, silently tapping the beat, or conducting.

Suggestion: To train the eye, write the first letter of each tonal syllable on a separate sheet of paper. Work for speed!

C. Dictation

   1. Listen as your instructor sings short melodic patterns on a neutral syllable and then notate using the short hand dictation method outlined in Appendix C. Focus on only one element (rhythm or tonal) at a time.

 Strategies for Successful Sight Singing

1. **Examine and analyze all musical elements prior to reading.**

   Pitch

   a. Determine the key. Does the melody begin on the tonic or another pitch?
   b. Scan the melody and locate all reference tones (1st, 3rd, and 5th scale degrees); if necessary circle them. Remember to relate all of the other pitches to these reference tones.
   c. Scan the melody again for skips and determine the interval and tonal syllables.
   d. What tonal pattern is in the first measure ... the sixth measure? Are there any repeated patterns, motives, sequences, or pitches? What is the tonal syllable of the accidental?

   Rhythm

   a. Determine the tempo (speed of beat) and the meter (simple or compound). What is the beat unit ... the beat division ... the beat subdivision?
   b. Scan the line for rhythm patterns. What rhythm pattern is in the third measure ... the fifth measure ... the last measure? Are there any repeated patterns? Is that a tie or a slur?

   Phrases

   a. Phrases have been marked in some of the exercises to serve as a guide for breathing. In exercises without phrase markings, determine and mark appropriate places to breathe.
   b. Analyze phrase structure and cadence types.

   Harmony

   a. Analyze the underlying harmonies implied by the melodic line. Look for chord tones and nonharmonic tones.
   b. Train the eye to look for musical markings: dynamic, expression, and articulation.

   Do not move from the inquiry period to the reading until all the concepts have been reviewed.

2. **Always establish tonality prior to reading.**

   a. Play the tonic note of the key on the piano or a pitch pipe. Sing the scale of the key and the tonic chord arpeggio that fits the range of the melody. If necessary, transpose the melody into a key that provides a more comfortable range. Transposition will not present a problem for students using the Moveable Do method.
   b. Find and sing the first note of the melody.

3. **Prepare and condition the ear, body, and mind prior to reading.**

   a. Sing vocal-pitch exercises that use the pitch skill(s) found in the exercise.
   b. Sing a scale or other vocal-pitch exercises integrating the rhythm patterns found in the exercise. For example, sing the scale using a dotted quarter-eighth pattern.

4. **Always establish meter prior to reading.**

   a. Set a tempo that is appropriate for your current skill level.
   b. Establish an internal feeling of the pulse by walking in place, silently tapping the beat using large arm movements or conducting for one to two measures before reading. Occasionally use a metronome.

   c. Feel the division of the beat (down-up principle). Focus on the rhythm patterns in relation to the micro and macro beat. <u>The beat should always be inaudible.</u>

5. **Silently read the exercise (audiation).**

   Prior to reading, silently read the exercise, preferably using hand signs, tapping the beat, or conducting.

6. **Sing all exercises *a cappella*.**

   To achieve independence, all exercises should be sung without accompaniment.

7. **Perform exercises from beginning to end.**

   a. Do not stop to correct pitches or rhythms. Always keep a steady beat!
   b. After the initial reading, return and drill the trouble spots.
   c. If necessary chant only the rhythm and then sing only the pitches. Do not sing repeated notes/one note per beat.

8. **Sing phrases as a musical entity rather than a series of individual notes.**

   Look ahead. The farther ahead one reads the more accurate, fluent, and musical one's sight singing will be.

9. **Do not write the tonal or rhythm syllables in the music.**

   Tonal and rhythm syllables should never be spelled out and read as symbols.

10. **After accurately singing an exercise on tonal syllables, repeat the exercise:**

    a. at a faster tempo;
    b. silently singing the even-numbered measures, or all the eighth notes, or all the mi's, or the second phrase;
    c. singing aloud until given an appropriate signal, at which time reading should be silent (audiation). After another appropriate signal, resume singing aloud; or
    d. on a neutral syllable, using hand signs, tapping the beat, or conducting. Symbolic systems should be discarded when one has developed the ability to recall the pitch and/or duration relationship.

Skill follows drill. Skills can be mastered only by consistent practice.

**Brief, but frequent, practice sessions are more beneficial
than occasional marathon sessions.**

Practice with a partner.

# Building Musicianship and Independence

Audiation, aural skills, dictation skills, and musical memory skills must be included throughout the learning process. Following are some suggested activities to aid in building these skills.

Audiation Skills (Inner Hearing)

"Silent singing" can be a useful tool for developing audiation, the ability to think musical sounds without external voicing. The following activities may be used to develop audiation skills:

1. Sing a scale and designate specific tonal syllables to be sung silently. Example: Sing the major scale; silently sing *re* in the ascending scale and *fa* in the descending scale.
2. When given an appropriate signal by your instructor, stop singing or chanting aloud but continue to read the exercise silently. After another appropriate signal, resume singing or chanting aloud. For example, during practice sessions silently sing or chant the first, third, and seventh measures, or silently sing or chant all of the eighth notes, or silently sing all the *mi's*, or silently sing the third phrase.

Aural Skills: Error Recognition

Your instructor should intentionally include tonal and/or rhythmic errors in the playing, singing, or chanting of a notated melody or rhythm. At first you should indicate whether the example was correct or incorrect. After this skill is mastered, you should indicate which measures were incorrect and then finally identify the exact nature of each discrepancy. To enhance independence, work with a partner; one student sings the exercise while the other student works on his/her error detection skills. Exchange tasks.

Musical Memory Skills

Musical memory skills are essential for dictation. The following activities may be used to develop musical memory:

1. Using only hand signs or the tonal ladder, the instructor or a student partner shows a 3 to 5 note tonal pattern; then, you should sing the pattern back using tonal syllables. When the tonal patterns have been mastered, progress to two-bar and four-bar melodies.
2. The instructor sings a melody or chants a four-bar rhythm using a neutral syllable. Sing the melody or chant the rhythm with tonal/rhythm syllables in canon one measure later.
3. The first student sings a single pitch on tonal syllables or chants a two-beat rhythm pattern with rhythm syllables. Without missing a beat, the second student repeats the first pitch or rhythm pattern and adds another pitch/rhythm. Then a third student repeats the first two pitches/rhythms and adds another pitch/rhythm. Continue until a student misses a pattern. Remember: It is important that parameters be established that reflect the tone-set or rhythm-pattern knowledge.
4. Divide the class into groups. Each group forms a line, one person behind the other. The instructor will hand the last person in each line a card containing a short rhythm pattern.

The student taps the pattern on the back of the student in front of them. This process continues until it reaches the student at the front of the line who then writes or chants the pattern. This activity can be done as a competitive game.

5. A four-measure melodic or rhythmic phrase is written on the board and read by the class or an individual. One measure is erased and then the phrase is read aloud again, including the erased measure. Another measure is erased, until nothing remains on the board and everything is committed to memory. Gradually increase the length from four-bar to eight-bar phrases, and so on.

Dictation Skills

The purpose of dictation is to produce a listener who can hear musical patterns. Dictation skills are directly related to the development of musical memory, inner hearing (audiation), and reading and writing skills. Rhythm and tonal should once again be taught separately and then combined. Initial dictation exercises should be based on familiar 3 to 5 note tonal patterns and 3 to 4 beat rhythm patterns. Using the shorthand method outlined in Appendix C can facilitate the learning process.

PART I

Rhythmic Reading

Chapter 1
Simple Meter
Quarter Note = Beat Unit;
Undivided Beat

I. Building Aural/Oral Skills

Beat: The steady, underlying pulse of the music is the *beat.*
To develop an internal feeling of the pulse, one must feel the space (distance) between the beats. Beat should always be inaudible—silent.

- Singing a familiar song (a) walk in place to the beat, shifting weight back and forth or side to side in a continuous, flowing manner, or (b) tap the beat (silently tap the thighs with one or both hands, using large arm movements that start from the shoulder). Feel the down-up motion of the hand on each beat. *Note: Clapping will not internalize beat because it doesn't involve changing/shifting body weight. Clapping however is a good way to check the accuracy of ensemble performance.*

Tempo: The speed of the beat (fast, moderate, and slow) is the *tempo.*

- Sing "Hot Cross Buns" or another familiar melody at a moderate tempo, then at a fast tempo and finally at a slow tempo.

Meter: An organization or grouping of rhythmic pulses by means of regular accents (strong and weak beats) is called *meter.*
Duple meter has an accented–unaccented (strong–weak) beat pattern: ▮ | ▮ |

Example:

	Hot	cross	buns,	———	Hot	cross	buns.	———
Meter:	▮	|	▮	|	▮	|	▮	|

- Practice performing the beat using tap–touch (silently touch the finger tips of both hands together) or two taps (one strong, one weak) while listening to or singing a variety of songs in duple meter. Suggested songs: "Old Joe Clark" and "Tidy-O."
- Practice singing each of the suggested songs while conducting the two-beat pattern.

Triple meter has a strong–weak–weak beat pattern: ▮ | | ▮ | |

Example:

	Rock -	a -	bye	ba -	by,	in	the	tree	top.	———
Meter:	▮	|	|	▮	|	|	▮	|	|	▮	|	|

- Practice performing the beat using tap–touch–touch while listening to or singing a variety of songs in triple meter. Suggested songs: "Lavender's Blue" and "O, How Lovely."
- Practice singing each of the suggested songs while conducting the three-beat pattern.

Quadruple meter, a strong–weak–semistrong–weak beat pattern, is a combination of two duple meters with a lesser accent on the third beat: ▮ | ▮ | ▮ | ▮ |

Example:

           Twin - kle, twin - kle, lit - tle star. ——— How I won - der what you are. ———
Meter: ▮ | ▮ | ▮ | ▮ | ▮ | ▮ | ▮ | ▮ |

- Practice performing the beat using tap–touch–out (tap in air just above the thighs)–touch while listening to or singing a variety of songs in quadruple meter. Suggested songs: "Hymn to Joy," "Frére Jacques," and "Yankee Doodle."
- Practice singing each of the suggested songs while conducting the four-beat pattern.

Rhythm: Rhythm is defined as longer and shorter sounds and silences (duration) that overlay the steady beat.

- Chant the rhythm of familiar songs on a neutral syllable while your instructor overlays the steady beat. Suggested songs: "Happy Birthday," and "London Bridge."
- After chanting the rhythm to a familiar song, half of the class should chant the rhythm while the other half claps the beat; repeat with the two groups exchanging their tasks. Now chant the rhythm while walking to the beat.

Reading Readiness Rhythm Patterns

- Listen as your instructor chants a variety of rhythm patterns on rhythm syllables; echo each pattern while (a) quietly tapping the beat, (b) conducting, or (c) using the appropriate metric motion (tap–touch).[1] Focus on the rhythm pattern in relation to the beat and meter pattern. See Appendix A for a description of Beat Function Syllables (Gordon or Takadimi) and Time Value Syllables (Kodály).

Reading Readiness Aural Skills

- Listen as your instructor demonstrates two short rhythm patterns on a neutral syllable. Determine if the patterns were the same, different, or similar.
- Listen as your instructor sings a song and then determine the meter of the song. Use the tap–touch movements to help you determine the meter.
- Listen as your instructor demonstrates two short examples and determine which example has a faster tempo.

II. Symbolic Association

Score Notation: The visual representation of music is called *score notation.* Its main purpose is to indicate pitch and the duration of each tone.

Notes: The written symbols for sound in music are notes.

Types of notes:

	Whole Note	**Half Note**	**Quarter Note**	
Takadimi Rhythm Syllables	ta	ta	ta	(Beat Function System)
Kodály Rhythm Syllables	toh	too	ta	(Time Value System)

---

[1] Note to instructors: The rhythm patterns are found in Section III of this chapter. These patterns should be taught by rote using the two-step process outlined in the Musical Literacy Process section of the Preface.

Parts of a note:  ↔ stem   Stems are attached to the note head and extend
up on the right or down on the left.
↔ head   Noteheads are oval in shape.
Noteheads are open for whole notes and half notes
and solid for quarter notes.

Rests: The written symbols for silence in music are rests.

Types of rests:

Whole Rest   **Half Rest**   **Quarter Rest**

Identify the type of note or rest.

1. ___   2. ___   3. ___   4. ___   5. ___   6. ___   7. ___   8. ___

Meter Signature: A *meter signature* is used to designate the pattern (duple, triple, quadruple) in which a steady succession of rhythmic pulses is organized. In simple meter the top number indicates the number of beats per pattern and the bottom number indicates the kind of note that receives one beat.

2 → two beats in each pattern	3 → three beats in each pattern
4 → the quarter note is the beat unit	4 → the quarter note is the beat unit

Vertical lines called *bar lines* are used to organize the basic beat patterns. One complete pattern is termed a *measure* and is enclosed between two bar lines. A *double bar line* is used to indicate the end of a section or the composition.

$$\frac{2}{4} \qquad\qquad \frac{3}{4} \qquad\qquad \frac{4}{4}$$

←——measure——→   bar line ↑   double bar line ↑

III. Rhythm Patterns

* Determine the meter, set an appropriate tempo and then establish meter by silently tapping or conducting the beat for one measure.
* Using the rhythm syllables designated by your instructor (see Appendix A for a description of beat function syllables and time value syllables), chant the written notation of each of the rhythm patterns A1–A40. Focus on the rhythm pattern in relation to the beat and meter. Always silently tap the beat with the dominant hand or conduct, and if necessary, track the notes on the score with the other hand.

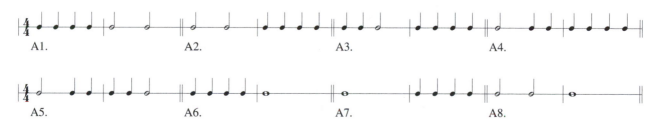

A1.   A2.   A3.   A4.

A5.   A6.   A7.   A8.

(Continued)

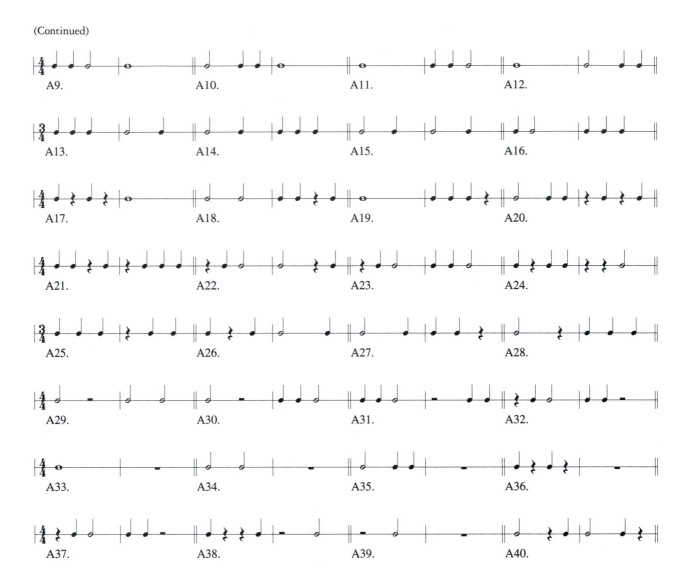

IV. Exercises

- Determine the meter and then scan each exercise for rhythm patterns.
- Determine the phrasing and mark it.
- Set an appropriate tempo, establish meter by tapping the beat or conducting for one measure. Then chant the exercise on rhythm syllables from beginning to end without breaking the tempo. Always silently tap the beat with the dominant hand and if necessary, track the notes on the score with the other hand.
- Remember to hold every note for the correct number of beats. A note ends exactly when the next note begins.
- After the initial reading, isolate problematic patterns or measure(s) and practice them more slowly. Then perform the problematic pattern/measure(s) and the previous measure/pattern. After the patterns/measures have been chanted accurately, read and chant the exercise again.
- After the exercise has been chanted accurately, repeat the exercise first at a faster tempo and then chant on a neutral syllable. Always silently tap the beat or conduct.
- Occasionally use a metronome to check for steadiness of tempo.

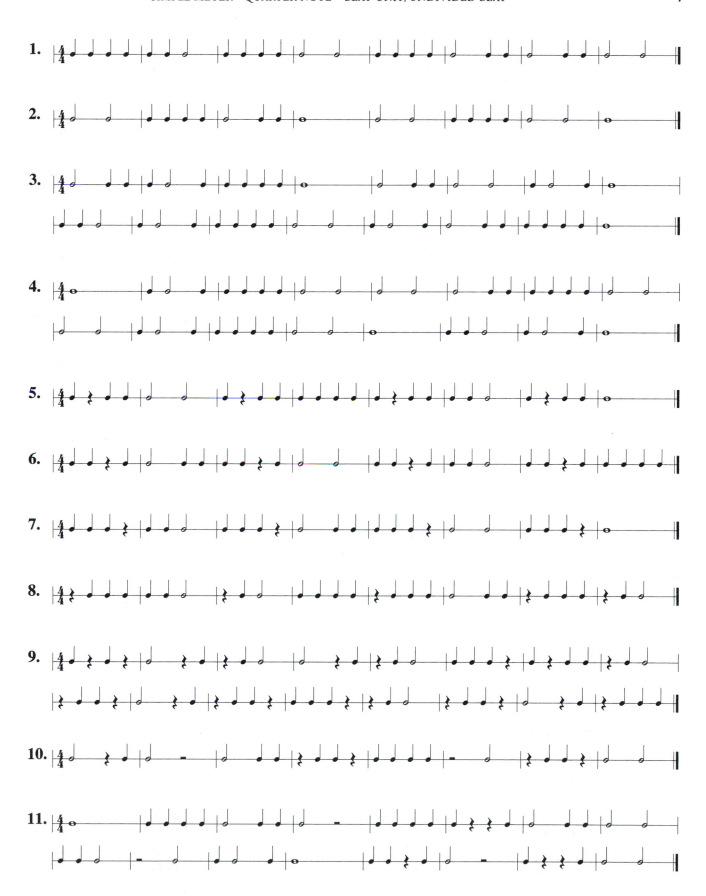

The symbol in measures two and four has two meanings. In example A the symbol is a whole note rest and in example B the symbol signifies a whole-measure rest in any meter.

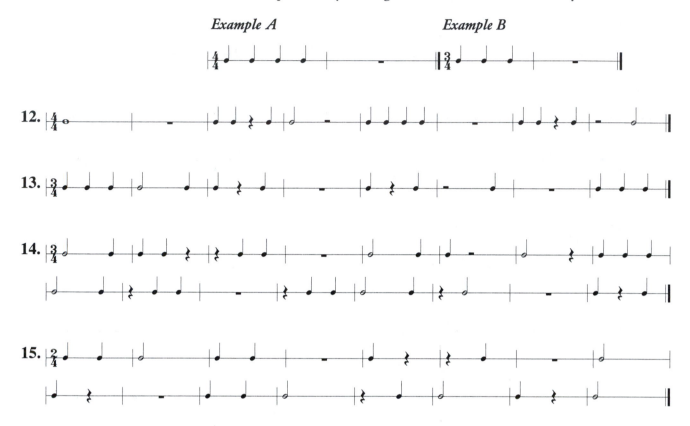

Example A   *Example B*

The exercises can be performed as a two-, three-, or four-part ensemble by simultaneously performing exercises with the same meter signature and same number of measures or they can also be performed as a *canon* or *retrograde canon* (also known as a crab canon). In a canon, two or more voices perform identical rhythms; each voice enters one measure after the previous voice has begun. In a retrograde canon, one voice enters with the last note and reads backward; simultaneously the second voice enters at the beginning.

Meter Changes

Changes in meter can produce a unique effect, because stressed beats occur at irregular intervals. When the meter changes within an exercise, stress the appropriate beats for each meter.

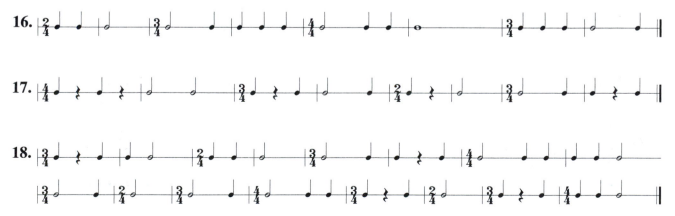

Anacrusis

Compositions sometimes begin with an incomplete measure called an *anacrusis*. The notes that complete the initial measure appear at the end of the composition. Measure numbering begins with the first complete measure. An anacrusis is also known as an upbeat or pickup. Sing familiar songs that begin with an anacrusis. Suggested songs: "The Star-Spangled Banner," "O Come All Ye Faithful," and "We Wish You a Merry Christmas."

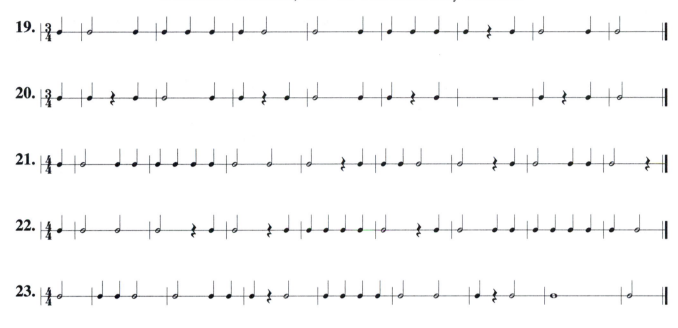

Ensemble Exercises

Two different staves are usually used to indicate two voice parts. The staves are connected on the left side by a *bracket*. Divide the class into two groups or team up with another student to perform these exercises.

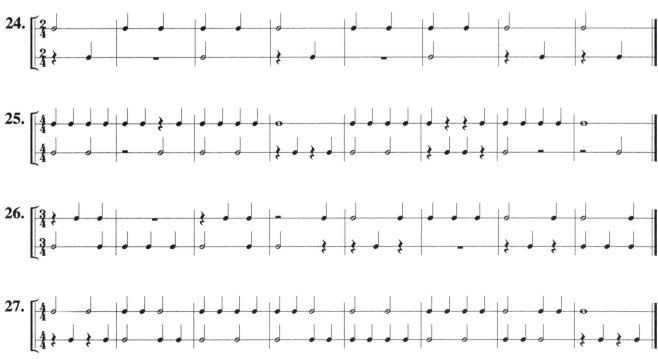

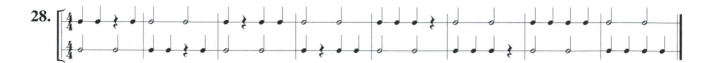

Two-Part Exercises for One Person

These exercises are designed to improve an individual's ability to read two lines simultaneously.

Perform these exercises either individually or with the entire class in the following manner:

- Tap each part with a different hand.
- Tap one part and chant the other part on rhythm syllables.
- Using two different keys on the piano, play each part with a different hand.
- Chant one part on rhythm syllables and play the other part on the piano.

Notice that when two parts share the same staff, the stems of the upper voice point upward while the stems of the lower voice point downward.

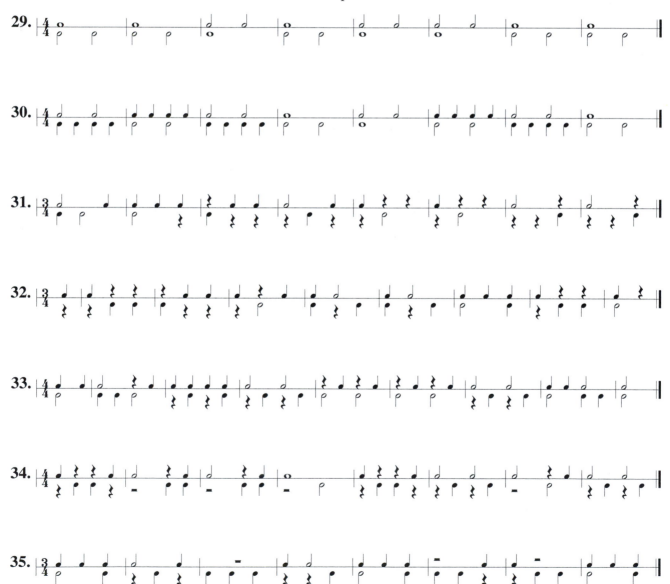

36.

37.

Dictation Skills

Dictation skills are directly related to the development of musical memory, audiation, and reading and writing skills. Using a shorthand method can facilitate the learning process. See Appendix C for detailed information.

• Listen as your instructor or student partner plays or chants a neutral syllable rhythm pattern from Section III (in this chapter) and then notate the rhythm. As your skills improve gradually increase the length of each dictation exercise. All or part of each exercise in Section IV (in this chapter) can be used for dictation.

Chapter 2
Simple Meter
Quarter Note = Beat Unit;
Divided Beat

I. Building Aural/Oral Skills

Beat: Beats can be divided into smaller groups of twos (down–up motion of each beat).

- Alternate chanting the *macro beats* and *micro beats* on a neutral syllable or the rhythm syllables advocated by your instructor. Feel, see, and hear that there is only one sound for a macro beat and two sounds for the micro beat.

	Macro Beat		**Micro Beat**	
Takadimi Syllables	ta		ta	di
Kodály Syllables	ta		ti	ti
	↓	↑	↓	↑

- While your instructor claps the micro beat, sing a familiar song and tap the beat. Feel the down–up motion of each beat. Suggested songs: "It Ain't Gonna Rain" and "Polly-Wolly Doodle".

Meter: Meter as indicated by a meter signature is identified as "simple" or "compound" according to the micro beat (divided beat). The beat is usually divided into two equal parts in simple meter and three equal parts in compound meter.
Compound meter will be discussed in detail in Chapter 5.

- Sing a variety of songs in simple meters. Divide the class into two groups. One group should sing and tap the beat while the other group uses the metric motions (tap—touch) and chants the micro beat rising rhythm syllables. Feel, see, and hear that there are two sounds on each beat, one on the down motion and one on the up motion of each beat. Suggested songs: "Down in the Valley", "Old Joe Clark", "This Old Man", "She's Like the Swallow", "Scarborough Fair", "All the Pretty Little Horses", and "Simple Gifts". Repeat with the two groups exchanging their tasks.

Example:

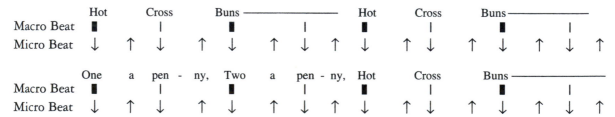

12

Rhythm: Rhythm is defined as longer and shorter sounds and silences (duration)

- Sing a variety of songs in simple meters. Divide the class into two groups: half of the class should chant the rhythm on a neutral syllable while the other half claps the beat; repeat with the two groups exchanging their tasks. Suggested songs: "Deck the Halls", "Skip to My Lou", and "Do Lord".

Rhythm Patterns (Motives): A pattern or *motive* is a minimal rhythm unit that adds to the unity and variety of music.

- Sing "Hot Cross Buns" and tap the rhythm. Notice that the first rhythmic pattern is repeated twice. This rhythm pattern helps to unify the melody.

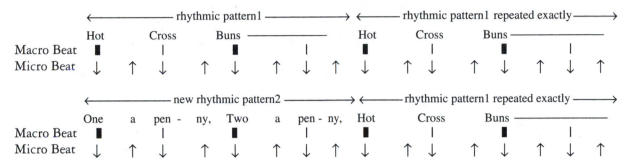

- Sing a known song and tap the rhythm. Now analyze the rhythm patterns. Suggested songs: "Skip to My Lou", "Silent Night", and "Drunken Sailor". The aural and visual recognition of patterns (motives) is essential in developing sight-singing skills.

Reading Readiness Rhythm Patterns

- Listen as your instructor chants a variety of rhythm patterns; echo each pattern while (a) quietly tapping the beat, (b) conducting, or (c) using the appropriate metric motion (tap–touch).[1] Focus on the rhythm pattern in relation to the beat and meter pattern.

Reading Readiness Aural Skills

- Listen as your instructor demonstrates two short rhythm patterns on a neutral syllable. Determine if the patterns were the same, different, or similar.
- Listen as your instructor demonstrates two short examples and determine which example has a slower tempo.
- Walk in place to the beat while your instructor chants macro beats or micro beats on a neutral syllable. Raise one hand when you hear macro beats and two hands when you hear micro beats.

II. Symbolic Association

Notes and Rests:

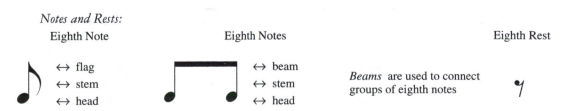

Eighth Note   Eighth Notes   Eighth Rest

↔ flag   ↔ beam
↔ stem   ↔ stem   *Beams* are used to connect groups of eighth notes
↔ head   ↔ head

---

[1]Note to instructors: The rhythm patterns are found in Section III of this chapter. These patterns should be taught by rote using the two-step process outlined in the Musical Literacy Process section of the Preface.

The macro beat is represented by quarter notes and micro beat is represented by eighth notes.

Rhythm Motives: A motive is a minimal rhythm unit that adds to the unity and variety of music.

- Sing "Polly-Wolly Doodle" while tapping the rhythm. Analyze the rhythm patterns in the song.

III. Rhythm Patterns

- Using rhythm syllables, chant the written notation of each of the rhythm patterns A1–A38. Always conduct or silently tap the beat with the dominant hand, and if necessary, track the notes on the score with other hand.

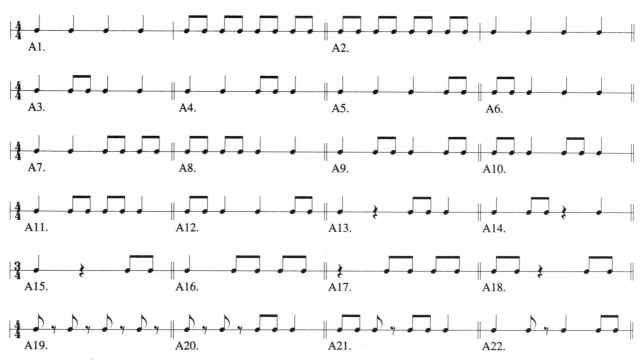

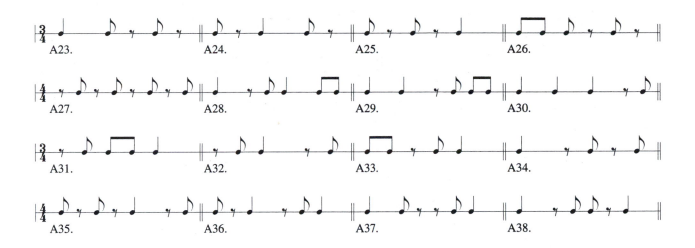

IV. Exercises

Remember to

- chant each exercise on rhythm syllables from beginning to end without breaking the tempo;
- perform these exercises as a canon, or retrograde canon;
- perform exercises with the same meter signature and same number of measures as a two-, three-, or four-part ensemble.

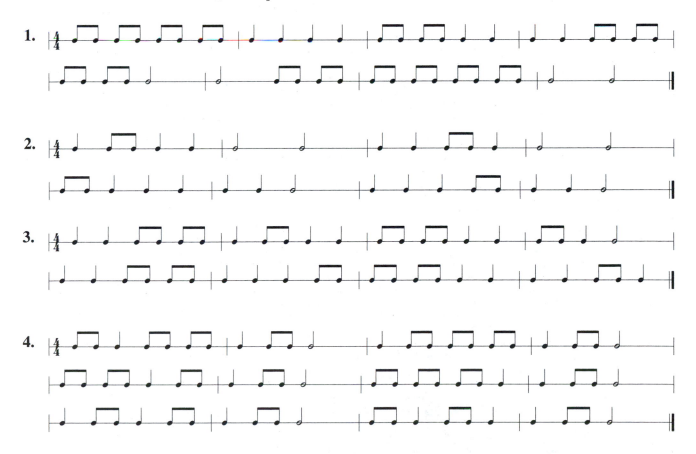

5.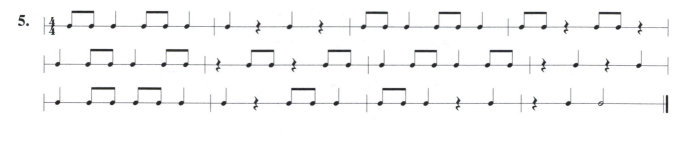

6.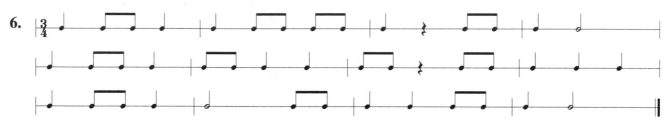

Common Time

The symbol **c** signifies common time and is the equivalent of the meter signature $\frac{4}{4}$. The symbol **c** is not an abbreviation for common time; it is a relic from a system of notation used during the Middle Ages. During this time the geometrically "perfect" circle stood for triple meter, the number three representing the "perfection" of the Holy Trinity. An "imperfect" half-circle stood for duple or quadruple meter.

7.

8.

9.

10.

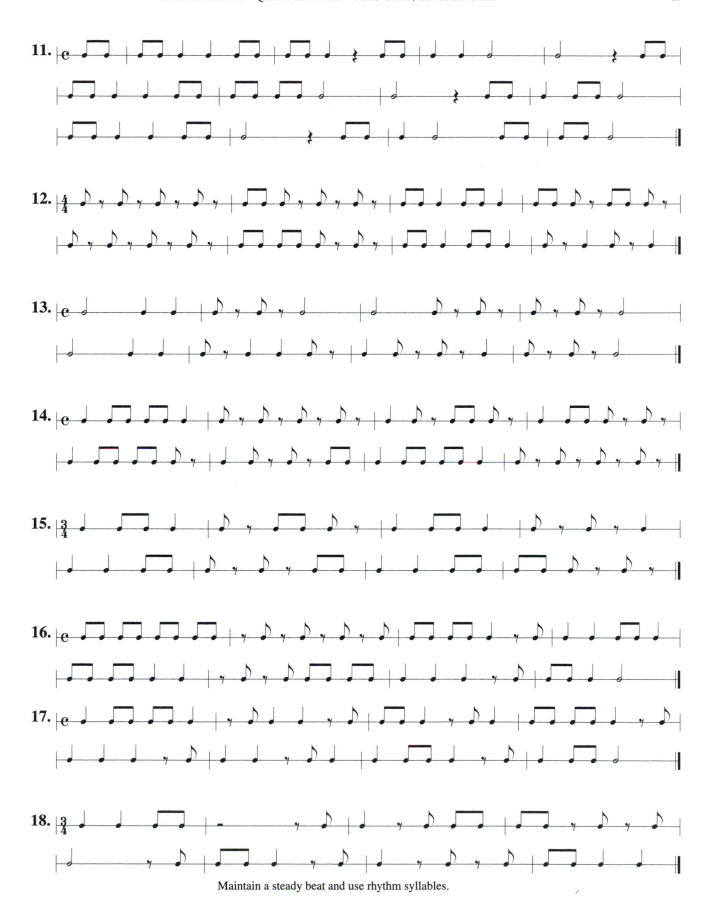

Maintain a steady beat and use rhythm syllables.

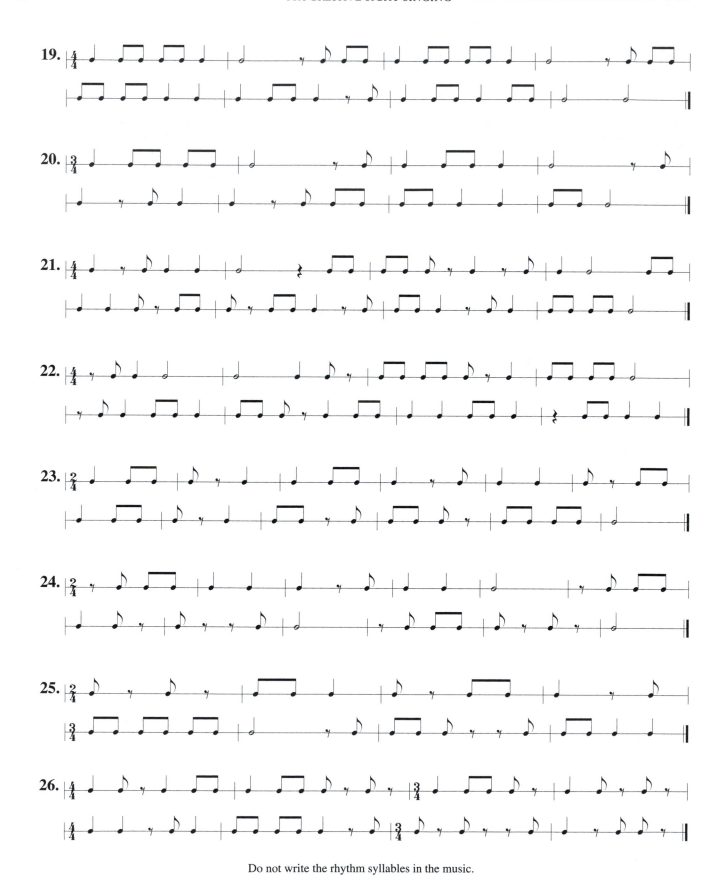

Do not write the rhythm syllables in the music.

Remember to practice your dictation skills.

Ensemble Exercises

(Continued)

Two-Part Exercises for One Person

33.

34.

35.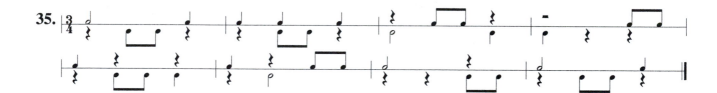

36.

37.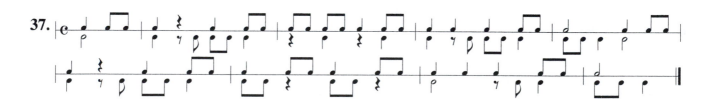

38.

Chapter 3
Simple Meter
Quarter Note = Beat Unit
Slur, Tie, and Extension Dot

I. Building Aural/Oral Skills

Reading Readiness Rhythm Patterns

- Listen as your instructor chants a variety of rhythm patterns on rhythm syllables; echo each pattern on the rhythm syllables while (a) quietly tapping the beat, (b) conducting or (c) using the appropriate metric motion (tap–touch).[1]

II. Symbolic Association

The duration of a pitch may be extended by the notational symbols of the tie and the extension dot.

Tie: The *tie* (bind) is a curved line that connects two or more consecutive notes of the same pitch. The second note is not articulated and the result is one sustained unbroken sound that lasts the combined duration of both notes. Ties are often used to notate a duration that extends over a bar line.

Extension Dot: An *extension dot* (also called *augmentation dot*) is written to the right of a note head and increases the duration of a note by half of its original value. The extension dot eliminates the necessity of writing the tie and the extra note value it represents. Extension dots are not used to extend a duration over a bar line.

Extension dots are sometimes added to rests. Dotted rests are seldom used in simple meter. However, they are common in compound meter. Compound meter will be discussed in Chapter 5.

---

[1]Note to instructors: The rhythm patterns are found in Section III of this chapter. These patterns should be taught by rote using the two-step process outlined in the Musical Literacy Process section of the Preface.

The Tie versus the Slur: A tie is identical in appearance to a *slur*. While a tie connects two or more consecutive notes on the same pitch, a slur connects (a) two or more notes on different pitches, or (b) nonconsecutive notes on the same pitch.

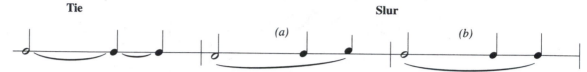

A slur indicates (a) that the notes are to be performed *legato* (in a smooth and connected manner), (b) that the notes are to be sung to a single syllable, or (c) a *phrase* (a complete musical statement).

III. Rhythm Patterns

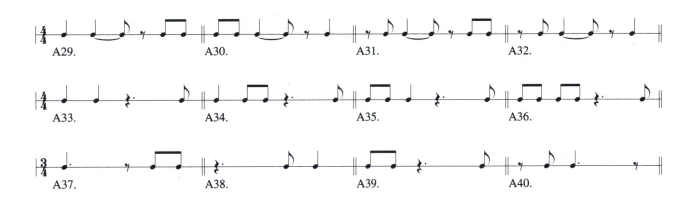

IV. Exercises

Maintain a steady beat and use rhythm syllables.

Remember to perform these exercises as a canon, retrograde canon, or as a two-, three-, or four-part ensemble.

Remember to use these exercises to practice your dictation skills.

Two-Part Exercises for One Person

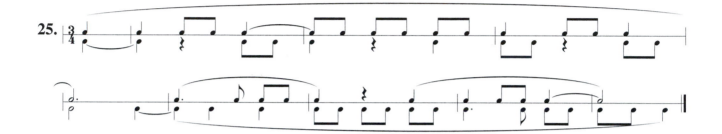

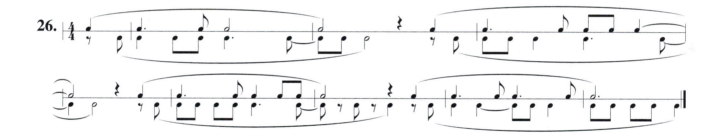

Ensemble Exercises

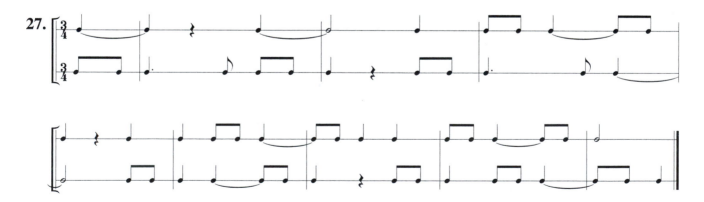

28.

Chapter 4
Terms and Symbols

I. Symbolic Association: Performance Markings

Performance Instructions: Composers usually include instructions or markings to guide the performer(s). These markings usually include beat interruption, tempo, dynamics, and articulation.

Interruptions in the Beat: A variety of symbols may be used to indicate an interruption of the beat.

Interruptions in the Beat		
breath mark	,	short pause; usually an indication of phrasing or breathing
fermata	⌢	placed over a note or rest to indicate that it is to be lengthened or prolonged to about twice its value; also called a pause or hold
tenuto	ten.	placed over a note to indicate a hold of shorter duration than a fermata
caesura	//	indicates silence
General Pause	G. P.	indicates a silence of significant length

Using rhythm syllables chant the following rhythm patterns. Remember to observe all markings.

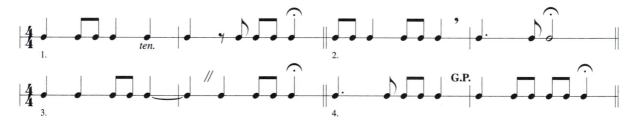

Tempo Markings:

    a. Beats in music can move at different speeds. The speed of beat is indicated by a *tempo marking* written above the staff at the beginning of the composition. Tempo is usually indicated by Italian terms: however, French, German, and English terms may also be used.

Tempo Terms				
	Slow	**Moderate**		**Fast**
Adagio	*Andante*	*Moderato*	*Allegretto*	*Allegro*
slow, at ease	walking speed	moderate speed	moderately fast, light and cheerful	fast, quick, lively

Sing a major scale or a familiar song using each of the indicated tempo markings.

Tempo may be indicated precisely by a *metronome*, a mechanical apparatus that can be adjusted to sound any number of beats per minute. For example a metronome marking of M.M. ♩ = 60 indicates that the tempo of the music is sixty quarter-note beats per minute, or one per second.

The initials M.M. stand for "Maelzel's Metronome." Johann Nepomuk Maelzel (1772–1838) patented the apparatus as a metronome in 1816, however, the metronome was invented around 1812 by Dietrich Nikolaus Winkler (c. 1780–1826).[1]

b. Tempo can change either suddenly or gradually in music.

Gradual Changes in Tempo	Other Terms for Tempo
ritardando or *ritenuto (rit.)* • gradually decrease tempo *accelerando (accel.)* • gradually increase tempo	*a tempo* • return to previous tempo *poco* • little *poco a poco* • little by little

- Using rhythm syllables chant the following rhythm patterns. Observe all markings.

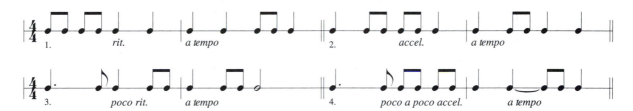

Dynamics: Dynamics are the degrees of loudness or intensity in musical sound.

a. Music can be louder or softer. Dynamics are indicated mainly through the following Italian terms and abbreviations.

Dynamic Markings						
Soft				**Loud**		
pp	*pianissimo*	very soft	softer	*mf*	*mezzo forte*	moderately loud
p	*piano*	soft	↓	*f*	*forte*	loud
mp	*mezzo piano*	moderately soft	louder	*ff*	*fortissimo*	very loud

- Sing a major scale or a familiar song incorporating a variety of dynamic levels.
- Using rhythm syllables chant the following rhythm patterns. Observe all markings.

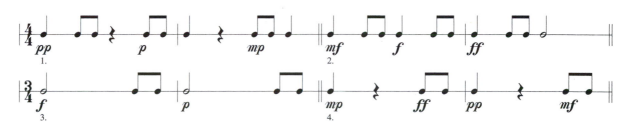

[1]Don Michael Randel, ed. *The New Harvard Dictionary of Music* (Cambridge, MA: The Belknap Press of Harvard University Press, 1986), 489.

b. Dynamics can change gradually.

Gradual Changes in Dynamics			Dynamic Spectrum
cresc.	*crescendo*	gradually louder	
decresc.	*decrescendo*	gradually softer	
dim.	*diminuendo*	gradually softer	

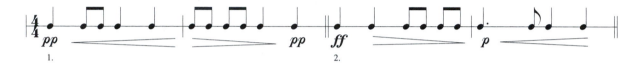

- Sing a major scale incorporating a *crescendo* as the scale ascends and a *decrescendo/diminuendo* as the scale descends.
- Using rhythm syllables chant the following rhythm patterns. Observe all markings.

Articulation: The act of attacking and releasing notes is called articulation.

Articulation		
legato	*leg.*	smooth and connected style; a slur is often used to show legato groups of notes (See Chapter 3, page 22 for more information.)
staccato	*stacc.* or	detached manner; opposite of legato; indicated by a dot above or below the note head
accent	> or —	a sudden strong stress; symbol is placed above or below the note head

- Sing a major scale using the indicated articulation.

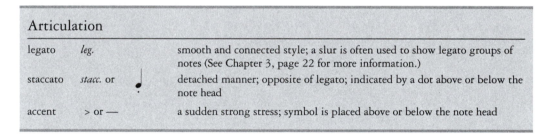

- Using rhythm syllables chant the following rhythm patterns. Observe all markings.

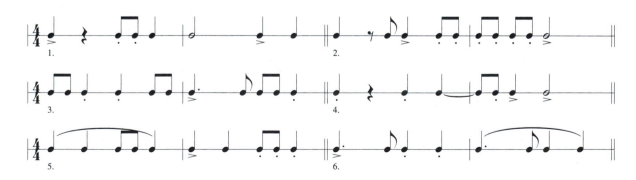

Technical Terms

Repeat Sign: A *repeat sign* is made up of a double bar preceded by two dots.

a. Repeat Sign at the End of a Measure. Repeat the music preceding the sign. Upon reaching the repeat sign the second time, continue on to the next measure.

b. Repetition of a Section within a Composition. Notice that the section to be repeated is enclosed by double bars, the first with dots to the right of the double bar and the second with dots to the left of the double bar. Upon reaching the repeat sign the second time, continue on to the next measure.

c. Repeat Sign within a Measure. Repeat the music preceding the sign. Upon reaching the repeat sign the second time, continue on to the next measure.

First and Second Endings: The first ending indicates (a) a repeat to the beginning, or (b) a return to a previous repeat sign. During the repetition, the music of the first ending is skipped and the piece continues with the second ending.

a. Repeat to the beginning.

b. Return to a previous repeat sign.

c. Multiple endings.

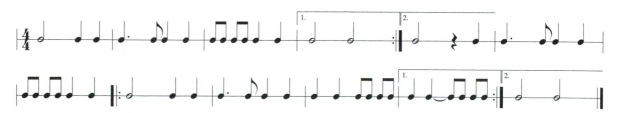

II. Exercises

Remember to observe all dynamic, articulation, tempo, and notation markings.

Maintain a steady beat and use rhythm syllables.

Two-Part Exercises for One Person

Ensemble Exercises

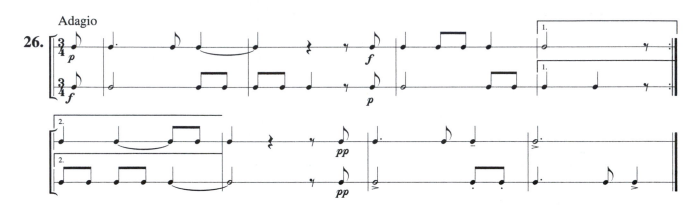

Chapter 5

Compound Meter
Dotted Quarter = Beat Unit;
Divided Beats

I. Building Aural/Oral Skills

Beat: Beats can be divided into smaller groups of two or three equal parts.

- Quietly tap the beat using a circular arm movement rather than a down/up movement. Alternate chanting the beat (dotted quarter) and the divided beat (three eighth notes) using rhythm syllables. Feel, see, and hear that there are three sounds (ta-ki-da) on a beat for three eighth notes and only one sound (ta) for a dotted quarter note.

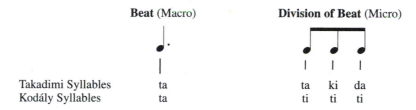

	Beat (Macro)	**Division of Beat** (Micro)
Takadimi Syllables	ta	ta ki da
Kodály Syllables	ta	ti ti ti

Meter: Meter is described as *simple* if the beat divides into two equal parts and *compound* if the beat divides into three equal parts. As with simple meters, compound meters may be *duple*, *triple*, or *quadruple* with the same patterns of accented and unaccented beats.

- Perform each of the six types of meters in the following manner:
- Tap the beat with one hand and the divided beat with the other hand.
- Tap the beat and chant the divided beat using rhythm syllables.
- Chant the beat using rhythm syllables and tap the divided beat.

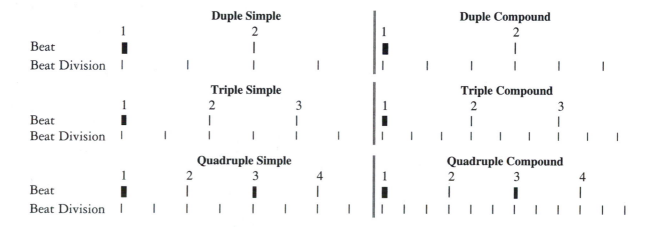

---

[1]Note to instructors: The rhythm patterns are found in Section III of this chapter. These patterns should be taught by rote using the two-step process outlined in the Musical Literacy Process section of the preface.

Reading Readiness Rhythm Patterns
- Listen as your instructor chants a variety of rhythm patterns using rhythm syllables; echo each pattern while (a) quietly tapping the beat, (b) conducting, or (c) using the appropriate metric motion.[1]

II. Symbolic Association

Compound Meter Signature: In compound meter the beat is a dotted note that divides into three equal parts. Because there isn't a number that corresponds to a dotted note, the bottom number of a compound meter signature indicates the rhythmic value of the <u>division of the beat</u>, not the rhythmic value of the beat as in simple meter.

$\frac{6}{8}$ eighth note is the division unit   ♪. = beat unit

The top number of a compound meter signature indicates the number of divisions in each measure. The upper number is usually 6, 9, 12, or another multiple of three.
To determine the number of beats in each measure, divide the top number by three.

$\frac{6}{8}$ six divisions in each measure   2 beats per measure

Memorize that $\frac{6}{8}$, $\frac{9}{8}$, and $\frac{12}{8}$ meter signature are duple, triple, and quadruple patterns, respectively.

Duple compound*	$\frac{6}{8}$	six divisions in each measure	2 beats per measure
		eighth note is the division unit	♪. = 1 beat
Triple compound	$\frac{9}{8}$	nine divisions in each measure	3 beats per measure
		eighth note is the division unit	♪. = 1 beat
Quadruple compound	$\frac{12}{8}$	twelve divisions in each measure	4 beats per measure
		eighth note is the division unit	♪. = 1 beat

*$\frac{6}{8}$ is the most common compound meter signature.

- Following are excerpts of songs in compound meter. Divide the class into two groups. One group should sing and tap the meter while the other group sings and taps the divided beat.

Rhythm Motives: Rhythms may be organized into patterns or motives that add to the unity and variety of music.
- Sing "Row, Row, Row Your Boat" and tap the rhythm. Notice that there are three different rhythm patterns with the second rhythm pattern repeated at the end. This repeated rhythm pattern helps to unify the melody.

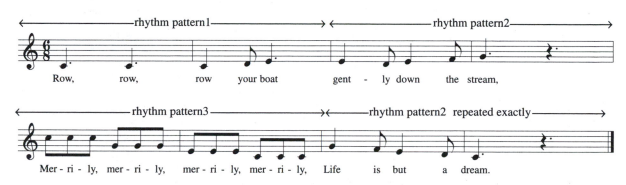

Row, row, row your boat gent - ly down the stream,

Mer - ri - ly, mer - ri - ly, mer - ri - ly, mer - ri - ly, Life is but a dream.

- Sing a known song in compound meter and tap the rhythm. Analyze the rhythm patterns in the song. Suggested songs: "Home on the Range", "Looby Loo", "Lavender's Blue", "Bonavist' Harbour", "I's the B'y", "Drink to Me Only with Thine Eyes", "I Saw Three Ships", "It Came upon a Midnight Clear", and "Bring a Torch", "Jeannette", "Isabella".

III. Rhythm Patterns

IV. Exercises

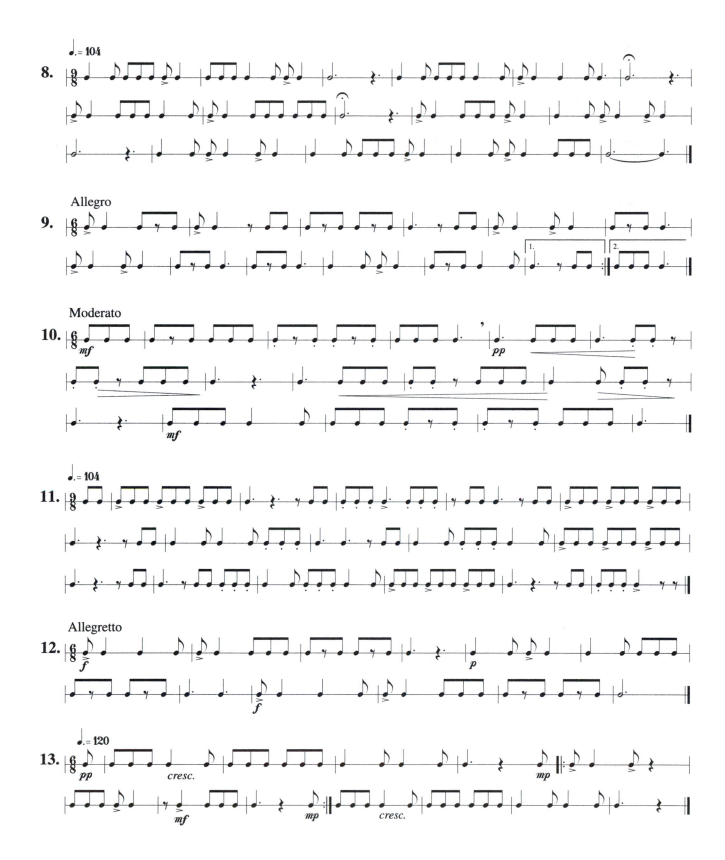

Remember to perform these exercises as a canon, retrograde canon, or as a two-, three-, or four-part ensemble.

Maintain a steady beat and use rhythm syllables.

Two-Part Exercises for One Person

Ensemble Exercises

Chapter 6
Simple Meter Quarter Note = Beat Unit; Borrowed Division

I. Building Aural/Oral Skills

Beat—Borrowed Division: The beat in simple meters usually divides into two equal parts (downbeat-upbeat) and the beat in compound meter usually divides into three equal parts (circular pattern). Either meter can borrow the other meters beat division for use on a temporary basis. Remember to use the rhythm syllables advocated by your instructor.

Beat Divided into Two Equal Parts			*Beat Divided into Three Equal Parts*			
Natural Division			**Borrowed Division**			
Beat	▮		Beat	▮		
Beat Division	|	|	Beat Division	|	|	|
Takadimi	ta	di		ta	ki	da
Kodály	ti	ti		tri	o	la

- Tap the beat, chanting the beat divided into three (*triplet*). Feel, see, and hear that there are three sounds and a circular motion on a beat for triplet eighth notes.
- Tap the beat, chanting the beat divided into two (*duplet*). Feel, see, and hear that there are two sounds and a downup motion on the beat for duplet eighth notes.
- Alternate between chanting triplet and duplet eighth notes.

Reading Readiness Rhythm Patterns

- Listen as your instructor chants a variety of rhythm patterns on rhythm syllables; echo each pattern while (a) quietly tapping the beat, (b) conducting, or (c) using the appropriate metric motion.[1]

II. Symbolic Association

Beat—Borrowed Division: In simple meter, the borrowed division is the triplet, which divides the beat into three. The numeral 3 is place over the figure to indicate this borrowed division.

Natural Division

ta - di
ti - ti
Beat Divided Into Two Equal Parts

Borrowed Division

ta-ki-da
tri-o-la
Beat Divided into Three Equal Parts

---

[1]Note to instructors: The rhythm patterns are found in Section III of this chapter. These patterns should be taught by rote using the two-step process outlined in the Musical Literacy Process section of the Preface.

Rhythm: Rhythms may be organized into *cross-rhythms* where two different beat divisions occur simultaneously.

- Divide the class into two groups. One group should tap the beat, chanting the beat divided into three (triplet) while the other group taps the beat, chanting the beat divided into two (duplet). Feel, see, and hear that there are three sounds (ta-ki-da or tri-o-la) and a circular motion on a beat for triplet eighth notes, and two sounds (ta-di or ti-ti) and a down-up motion on the beat for duplet eighth notes. Exchange tasks.

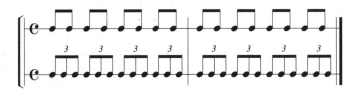

- Rhythms may be organized into patterns or motives. Sing "Heavenly Sunshine" and tap the beat or conduct. Analyze the rhythm patterns in the song. Feel, see, and hear the difference between the triplet and the duplet eighth note patterns.

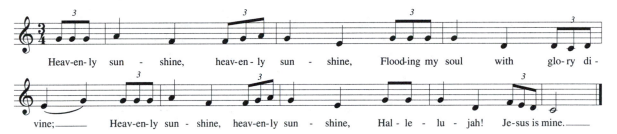

- Sing "Juanita", a Spanish folk song, and tap the beat or conduct. Analyze the rhythm patterns in the song.

III. Rhythm Patterns

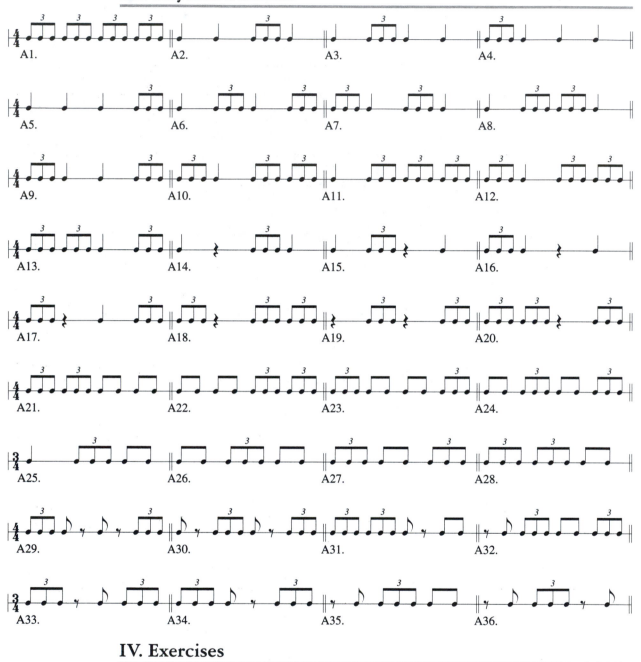

A1. A2. A3. A4.

A5. A6. A7. A8.

A9. A10. A11. A12.

A13. A14. A15. A16.

A17. A18. A19. A20.

A21. A22. A23. A24.

A25. A26. A27. A28.

A29. A30. A31. A32.

A33. A34. A35. A36.

IV. Exercises

1. Andante

Perform these exercises as a canon, retrograde canon, or as a two-, three-, or four-part ensemble.

Remember to practice your dictation skills.

Two-Part Exercises for One Person

Ensemble Exercises

Chapter 7
Simple Meter
Quarter Note =
Beat Unit; Syncopation

I. Building Aural/Oral Skills

Reading Readiness Rhythm Patterns

- Listen as your instructor chants a variety of rhythm patterns on rhythm syllables; echo each pattern while (a) quietly tapping the beat, (b) conducting, or (c) using the appropriate metric motion (tap–touch).[1]

II. Symbolic Association

Syncopation is the "momentary contradiction of the prevailing meter."[2] When an accent is placed on a unstressed beat or unstressed beat division, a syncopation occurs. For a syncopation to occur, it is essential that the prevailing meter is maintained.

Types of Syncopation

a. Accent on an unstressed beat. A note that is louder than nearby notes is a dynamic accent.

Dynamic accent on an unstressed beat

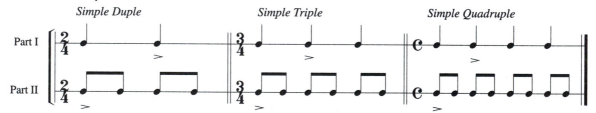

- Divide the class into two groups. One group should quietly tap and chant the beat accenting the unstressed beat as indicated in the first measure of Part I while the other group taps the beat and chants the beat division accenting the beat of the traditional simple duple meter as indicated in Part II. Exchange tasks. Repeat using simple triple and simple quadruple meter.
- For examples see Chapter 4, exercises 1, 2, and 21.

An accent is also perceived on a note that follows a rest (Example A) or a tied note (Example B) that ends on a beat. The syncopated notes are indicated with an asterisk (*).

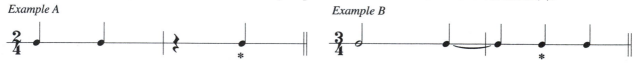

---

[1]Note to instructors: The rhythm patterns are found in Section III of this chapter.
[2]Don Michael Randel, ed. *The New Harvard Dictionary of Music* (Cambridge, MA: The Belknap Press of Harvard University Press, 1986), 827.

- Perform each example shown.
- For examples see Chapter 3, exercises 1, 4, 5, 6, and 7.

Agogic accent: agogic accent (or durational accent) is when a weak beat extends over a strong beat.

- Sing "My Lord, what a Morning" while tapping the beat or conducting. An asterisk (*) indicates the agogic accent.

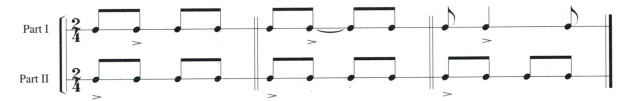

- For examples see Chapter 4, exercises 4 and 16.

b. Accent on Unstressed Beat Division.

- Perform each measure of syncopation in Part I.
- Divide the class into two groups. One group should tap and chant the division of the beat as indicated in the first measure of Part I while the other group taps the division of the beat, accenting the first in each group as indicated in Part II. Feel, see, and hear the unexpected accent on the upbeat. Exchange tasks. Repeat using the division of the beat indicated in the second and then in the third measure.

Sing "I Gave My Love a Cherry" while tapping or conducting the beat.

Rhythm Motives

- Sing the round "I Got a Letter" (Example A) and the spiritual "Nobody Knows the Trouble I've Seen" (Example B) while tapping the beat or conducting. Analyze the rhythmic motives and locate the syncopated notes. Notice that the point of syncopation occurs on the beat division and is not articulated through conducting and/or tapping the beat.

Example A

I got   a let-ter this   morn - in',   O   yes,

I got   a let-ter this   morn - in',   O   yes.

Example B

No-bod - y knows   the trou-ble I've seen,   No-bod- y knows   but Je - sus.

No-bod- y knows   the trou-ble I've seen,   Glo   - ry Hal - le - lu - jah!

III. Rhythm Patterns

IV. Exercises

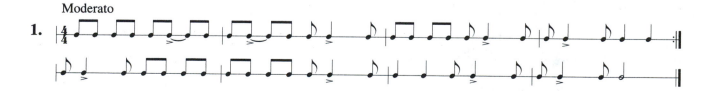

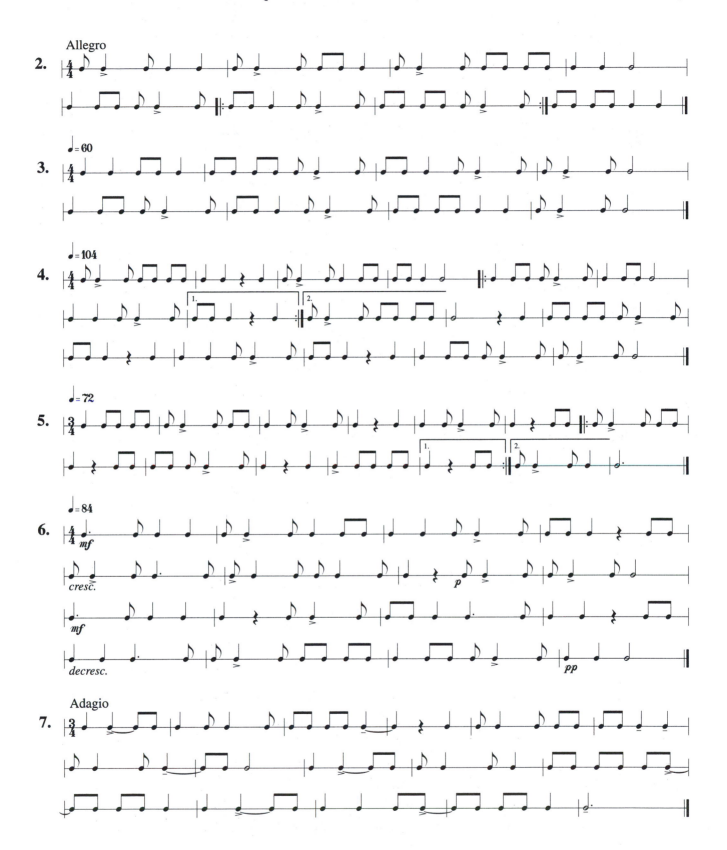

Perform these exercises as a canon, retrograde canon, or as a two-, three-, or four-part ensemble.

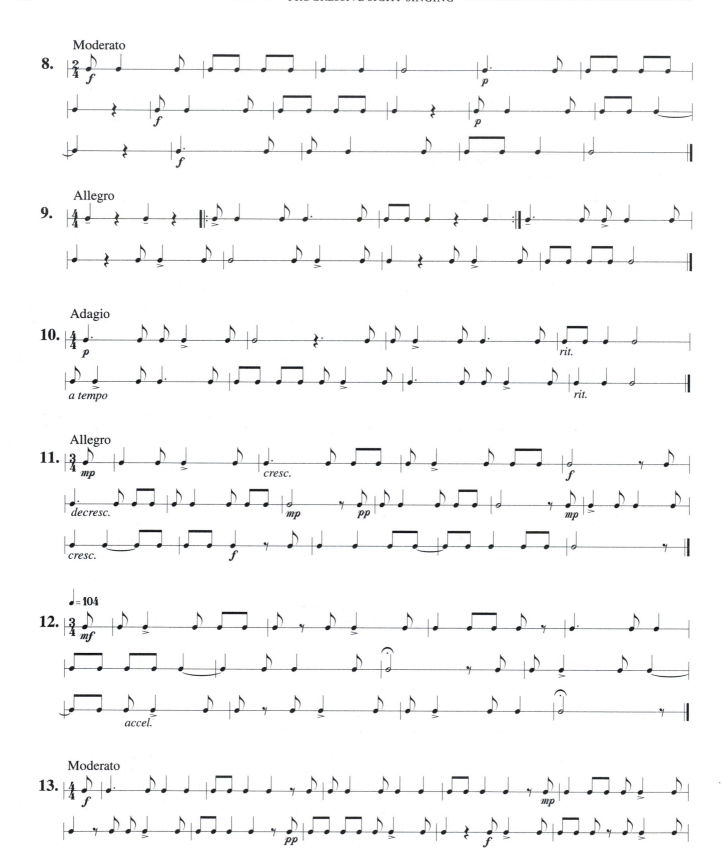

These exercises can be used to practice dictation skills.

Two-Part Exercises for One Person

Moderato

20.

Ensemble Exercises

21.

22.

Chapter 8
Simple Meter
Quarter Note =
Beat Unit; Subdivided Beats

I. Building Aural/Oral Skills

Beat Division and Subdivision: In simple meter, the beat division (down-up motion) itself can be subdivided into two equal parts.

	Beat		Divided Beat		Subdivided Beat			
	↓	↑	↓	↑	↓		↑	
Takadimi Syllables	ta		ta	di	ta	ka	di	mi
Kodály Syllables	ta		ta	ti	ti	ka	ti	ka

* Tap the beat, chanting the beat on rhythm syllables, then switch to the divided beat, and finally to the subdivided beat. Feel, see and hear that there is one sound on the beat, two sounds (one on downbeat and one on upbeat) in the divided beat, and four sounds (two on the down motion and two on the up motion) in the subdivided beat.
* Divide the class into two groups. One group taps the beat and chants the beat division while the other group taps the beat and chants the beat subdivision. Exchange tasks.

Reading Readiness Rhythm Patterns

* Listen as your instructor chants a variety of rhythm patterns on rhythm syllables; echo each pattern while (a) quietly tapping the beat, (b) conducting, or (c) using the appropriate metric motion (tap–touch).[1]

II. Symbolic Association

Rhythm:

a. Rhythms may be organized into patterns or motives.

* Perform the following rhythm patterns containing beat division and beat subdivision using rhythm syllables. Treat each pattern as its own entity rather than reading note-to-note.

1.   2.   3.    4.    5.

---

[1]Note to instructors: The rhythm patterns are found in Section III of this chapter.

- Portions of songs are presented that include beat division and beat subdivision. Analyze the rhythm patterns and then sing each of the songs while (a) tapping the beat, (b) tapping the beat division, (c) tapping the beat subdivision, and/or conducting. Feel, hear, and see the divided and subdivided beats. Other suggested songs: "Clementine", "Working on the Railroad", "This Old Man", "Blue-Tail Fly", "Cedar Swamp", "Drunken Sailor", "How Many Miles to Babylon?", and "Shoo, Fly".

1. *Paw Paw Patch*

2. *Skip to My Lou*

3. *Battle Hymn of the Republic*

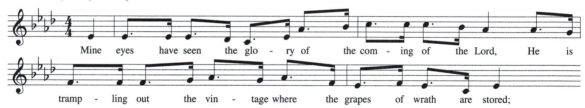

b. Rhythms may be organized into cross rhythms where two or three different beat divisions occur simultaneously.

- Divide the class into three groups. The first group taps the beat and chants the divided beat—beat divided into two (duplet); the second group taps the beat and chants the borrowed divided beat—beat divided into three (triplet); and the third group taps the beat and chants the subdivided beat—beat divided into four (quadruplet). Feel, see, and hear that there are two sounds and a down-up motion on the beat for the divided beat, three sounds and a circular motion on a beat for the borrowed beat division, and four sounds and a down-up motion on the beat for the subdivided beat. Exchange tasks.

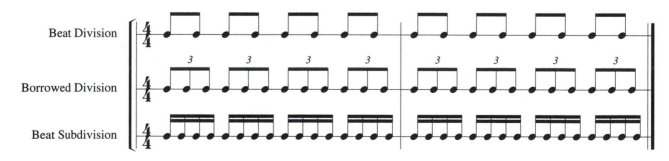

III. Rhythm Patterns

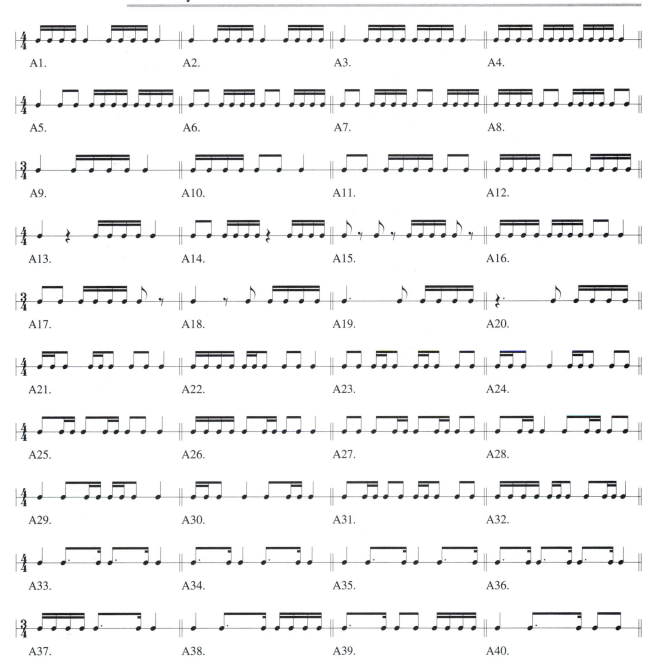

IV. Exercises

Maintain a steady pulse and use rhythm syllables.

Remember to perform these exercises as a canon, retrograde canon, or as a two-, three-, or four-part ensemble.

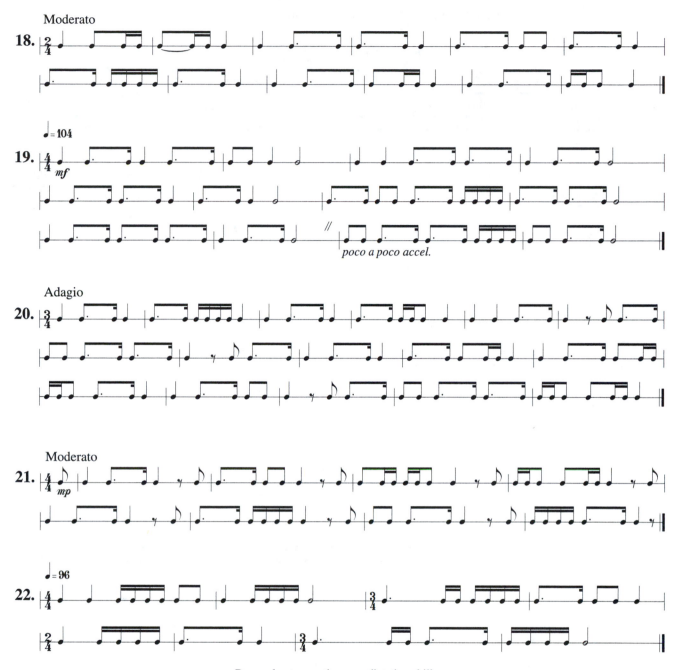

Remember to practice your dictation skills.

Two-Part Exercises for One Person

Ensemble Exercises

Chapter 9
More Terms and Symbols

I. Symbolic Association: Performance Markings

Performance Instructions: Effective musical communication requires an in-depth knowledge of the meaning of musical terms and symbols and the ability to apply them.

Tempo: The speed of the beat is the tempo

   a. Additional tempo markings:

Additional Tempo Terms

Very Slow		Very Fast	
Largo	Lento	Vivace	Presto
• Very slow	• Slow	• Lively	• Very quick

Tempo Marking Spectrum

Very Slow	Slow	Moderate	Fast	Very Fast
Largo	Adagio	Moderato	Allegro	Presto
Lento	Andante		Allegretto	Vivace

Sing a major scale or a familiar song using each of the tempo markings presented.

   b. The tempo can change either suddenly or gradually in music.

Gradual Changes in Tempo	Other Terms for Tempo
rallentando (rall.) • to gradually decrease tempo	*con moto* • with motion
rubato • to make the tempo flexible by accelerating or slowing down the tempo	*meno mosso* • less motion

Using rhythm syllables chant the following rhythm patterns. Observe all markings.

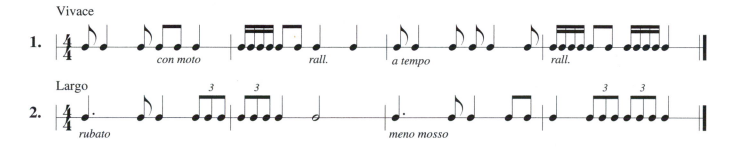

Character Terms: Character terms are used to express a definite mood or idea.

Character Terms				
cantabile	*dolce*	*maestoso*	*con brio*	*agitato*
• in a singing style	• sweetly	• majestic	• with spirit	• agitated

Dynamics: Dynamics are the degrees of loudness or intensity in musical sound.

Other Dynamic Marks		
sfz or *sf*	*sforzando* or *sforzato*	a sudden, strong, forced (often loud) accent
sfp	*sforzando-piano*	a sudden (often loud) accent followed immediately
fp	*forte piano*	by soft loud, immediately soft

Sing a major scale or a familiar song incorporating different dynamic levels. See the following example.

Using rhythm syllables chant the following rhythm patterns. Observe all markings.

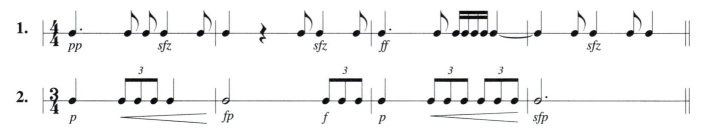

Articulation: The act of attacking and releasing notes is called articulation.

Articulation			
marcato	*marcato*		stressed, marked, emphasized
legato	*leg.*		smooth and connected style
staccato	*stacc.* or		detached manner; opposite of legato; indicated by a dot above or below the note head
accent	> or —		a sudden strong stress; symbol is placed above or below the note head

Sing a major scale using the indicated articulation.

Using rhythm syllables chant the following rhythm patterns. Observe all markings.

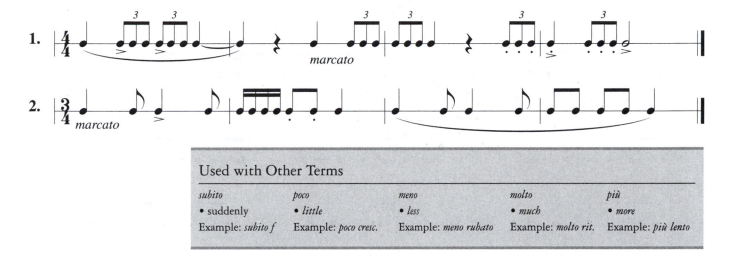

1. *marcato*

2. *marcato*

Used with Other Terms

subito	*poco*	*meno*	*molto*	*più*
• suddenly	• little	• less	• much	• more
Example: *subito f*	Example: *poco cresc.*	Example: *meno rubato*	Example: *molto rit.*	Example: *più lento*

Technical Terms: Musical repeat devices

Additional Devices for Musical Repeats

Da Capo	D.C.	• Italian, "from the head" • a repeat from the beginning	*Fine*	*fine*	• Italian, " end" (FEE-nay) • indicates where the composition ends after a D.C. or D.S.
Dal Segno *Sign*	D.S. 𝄋	• Italian, "from the sign" • indicates a repeat from the sign	*Coda*	⊕	• Italian, "tail" • concluding portion of a composition

Example A: Da capo al fine

Fine

D.C. al Fine.

Example B: Dal segno al fine

Fine

D.S. al Fine

Example C: Da capo al coda

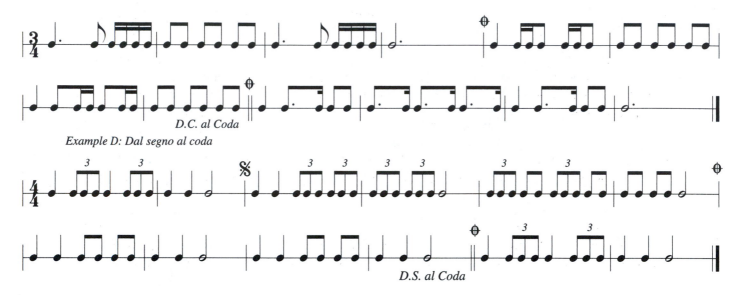

D.C. al Coda

Example D: Dal segno al coda

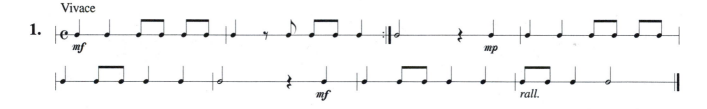

D.S. al Coda

II. Exercises

Vivace

1.

Maestoso

2.

Cantabile ♩ = 88

3.

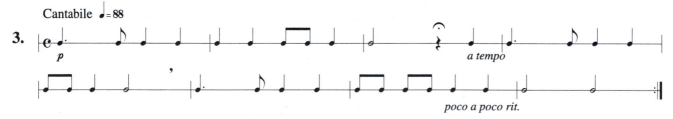

Lento

4.

Remember to practice your dictation skills.

22.

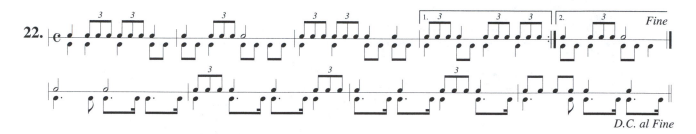

Fine

D.C. al Fine

Ensemble Exercises

23. Allegro

Fine

Fine

D.C. al Fine

D.C. al Fine

24. Moderato

Fine

Fine

D.S. al Fine

D.S. al Fine

Chapter 10
Simple Meter Quarter Note = Beat Unit; More Rhythms with Borrowed Beat Division

I. Building Aural/Oral Skills

Reading Readiness Rhythm Patterns

- Divide the class into two groups. The first group taps the beat and chants the borrowed beat (triplet); the second group taps the beat and chants the first rhythm pattern found in Section II that follows. Exchange tasks. Repeat using each of the patterns in Section II.
- Listen as your instructor chants a variety of rhythm patterns on rhythm syllables; echo each pattern while (a) quietly tapping the beat, (b) conducting, or (c) using the appropriate metric motion (tap—touch).[1]

II. Symbolic Association

- Divide the class into two groups. The first group taps the beat and chants the borrowed beat (triplet); the second group taps the beat and reads (chant using rhythm syllables) the first of the seven patterns listed. Exchange tasks. Repeat until all seven patterns have been read and chanted by each group.

Triplet Notes and Rests

Tied Triplets and Quarter/Eighth Triplet Combinations

---

[1]Note to instructors: The rhythm patterns are found in Section III of this chapter.

III. Rhythm Patterns

IV. Exercises

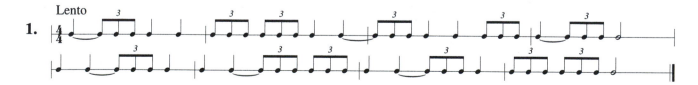

Maintain a steady pulse and use rhythm syllables.

Remember to practice your dictation skills.

These exercises can be performed as a canon, retrograde canon, or as a two-, three-, or four-part ensemble.

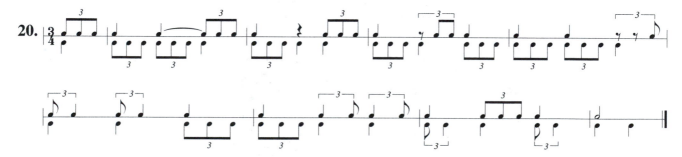

Two-Part Exercises for One Person

Ensemble Exercises

Chapter 11

Simple Meter
Quarter Note = Beat Unit;
More Rhythms with Syncopation

I. Building Aural/Oral Skills

Reading Readiness Rhythm Patterns

- •Divide the class into two groups. The first group taps the beat and chants a divided beat syncopation pattern; the second group taps the beat and chants the first rhythm pattern found in Section II that follows. Exchange tasks. Repeat using each of the patterns in Section II.

- Listen as your instructor chants a variety of rhythm patterns on rhythm syllables; echo each pattern while (a) quietly tapping the beat, (b) conducting, or (c) using the appropriate metric motion (tap–touch).[1]

II. Symbolic Association

- Divide the class into two groups. The first group taps the beat and chants the divided beat (micro); the second group taps the beat and reads (chant using rhythm syllables) the first pattern listed that follows. Exchange tasks. Repeat until all eight patterns have been read and chanted by each group.

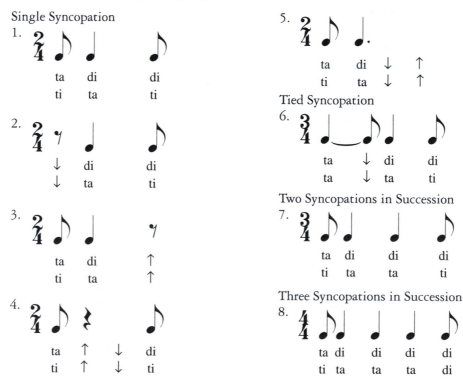

---

[1]Note to instructors: The rhythm patterns are found in Section III of this chapter.

82

III. Rhythm Patterns

IV. Exercises

Remember to practice your dictation skills.

These exercises can be performed as a canon, retrograde canon, or as a two-, three-, or four-part ensemble.

Two-Part Exercises for One Person

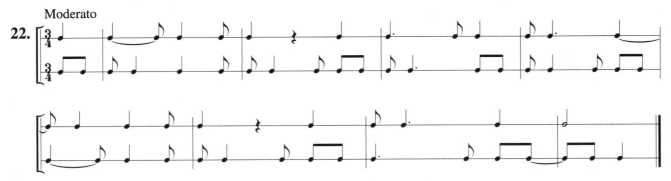

Ensemble Exercises

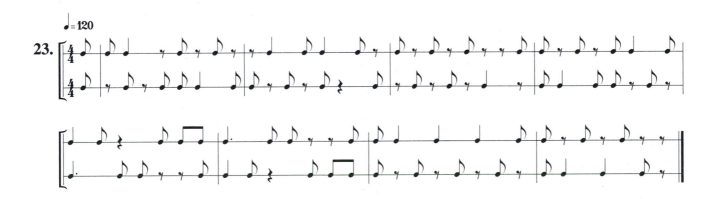

Chapter 12

Simple Meter
Quarter Note = Beat Unit;
More Rhythms with Subdivided Beats

I. Building Aural/Oral Skills

Reading Readiness Rhythm Patterns

* Divide the class into two groups. The first group taps the beat and chants the division of beat (eighths); the second group taps the beat and chants the first rhythm pattern found in Section II. Exchange tasks. Repeat using each of the patterns in Section II.

* Listen as your instructor chants a variety of rhythm patterns on rhythm syllables; echo each pattern while (a) quietly tapping the beat, (b) conducting, or (c) using the appropriate metric motion (tap–touch).[1]

II. Symbolic Association

* Divide the class into two groups. The first group taps the beat and chants the divided beat (micro); the second group reads the rhythm patterns on rhythm syllables while tapping the beat or conducting. Exchange tasks. Repeat until all of the patterns have been read and chanted by each group.

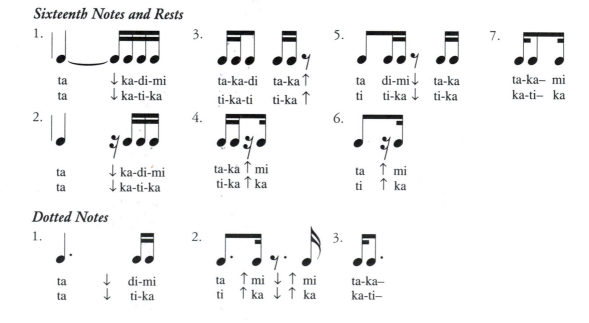

Sixteenth Notes and Rests

1.   ta   ↓ ka-di-mi   ta   ↓ ka-ti-ka
3.   ta-ka-di   ta-ka ↑   ti-ka-ti   ti-ka ↑
5.   ta   di-mi↓   ta-ka   ti   ti-ka ↓   ti-ka
7.   ta-ka– mi   ka-ti– ka

2.   ta   ↓ ka-di-mi   ta   ↓ ka-ti-ka
4.   ta-ka ↑ mi   ti-ka ↑ ka
6.   ta   ↑   mi   ti   ↑   ka

Dotted Notes

1.   ta   ↓   di-mi   ta   ↓   ti-ka
2.   ta   ↑ mi ↓ ↑ mi   ti   ↑ ka ↓ ↑ ka
3.   ta-ka–   ka-ti–

---

[1]Note to instructors: The rhythm patterns are found in Section III in this chapter.

III. Rhythm Patterns

IV. Exercises

1. Andante

Remember to practice your dictation skills.

Perform these exercises as a canon, retrograde canon, or as a two-, three-, or four-part ensemble.

Two-Part Exercises for One Person

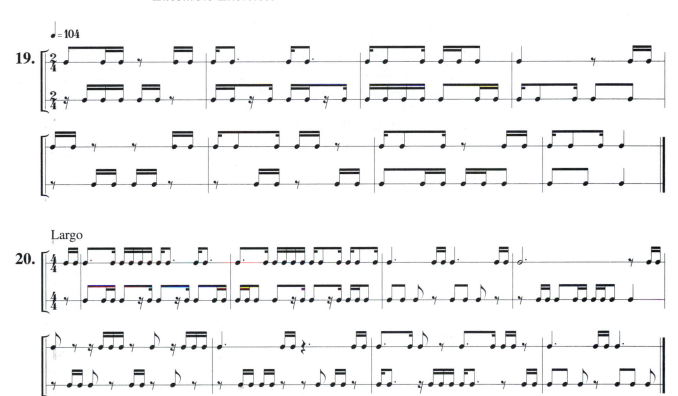

Ensemble Exercises

Chapter 13

Half Note = Beat Unit

I. Symbolic Association

Meter Signature: In previous chapters the quarter note or the dotted quarter note represented the beat. The half note can also be used to represent the beat. Duple simple meter is often called *alla breve* or *cut time* and may be represented by the symbol for Common Time with a vertical line drawn through it.

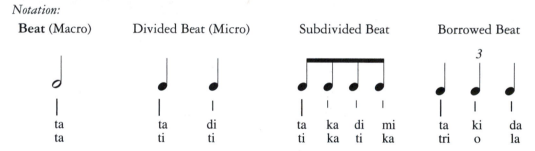

Duple Simple (*Alla breve*)	Triple Simple	Quadruple Simple
¢ or 2 → two beats per measure 2 → half note equals beat unit	3 → three beats per measure 2 → half note equals beat unit	4 → four beats per measure 2 → half note equals beat unit

Notation:

Beat (Macro)   Divided Beat (Micro)   Subdivided Beat   Borrowed Beat

ta	ta	di	ta	ka	di	mi	ta	ki	da
ta	ti	ti	ti	ka	ti	ka	tri	o	la

Notice that there are three new rhythmic symbols. A dotted whole note is used to fill three beats (E1) and a *double whole note/double whole rest* (A3) fills four beats of sound/silence.

A. Beat/Long Notes	B. Divided/Subdivided	C. Syncopation	E. Extension Dot
1.	1.	1.	1.
2. Double Whole Note Rest	2. Combination	D. Triplet	2.
3.	2.	1.	3.

- Read and perform each of the patterns (A1–E3) while (a) quietly tapping the beat, (b) conducting, or (c) using the appropriate metric motion (tap–touch).

Comparison of Simple Meters:

• Tap and chant each of the following equivalent patterns using rhythm syllables.

II. Rhythm Patterns

III. Exercises

Two-Part Exercises for One Person

Ensemble Exercises

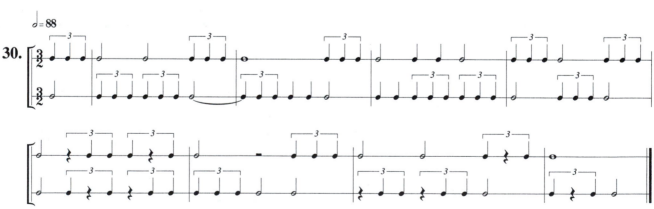

Chapter 14

Simple Meter—Eighth Note = Beat Unit

I. Symbolic Association

Meter Signature: In previous chapters the quarter note, dotted quarter note, and half note each represented the beat. The eighth note can also be used to represent the beat.

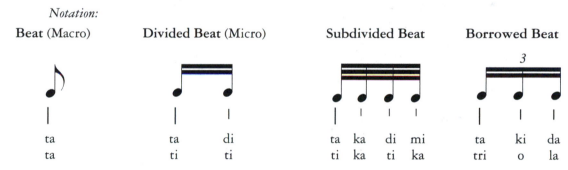

Duple Simple	Triple Simple	Quadruple Simple
2→two beats per measure	3→ three beats per measure	4→four beats per measure
8→eighth note equals beat unit	8→eighth note equals beat unit	8→eighth note equals beat unit

Notation:

Beat (Macro)	Divided Beat (Micro)	Subdivided Beat	Borrowed Beat
ta	ta di	ta ka di mi	ta ki da
ta	ti ti	ti ka ti ka	tri o la

Notice that the subdivision of the beat is represented by a new rhythmic symbol, a thirty-second note.

Comparison of Simple Meters:

- Chant each of the following equivalent patterns using rhythm syllables while tapping the beat or conducting. Focus on beats within the metric grid rather than on the flags/beams on the notes.

A. Quarter Note = Beat Unit

B. Eighth Note = Beat Unit

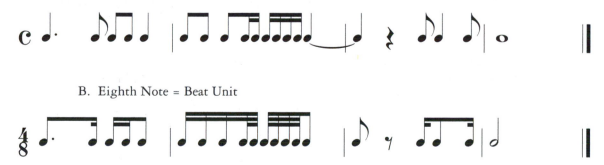

C. Half Note = Beat Unit

II. Rhythm Patterns

III. Exercises

Two-Part Exercises for One Person

Ensemble Exercises

Chapter 15

Compound Meter
More Rhythms

I. Building Aural/Oral Skills

Subdivided and Borrowed Beat in Compound Meter:

- Divide the class into two groups. The first group taps the beat and chants the division of beat (eighths); the second group taps the beat and chants the subdivided beat. Exchange tasks. Repeat with (a) one group chanting divided beat and the other group chanting borrowed beat; and (b) one group chanting subdivided beat and the other chanting borrowed beat. Exchange tasks.

Beat (Macro)   **Divided Beat (Micro)**   **Subdivided Beat**   **Borrowed Beat (Duplet*)**

ta	ta	ki	da	ta	va	ki	di	da	na	ta	di
ta	ti	ti	ti	ti	ka	ti	ka	ti	ka	ti	ti

*A duplet is a two-note group resulting from irregular division of a compound beat; borrowed from simple meter.

Reading Readiness Rhythm Patterns

- Listen as your instructor chants a variety of rhythm patterns using rhythm syllables; echo each pattern while (a) quietly tapping the beat, (b) conducting, or (c) using the appropriate metric motion (tap—touch).[1]

II. Symbolic Association

- Divide the class into two groups. The first group taps the beat and chants the divided beat (micro); the second group reads the rhythm patterns using rhythm syllables while tapping the beat or conducting. Exchange tasks. Repeat until all of the patterns have been read and chanted by each group.

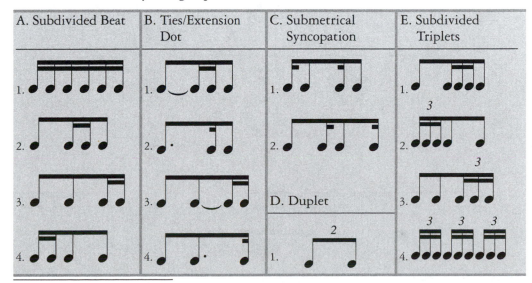

A. Subdivided Beat	B. Ties/Extension Dot	C. Submetrical Syncopation	E. Subdivided Triplets

[1]Note to instructors: The rhythm patterns are found in Section III of this chapter.

III. Rhythm Patterns

IV. Exercises

1. Allegretto

Two-Part Exercises for One Person

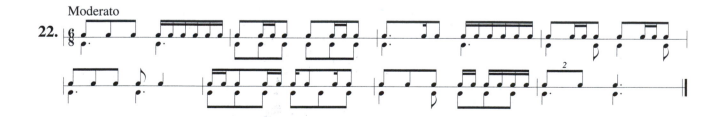

Ensemble Exercises

Chapter 16
Cross-Rhythms and Hemiola

I. Symbolic Association

Hemiola is a type of syncopation that results in a temporary shift in meter from simple to compound or vice versa. For example, the accents in a measure with six eighth notes is shifted from two groups of three eighth notes (compound duple) to three groups of two eighth notes (simple triple) or vice versa. Hemiola also results if a compound pattern (quarter/eighth) is superimposed on simple meter.

Three notes in the space of two beats   *Two-beat pattern in the space of three beats*

Notice that the division of the measure is changed rather than the division of the beat (duplet and triplet).

The hemiola pattern is most often three half notes in the time of two ¾ measures (one beat to a ¾ measure).

Two notes in the space of three beats

A *superduplet* is a cross-rhythm composed of two notes of equal value in the space of three beats. This figure is often referred to as "two against three" and may be notated in several different ways. Notice that the second version has the same visual appearance as a common pattern in compound meter.

Superduplet

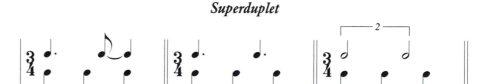

A *supertriplet* is a cross-rhythm composed of three notes of equal value in the space of two beats. This figure is often referred to as "three against two" and may be notated in several different ways. Think triplet eighth notes when performing this pattern.

Supertriplet

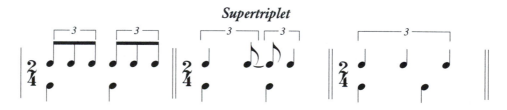

114

II. Exercises

Superduplet

Supertriplet

Hemiola

Two-Part Exercises for One Person

Ensemble Exercises

Chapter 17
Asymmetrical Meters

I. Symbolic Association

Asymmetrical or Composite Meter: Such unusual meters as quintuple (5 beats) or septuple (7 beats) are actually combination of groups of two and three beats within a measure. This produces an irregular accent pattern that is often indicated by accents or a dotted line within a measure.

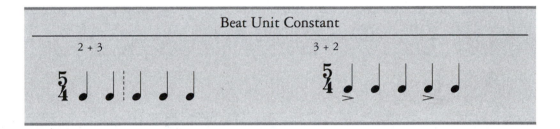

- Read and perform each of the $\frac{5}{4}$ patterns while quietly tapping the beat or conducting.

Asymmetrical meters can also combine simple and compound beat units. When this occurs the division unit rather than the beat unit remains constant. Notice that beams will usually make the groupings visible or the time signature may indicate the grouping.

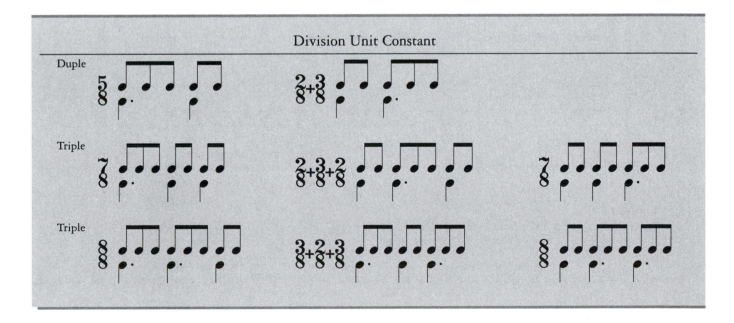

- Read and perform each of the duple and triple patterns while (a) quietly tapping the beat, (b) conducting, or (c) using the appropriate metric motion (tap—touch).

II. Rhythm Patterns and Exercises: Beat Constant

A. Rhythm Patterns

III. Rhythm Patterns and Exercises: Beat Division Constant

A. Rhythm Patterns

B. Exercises

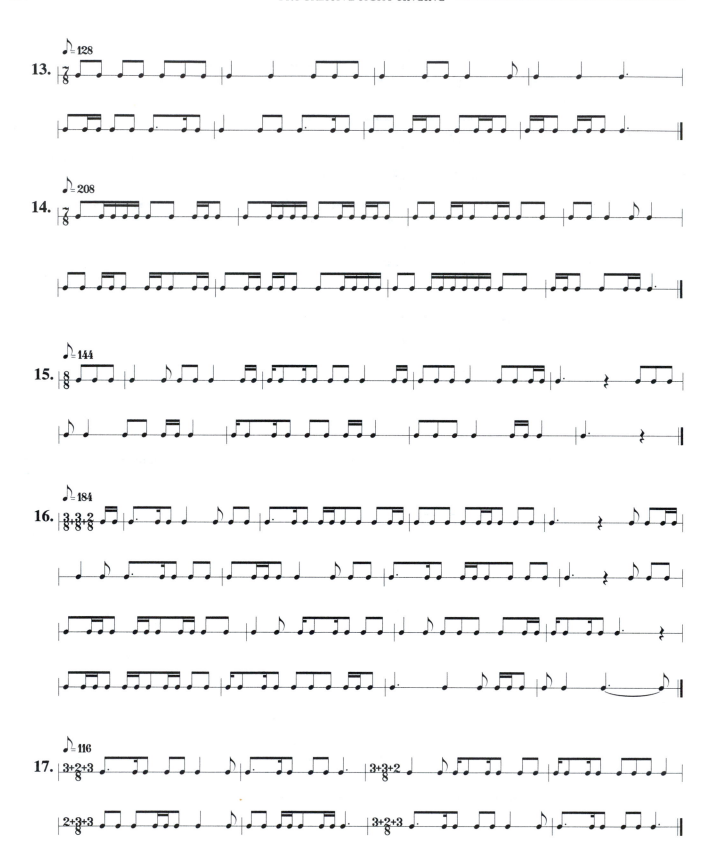

Changing Meters with Unequal Beats

Two-Part Exercises for One Person

Ensemble Exercises

Chapter 18

Mixed Meters

I. Symbolic Association

Mixed Meter

When simple and compound meters are mixed, either the beat or the division of the beat remains constant. The equivalence ($\flat$ = $\flat$ or $\downarrow$ = $\downarrow$.) is shown at the point of the change.

Division Constant: The speed of the eighth note remains constant throughout. Consequently, the beats are of unequal length. Tap the eighth note or use a metronome set to the eighth note to ensure the steadiness of the division as the meter changes. When conducting you will speed up when moving from compound to simple meter and slow down when moving from simple to compound meter.

Beat Constant: The quarter note in simple meter equals the dotted quarter note in compound meter. Consequently the speed of the eighth-note changes. Use a metronome to set the beat, conduct or tap the beat to keep the beat constant while chanting the rhythm using rhythm syllables. When the beat remains constant, your conducting will maintain a steady pulse.

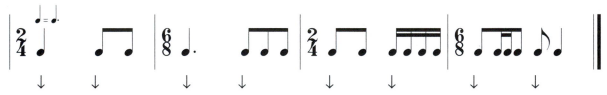

Mixed meter may also include symmetrical and asymmetrical meters.

II. Exercises

Division Constant

Normally the equivalence must be shown at the point of change; however, for these exercises the equivalence is shown at the beginnings.

Beat Remains Constant

Normally the equivalence must be shown at the point of change; however, for these exercises the equivalence is shown at the beginnings.

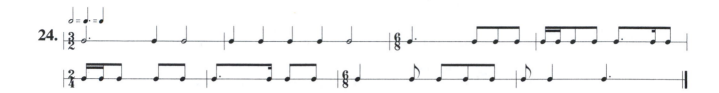

Symmetrical and Asymmetrical Meters

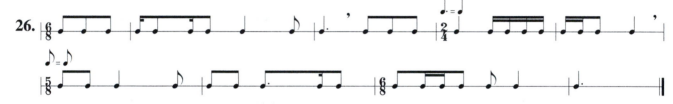

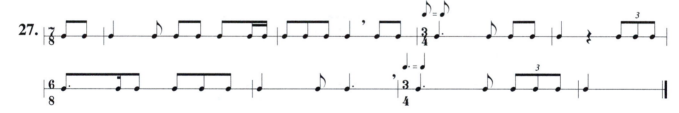

Two-Part Exercises for One Person

Ensemble Exercises

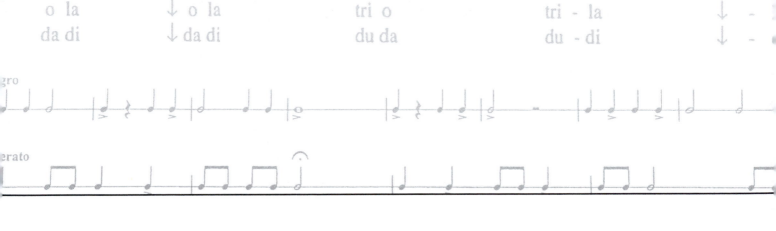

PART II

Melodic Reading

Chapter 1
Tonic Pentachord in Major Mode;
Simple Meters, Undivided Beat

I. Building Aural/Oral Skills: Diatonic Steps

Reading Readiness Tonal Patterns
- Listen as your instructor sings a variety of tonal patterns; echo each pattern. See Appendix B for a description of tonal reading systems and hand signs. The use of hand signs, tapping the beat or conducting is highly recommended.[1]

Vocal-Pitch Exercises: Sing each of the following drills daily.

Pentachord Scale
- Sing the ascending and descending *pentachord* (5 note) *scale* using tonal syllables. Start on various tonics and always maintain an even pulse.
  Solfège: do – re – mi – fa – so – fa – mi – re – do
  Numbers: 1 – 2 – 3 – 4 – 5 – 4 – 3 – 2 – 1
- Sing the ascending and descending additive pentachord scale using tonal syllables. Start on various tonics and always maintain an even pulse.

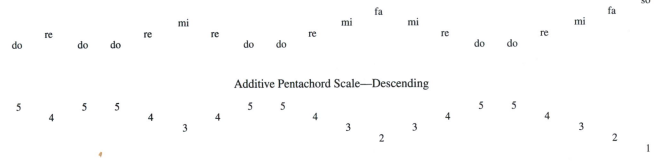

Additive Pentachord Scale—Ascending

Additive Pentachord Scale—Descending

Intervals: An *interval* is the distance in pitch between two tones; all intervals are identified numerically by counting both of the tones and the pitches spanned by the two tones.
- Sing the ascending intervals from the tonic and the descending intervals from the fifth scale degree. Verbally label the quantity of each interval prior to singing the interval. Begin to recognize these intervals by sound.
  - *Solfège*   Second: do – re – do; Third: do – mi – do; Fourth: do – fa – do; Fifth: do – so – do;
    Second: so – fa – so; Third: so – mi – so; Fourth: so – re – so; Fifth: so – do – so
  - *Numbers*   Second: 1 – 2 – 1; Third: 1 – 3 – 1; Fourth: 1 – 4 – 1; Fifth: 1 – 5 – 1;
    Second: 5 – 4 – 5; Third: 5 – 3 – 5; Fourth: 5 – 2 – 5; Fifth: 5 – 1 – 5

---

[1]Note to instructors: The tonal patterns are found in Section III of this chapter, and should be taught by rote using the two-step process outlined in the Musical Literacy Process section of the Preface.

- Sing the intervals of a third ascending from the tonic and descending from the fifth scale degree. Begin to recognize these intervals by sound.
  - *Preparation Exercise:*
    Solfège: do – re – mi – do – mi; re – mi – fa – re – fa; mi – fa – so – mi – so; so – fa – mi – so – mi; fa – mi – re – fa – re; mi – re – do – mi – do
    Numbers: 1 – 2 – 3 – 1 – 3; 2 – 3 – 4 – 2 – 4; 3 – 4 – 5 – 3 – 5; 5 – 4 – 3 – 5 – 3; 4 – 3 – 2 – 4 – 2; 3 – 2 – 1 – 3 – 1
  - Thirds Only
    Solfège: do – mi; re – fa; mi – so; so – mi; fa – re; mi – do
    Numbers: 1 – 3; 2 – 4; 3 – 5; 5 – 3; 4 – 2; 3 – 1

Tonic Triad: A *tonic triad* is a combination of three tones arranged in thirds (tertian) and built on the home tone or keynote; the lowest note is called the *root*, the middle note is called the *third*, and the top note is called the *fifth* of the triad.

- Sing the tonic triad as a *chord* (tones are sounded simultaneously creating *harmony*—the vertical aspect of music) and as an arpeggio (notes of a chord sung one at a time).
  Solfège: do – mi – so – mi – do
  Numbers: 1 – 3 – 5 – 3 – 1

Reading Readiness Aural Skills

- Listen as your instructor sings on a neutral syllable or plays two tonal patterns and then determine if the patterns were the same or different.
- Sing the tonal syllables indicated by your instructor either via hand signs or the tonal ladder.[2]
- Listen as your instructor sings a known tonal pattern on a neutral syllable, "notate" the pattern using the tonal syllable or scale degree numbers in graphic form to illustrate the melodic contour of the pattern.

Example:

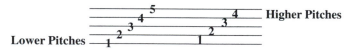

II. Symbolic Association: Diatonic Steps

Score notation: The visual representation of music is called *score notation*. Its main purpose is to indicate the pitch and duration of each tone.

Notation of pitch: Pitch is notated on a *staff* which consists of five parallel horizontal lines and four intervening spaces. The lines and spaces are numbered from the bottom to the top, from lower to higher pitch.

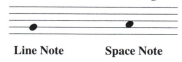

Notes: A *note* is a musical symbol which, when placed "on a line" or "in a space," indicates a specific pitch. A note is "on a line" if the line runs through the center of the note and a note is "in a space" if the outside of the note touches the surrounding lines.

Line Note   **Space Note**

---

[2]See Appendix B for hand signs and the tonal ladder.

- Determine the numerical number and position (line or space) of each note.

1. 4th space   2. 3rd line   3. _____   4. _____   5. _____   6. _____   7. _____   8. _____

- Tonal syllables can be used to name the notes. Using tonal syllables sing the following patterns, first following the tonal syllables and then following the notes on the staff.

■ = Tonic Keynote (*do*)

Intervals: All *intervals* are identified numerically by counting both of the tones and the lines and spaces spanned by the two tones. On the staff, a *second* moves from a space to a line or a line to a space; a *third* moves from a space to the next space or a line to the next line; a *fourth* moves from a space to line or line to a space skipping a line; a *fifth* moves from line to line or space to space skipping a line or space respectively.

Second   **Third**   **Fourth**   **Fifth**

- Determine the quantity (number) of each of the following intervals.

1. ____   2. ____   3. ____   4. ____   5. ____   6. ____   7. ____   8. ____

III. Tonal and Melodic Patterns: Diatonic Steps

A. Tonal Patterns: Symbolic Association

Using tonal syllables, read and sing the written notation of the tonal patterns A128. (See Appendix B for a description of tonal reading systems.)

- Establish tonality by singing a tonic chord arpeggio. If necessary transpose the pattern into a key that provides a comfortable range.
- Set an appropriate tempo, quietly tap several preparatory beats and then sing the pattern a cappella with one beat per notehead. Always silently tap the beat or conduct, and if necessary, track the notes on the score with the left hand.

■ = **Tonic keynote** (Clefs and key signatures will be deferred until basic reading skills have been acquired.)

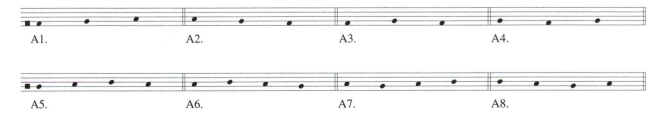

A1.   A2.   A3.   A4.

A5.   A6.   A7.   A8.

(Continued)

A9.   A10.   A11.   A12.

A13.   A14.   A15.   A16.

A17.   A18.   A19.   A20.

A21.   A22.   A23.   A24.

A25.   A26.   A27.   A28.

B. Melodic Patterns: Aural/Oral

1. Listen as your instructor sings a variety of melodic patterns (tonal + rhythm patterns); echo each pattern.[3]

2. Sing the five-note scale using tonal syllables integrating each of the following rhythm patterns. Use a variety of tonic pitches and silently tap the beat, conduct, or use hand signs.

a.

b.

C. Melodic Patterns: Symbolic Association

* Prior to reading from the written notation, scan the melodic pattern for tonal and rhythm patterns.

* Establish tonality by singing a tonic triad arpeggio. If necessary transpose the pattern into a key that provides a comfortable range.

* Set an appropriate tempo, tap, or conduct several preparatory beats and then silently read the pattern on tonal syllables while quietly tapping the beat, conducting or using hand signs.

* Sing the pattern a cappella using tonal syllables while silently tapping the beat, conducting, or using hand signs. If necessary, track the notes on the score with the left hand.

---

[3]Note to instructors: The melodic patterns are found in Section IIIC of this chapter.

■ = Tonic keynote

C1.   C2.   C3.   C4.

C5.   C6.

C7.   C8.

C9.   C10.

C11.   C12.

C13.   C14.

C15.   C16.

IV. Exercises: Diatonic Steps

- Determine the starting tonal syllable and then scan each exercise for tonal and rhythm patterns.
- Establish tonality by singing a tonic chord arpeggio that fits the range of the melody. If necessary transpose the exercise into a key that provides a more comfortable range.
- Set an appropriate tempo, tap or conduct several preparatory beats and then sing the exercise from beginning to end without breaking the tempo.
- After the initial reading, isolate problematic measures and practice them more slowly. Check to make sure that every note is held for its full duration. Sing the exercise again.
- After the exercise has been sung accurately, repeat the exercise—first at a faster tempo and then singing on a neutral syllable. All exercises should be sung a cappella.

■ = Tonic keynote

1.

2.

3.

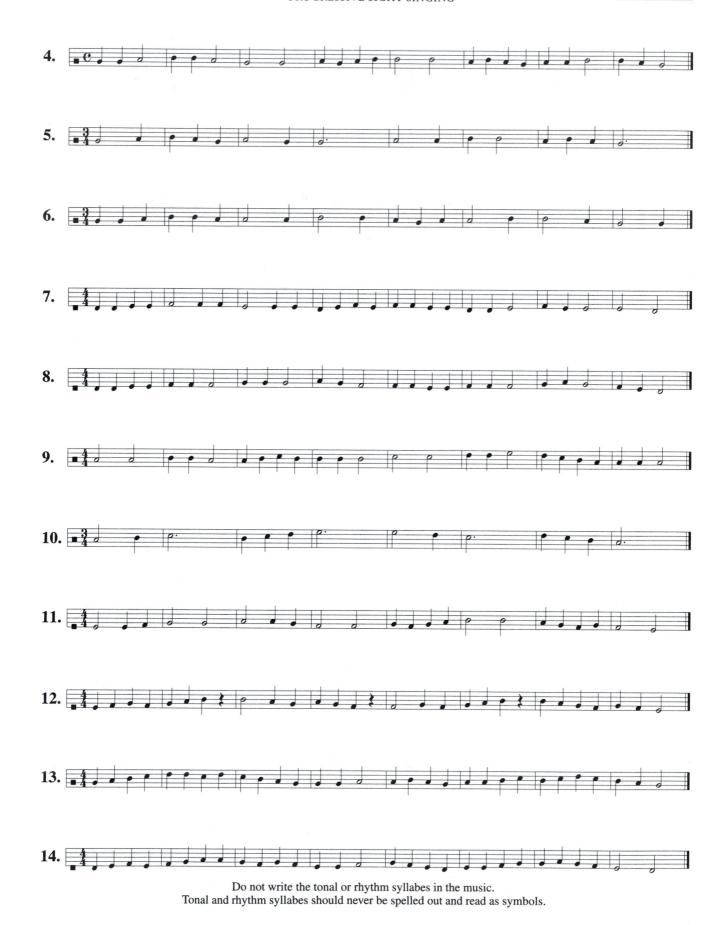

Do not write the tonal or rhythm syllabes in the music.
Tonal and rhythm syllabes should never be spelled out and read as symbols.

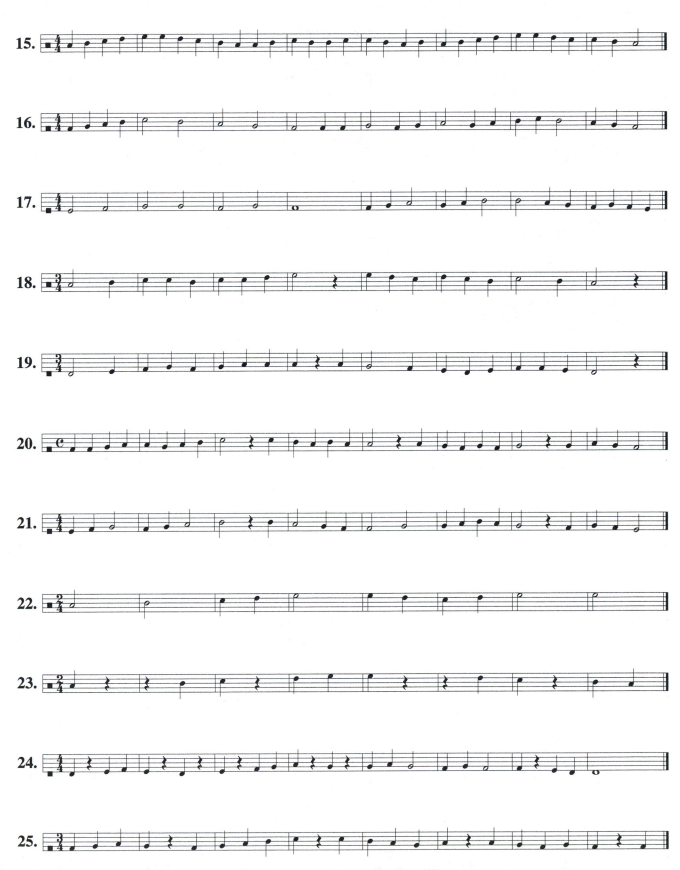

Remember to practice your dictation skills.
See Appendix C for helpful suggestions for tonal and melodic dictation.

Melodies that Begin on a Tone Other than the Tonic

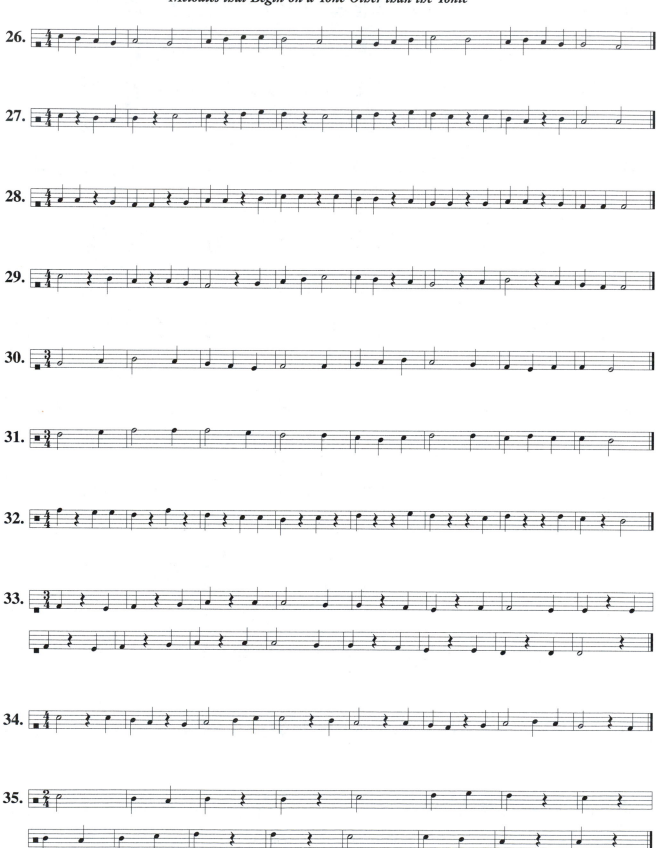

V. Building Aural/Oral Skills: Tonic Triad

Reading Readiness Tonal Patterns
- Listen as your instructor sings a variety of tonal patterns; echo each pattern. The use of hand signs, conducting, or quietly tapping the beat is highly recommended.[4]

Vocal–Pitch Exercises: Sing each of the following drills daily.

Pentachord Scale
- Sing the ascending and descending additive pentachord scale using tonal syllables. Start on various tonics and always maintain an even pulse. Sing the exercise again integrating a variety of rhythm patterns: quarter– quarter–half, and so on.

Intervals
- Sing the ascending intervals from the tonic and the descending intervals from the fifth scale degree. Verbally label the quantity of each interval prior to singing the interval.
- Sing the intervals of a third ascending from the tonic and descending from the fifth scale degree.

Tonic Triad: A tonic triad is three tones arranged in thirds (tertian); root, third, and fifth.
- Perform the tonic triad as a chord (tones are sounded simultaneously creating harmony—the vertical aspect of music) and as an arpeggio (notes of a chord sung one at a time).

Reading Readiness Aural Skills
- Sing the tonal syllables indicated by your instructor either via hand signs or the tonal ladder.
- Listen as your instructor demonstrates two tonal patterns on a neutral syllable. Determine if the patterns were the same, different, or similar.
- Listen as your instructor sings or plays a series of two pitches. Determine the quantity of each interval.
- Listen as your instructor sings a known pattern on a neutral syllable and then "notate" the pattern using the first letter of each tonal syllable or scale degree numbers in graphic form to illustrate the melodic contour of the pattern.

VI. Symbolic Association: Tonic Triad

A combination of three tones arranged in thirds (tertian) and built on the home tone or tonic is called the tonic triad. The lowest note of a triad is called the root, the middle note is called the third of the triad, and the top note is called the fifth of the triad. Notice that on the staff the tonic triad will appear either as space notes or as line notes. When all three tones of the tonic triad are performed simultaneously it is called a chord; when they are performed separately it is an arpeggio.

Tonic Triad   *Tonic Triad*

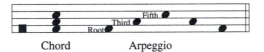   

   Chord   Arpeggio   Chord   Arpeggio

- Determine the position of each triad tone. Write R for the root, 3rd for the third, or 5th for the fifth of the tonic triad. Sing each pattern using tonal syllables.

VII. Tonal and Melodic Patterns: Diatonic Steps, Tonic Triad

A. Tonal Patterns: Symbolic Association

Using tonal syllables, read and sing the written notation of the tonal patterns A1–A40.

* Establish tonality by singing a tonic chord arpeggio. If necessary transpose the pattern into a key that provides a comfortable range.
* Set an appropriate tempo, silently tap or conduct several preparatory beats and then sing the pattern a cappella using tonal syllables with one beat per notehead. Always silently tap the beat, conduct, or use hand signs. If necessary, track the notes on the score with the left hand.

■ = Tonic keynote

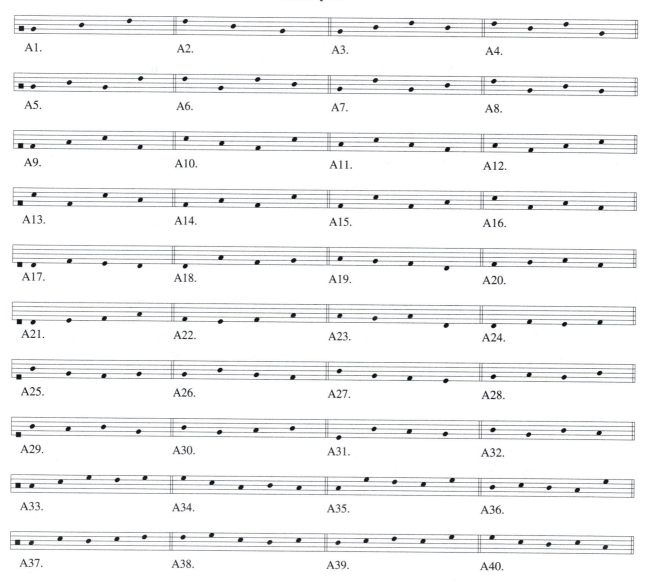

B. Melodic Patterns: Aural/Oral

1. Listen as your instructor sings a variety of melodic patterns (tonal + rhythm patterns); echo each pattern.[5]

---

[5]Note to instructors: The melodic patterns are located in Section VIC of this chapter.

2. Sing the ascending and descending tonic triad using tonal syllables integrating each of the following rhythm patterns. Use a variety of tonic pitches and silently tap the beat or conduct.

C. Melodic Patterns: Symbolic Association

- Prior to reading from the written notation, scan the melodic pattern for tonal and rhythm patterns.
- Establish tonality by singing a tonic triad arpeggio. If necessary transpose the pattern into a key that provides a comfortable range.
- Silently read the pattern using tonal syllables while silently tapping the beat, conducting, or using hand signs.
- Set an appropriate tempo, silently tap or conduct several preparatory beats and then sing the pattern a cappella using tonal syllables. Always silently tap the beat, conduct, or use hand signs.

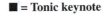

■ = Tonic keynote

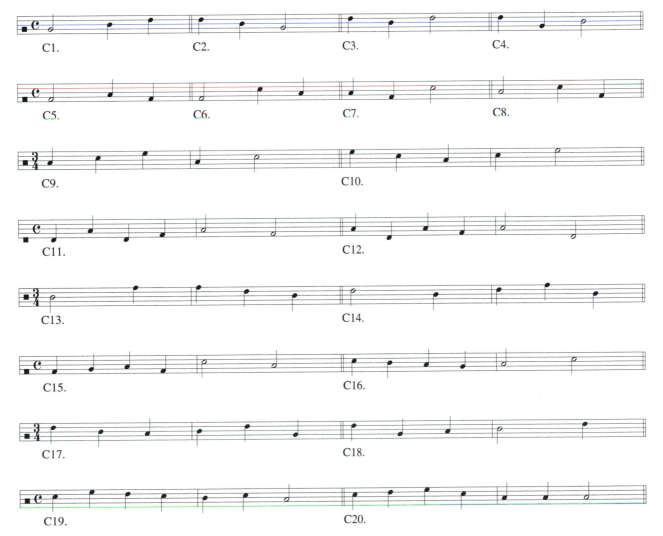

(Continued)

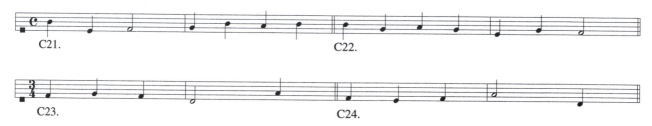

C21.
C22.

C23.
C24.

VIII. Exercises: Diatonic Steps, Tonic Triad

- Determine the starting tonal syllable and then scan each exercise for tonal and rhythm patterns.
- Establish tonality by singing a tonic triad arpeggio that fits the range of the melody. If necessary transpose the exercise into a key that provides a more comfortable range.
- Set an appropriate tempo, establish the meter by quietly tapping the beat for one measure and then sing the exercise from beginning to end without breaking the tempo. Always quietly tap the beat.
- After the initial reading isolate problematic measures and practice them more slowly. Check to make sure that every note is held for its full duration. Sing the exercise again.
- After the exercise has been sung accurately, repeat the exercise, first at a faster tempo and then sing using a neutral syllable while tapping the beat. All exercises should be sung a cappella.

■ = Tonic keynote

1.

2.

3.

4.

5.

6.

7.

Clef Signs

A symbol called a *clef* is placed at the beginning of the staff to indicate the pitch of the notes. Music for high voices and instruments will usually be written in *treble clef* or *G clef*. The symbol is an ornamented letter G used in early notation; the final curve of the symbol indicates the pitch "g" on the second line. Music for low voices and instruments will usually be written in *bass clef* or *F clef*. The symbol is an ornamented letter F used in early notation; the beginning of the curve, guarded by the two dots, indicates the pitch "f" on the fourth line.

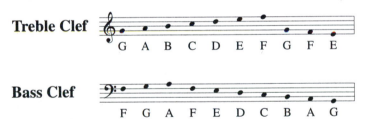

The *musical alphabet* consists of A, B, C, D, E, F, and G. Notice that each line and space represents a basic pitch of the music alphabet. As notes ascend on the staff, the pitch names move forward in the musical alphabet. As notes descend, the pitch names move backward. Avoid the use of old devices like "Every Good Boy Does Fine" as this results in slow readers and defeats the intent of the staff (sequential hierarchy of pitch from low to high). Drill the names of lines and spaces from bottom to top and top to bottom.

■ = **Tonic keynote**

Remember to practice your dictation skills.

Key Signature

A *key signature* is a grouping of the sharps or flats placed at the beginning of a staff to indicate the key or tonality in which the music is written. The rules for finding the starting tonal syllable from a key signature are as follows:

* For sharp key signatures, call the sharp farthest to the right *ti* or 7; assign a tonal syllable to each line and space until the starting pich is reached

* For flat key signatures, call the flat farthest to the right *fa* or 4; assign a tonal syllable to each line and space until the starting pitch is reached.

* If there are no flats or sharps, then C is *do*; assign a tonal syllable to each line and space until the starting pich is reached.

37.

38.

39.

40.

41. French

Canon: 4 voices

42. [1] [2] [3] [4] Traditional

Hocket

Related to the Latin word *hoquetus* meaning "hiccup," a *hocket* is a rhythmic device in which a single melody is split between two voices; each voice sings only short fragments of the melody. Sing each part and then divide the class into two groups and perform the two parts simultaneously. The challenge of performing such works is to listen to each other and ensure that the melody sounds seamless as it moves from one part to the other.

43.

Chapter 2

Diatonic Steps and Tonic Triad in the Major Scale; Simple Meters, Undivided Beat

I. Building Aural/Oral Skills: Diatonic Steps

Reading Readiness Tonal Patterns
- Listen as your instructor sings a variety of tonal patterns; echo each pattern, use hand signs, tap the beat, or conduct.[1]

Vocal–Pitch Exercises: Sing each of the following drills daily.

Major Scale: A *major scale* is an organized series of eight pitches; the pitches employed within a given scale are *diatonic*; pitches outside a scale are *nondiatonic*
- Basic: Sing the major scale using all quarter notes or a half–quarter–quarter rhythm pattern.
  - Solfège: do – re – mi – fa – so – la – ti – do' – ti – la – so – fa – mi – re – do
  - Numbers: 1 – 2 – 3 – 4 – 5 – 6 – 7 – 1' – 7 – 6 – 5 – 4 – 3 – 2 – 1
- Extended: Sing the extended major scale using all quarter notes or a quarter—quarter—half rhythm pattern.
  - Solfège: do – re – mi – fa – so – la – ti – do' – re' – do' – ti – la – so – fa – mi – re – do – ti₁ – la₁ – so₁ – la₁ – ti₁ – do
  - Numbers: 1 – 2 – 3 – 4 – 5 – 6 – 7 – 1' – 2' – 1' – 7 – 6 – 5 – 4 – 3 – 2 – 1 – 7₁ – 6₁ – 5₁ – 6₁ – 7₁ – 1
- Additive: Sing the additive major scale using a half—quarter—quarter or quarter—quarter—half rhythm pattern.
  - Solfège:
    Ascending: do – re – do; do – re – mi – re – do; do – re – mi – fa – mi – re – do; etc.
    Descending: do' – ti – do'; do' – ti – la – ti – do'; do' – ti – la – so – la – ti – do'; etc.
  - Numbers:
    Ascending: 1 – 2 – 1; 1 – 2 – 3 – 2 – 1; 1 – 2 – 3 – 4 – 3 – 2 – 1; etc.
    Descending: 1' – 7 – 1'; 1' – 7 – 6 – 7 – 1'; 1' – 7 – 6 – 5 – 6 – 7 – 1'; etc.

---

[1]Note to instructors: The tonal patterns are found in Section III in this chapter.

- Pentachord Major Scale: Sing the pentachord major scale using a variety of rhythm patterns.

	Solfège	Numbers
↑	ti – do' – re' – mi' – fa' – mi' – re' – do' – ti – do'	7 – 1' – 2' – 3' – 4' – 3' – 2' – 1' – 7 – 1'
	la – ti – do' – re' – mi' – re'– do' – ti – la;	6 – 7 – 1' – 2' – 3' – 2' – 1' – 7 – 6;
	so – la – ti – do' – re' – do' – ti – la – so;	5 – 6 – 7 – 1' – 2' – 1' – 7 – 6 – 5;
	fa – so – la – ti – do' – ti – la – so – fa;	4 – 5 – 6 – 7 – 1' – 7 – 6 – 5 – 4;
	mi – fa – so – la – ti – la – so – fa – mi;	3 – 4 – 5 – 6 – 7 – 6 – 5 – 4 – 3;
	re – mi – fa – so – la – so – fa – mi – re;	2 – 3 – 4 – 5 – 6 – 5 – 4 – 3 – 2;
start	do – re – mi – fa – so – fa – mi – re – do;	1 – 2 – 3 – 4 – 5 – 4 – 3 – 2 – 1;

Tonic Triad in the Major Scale

- Root Position: Sing the tonic chord as an arpeggio using a variety of rhythm patterns.
  Solfège: do – mi – so – mi – do   Numbers: 1 – 3 – 5 – 3 – 1

- Sing the extended arpeggio using a variety of rhythm patterns.
  Solfège: do – mi – so – do' – so – mi – do – so, – do
  Numbers: 1 – 3 – 5 – 1' – 5 – 3 – 1 – 5, – 1

Intervals from Tonic in the Major Scale

- Sing the ascending and descending intervals from the tonic.

Solfège	Numbers
Ascending: do – do; do – re; do – mi; do – fa; do – so; etc.	Ascending: 1 – 1; 1 – 2; 1 – 3; 1 – 4; 1 – 5; 1 – 6; etc.
Descending: do' – do'; do' – ti; do' – la; do' – so; do' – fa; etc.	Descending: 1' – 1'; 1' – 7; 1' – 6; 1' – 5; 1' – 4; etc.

- Verbally label the quantity of each interval prior to singing the interval. When two pitches are identical, the interval is termed a *unison* or *prime*; when two pitches are identical but eight tones apart, the interval is termed an *octave* (*do* to *do'* or 1 to 1').
  Example: unison—do-do; 2—do-re; 3—do-mi; 4—do-fa; 5—do-so; 6—do-la; 7—do-ti; octave—do-do'

Intervals of a Third in the Major Scale

- Preparation Exercise

Solfège	Numbers
Ascending: do – re – mi – do – mi; re – mi – fa – re – fa; mi – fa – so – mi – so; fa – so – la – fa – la; so – la – ti – so – ti; la – ti – do' – la – do' ; ti – do' – re' – ti – re' ; do'	Ascending: 1 – 2 – 3 – 1 – 3; 2 – 3 – 4 – 2 – 4; 3 – 4 – 5 – 3 – 5; 4 – 5 – 6 – 4 – 6; 5 – 6 – 7 – 5 – 7; 6 – 7 – 1' – 6 – 1' ; 7 – 1' – 2' – 7 – 2' ; 1'
Descending: do' – ti – la – do' – la; ti – la – so – ti – so; la – so – fa – la – fa; so – fa – mi – so – mi; fa – mi – re – fa – re; mi – re – do – mi – do; re – do – ti, – re – ti, ; do	Descending: 1'–7 – 6 – 1'– 6; 7 – 6 – 5 – 7 – 5; 6 – 5 – 4 – 6 – 4; 5 – 4 – 3 – 5 – 3; 4 – 3 – 2 – 4 – 2; 3 – 2 – 1 – 3 – 1; 2 – 1 – 7, – 2 – 7, ; 1

- Thirds Only

Solfège	Numbers
Ascending: do–mi; re–fa; mi–so; fa–la; so–ti; la–do' ; ti–re' ; do'	Ascending: 1–3; 2–4; 3–5; 4–6; 5–7; 6–1'; 7–2' – 1'
Descending: do' –la; ti–so; la–fa; so–mi; fa–re; mi–do; re–ti,; do	Descending: 1' –6; 7–5; 6–4; 5–3; 4–2; 3–1; 2–7, – 1

Reading Readiness Aural Skills
- Sing the tonal syllables indicated by your instructor either via hand signs or the tonal ladder.
- Listen as your instructor sings or plays a series of two pitches. Determine the quantity of each interval.
- Listen as your instructor sings a known pattern on a neutral syllable and then "notate" the pattern using the first letter of each tonal syllable or scale degree number in graphic form to illustrate the melodic contour of the pattern.

II. Symbolic Association: Diatonic Steps

Major Scale: The notes of the scales are numbered (counting up from the tonic); these numbers are called *scale degrees* and show the relationship between the tonic and another given pitch in the scale. Each degree of the scale also has a specific name describing its function in melodies and harmonies.

Number	Solfège	Scale Tone Names	Scale Degree
1'	do'	tonic	8th scale degree or octave
7	ti	leading tone	7th scale degree
6	la	submediant	6th scale degree
5	so	dominant	5th scale degree
4	fa	subdominant	4th scale degree
3	mi	mediant	3rd scale degree
2	re	supertonic	2nd scale degree
1	do	tonic	1st scale degree

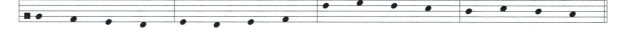

Degree #	1st	2nd	3rd	4th	5th	6th	7th	8th or octave
Solfège	do	re	mi	fa	so	la	ti	do'
Number	1	2	3	4	5	6	7	1'
Name	tonic	supertonic	mediant	subdominant	dominant	submediant	leading tone	tonic

- Consult the tonic keynote and then write (a) the scale degree number, (b) the scale degree name, and (c) the tonal syllable for each of the notes. Sing each pattern using tonal syllables

Degree #

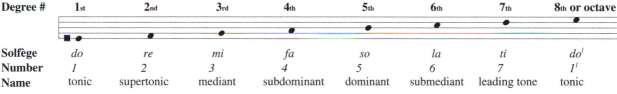

Syllable
Name

Intervals:
- Sing each of the following intervals using tonal syllables.

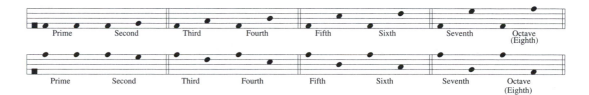

• Determine the quantity (number) of each of the following intervals. Remember to count both tones and the lines and spaces spanned by the two tones. Sing each of the following intervals using tonal syllables.

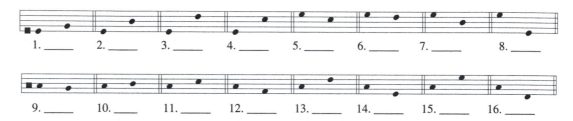

1. ____   2. ____   3. ____   4. ____   5. ____   6. ____   7. ____   8. ____

9. ____   10. ____   11. ____   12. ____   13. ____   14. ____   15. ____   16. ____

III. Tonal and Melodic Patterns: Diatonic Steps

A. Tonal Patterns: Symbolic Association

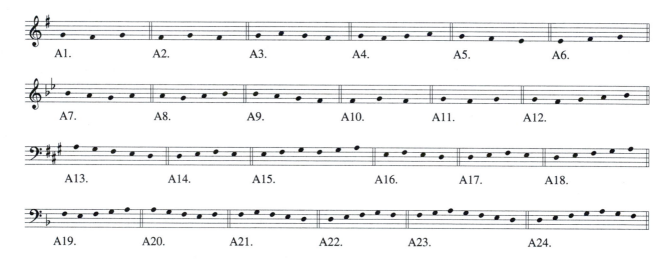

A1.   A2.   A3.   A4.   A5.   A6.

A7.   A8.   A9.   A10.   A11.   A12.

A13.   A14.   A15.   A16.   A17.   A18.

A19.   A20.   A21.   A22.   A23.   A24.

B. Melodic Patterns: Aural/Oral

1. Listen as your instructor strings a variety of melodic patterns (tonal + rhythm patterns); echo pattern.[2]

2. Sing the extended major scale using tonal syllables and integrate the following rhythms. Use a variety of tonic piches and remember to silently tap the beat or conduct.

a.

b.

_____

[2]Note to instructors: The melodic patterns are found in Section IIIC of this chapter.

C. Melodic Patterns: Symbolic Association

IV. Exercises: Diatonic Steps

Ledger Lines

The staff may be extended with ledger lines, short horizontal lines placed above or belove the staff. Both the ledger lines and the spaces between the lines represent piches. <u>Notice</u> that notes in spaces immediately below or above the staff do not require ledger lines and the ledger lines are never connected to one another.

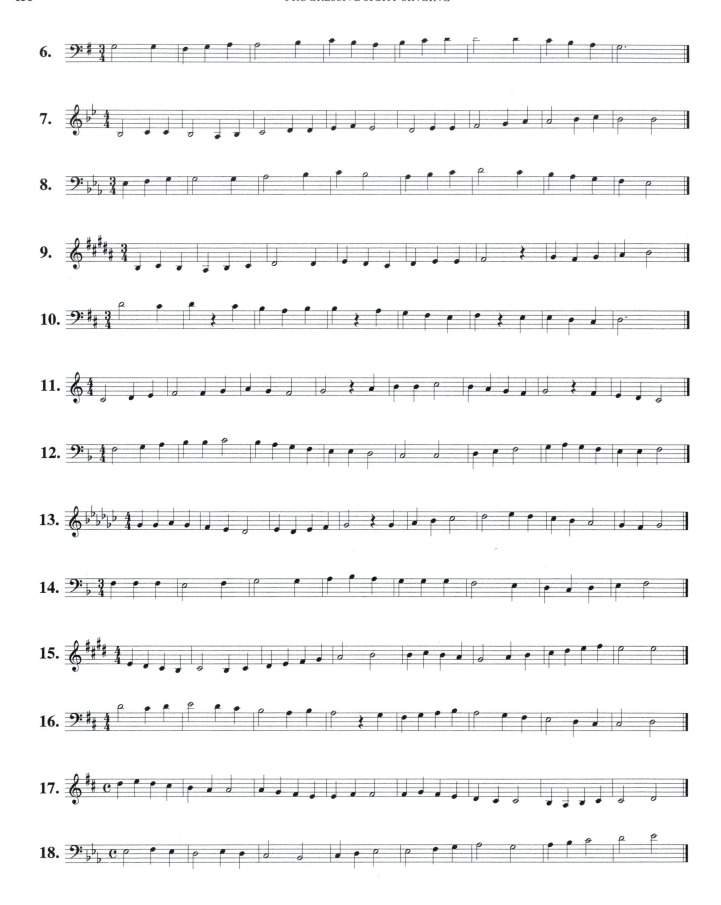

V. Building Aural/Oral Skills: Diatonic Steps, Tonic Triad

Reading Readiness Tonal Patterns

- Listen as your instructor sings a variety of tonal patterns; echo each pattern, use hand signs, tap the beat, or conduct.[3]

Vocal–Pitch Exercises: Sing each of the following drills daily.

Major Scale: A major scale is a series of seven tones in a specific pattern of whole and half steps. The smallest distance between two tones is a *half step* or *semi-tone*. Half steps occur between mi – fa (3–4) and ti – do (7–1'). Two half steps combine to form a *whole step*. Whole steps occur between do – re – mi (1 – 2 – 3) and fa – so – la – ti (4 – 5 – 6 – 7). The major scale pattern is whole, whole, half, whole, whole, whole, half.

- Sing the basic major scale. Listen for the half steps and whole steps.
- Sing the extended major scale using all quarter notes or a quarter–quarter–half rhythm pattern.

---

[3]Note to instructors: The tonal patterns are found in Section VIIA of this chapter.

- Sing the additive major scale using a half–quarter–quarter or quarter–quarter–half rhythm pattern.
- Sing the pentachord major scale using a variety of rhythm patterns.

Root-Position and Inverted Tonic Triads

When the root of a triad is the lowest-sounding pitch, the triad is in root position; when the third of the triad is the lowest-sounding pitch, the triad is in first inversion; when the fifth is the lowest-sounding pitch, the triad is in second inversion.

- Sing each of the following as an arpeggio (one tone at a time) and as a chord (three notes simultaneously).

a. Root Position:	b. First inversion:	c. Second inversion:
• do – mi – so – mi – do	• mi – so – do' – so – mi	• so – do' – mi' – do' – so
• 1 – 3 – 5 – 3 – 1	• 3 – 5 – 1' – 5 – 3	• 5 – 1' – 3' – 1' – 5

- Practice the extended arpeggio using a variety of rhythm patterns.

Intervals from Tonic in the Major Scale

- Verbally label the quantity of each ascending and descending intervals from the tonic and then sing the interval.
- Sing the intervals using a variety of rhythm patterns.

With enough drill, each interval should be automatically recognized via the connection between the sound and the tonal syllables.

Intervals of a Third in the Major Scale

- Sing the ascending and descending thirds in a major scale.

Intervals of a Fourth in the Major Scale

- Sing the ascending and descending fourths in a major scale.

Solfège	Numbers
Ascending: do–fa; re–so; mi–la; fa–ti; so–do'; la–re'; ti–mi'; do'	Ascending: 1–4; 2–5; 3–6; 4–7; 5–1'; 6–2'; 7–2'–1'
Descending: do'–so; ti–fa; la–mi; so–re; fa–re; mi–ti₁; re–la₁; do	Descending: 1'–5; 7–4; 6–3; 5–2; 4–1; 3–7₁; 2–6₁–1

Reading Readiness Aural Skills

- Sing the tonal syllables indicated by your instructor either via hand signs or the tonal ladder.
- Listen as your instructor demonstrates two tonal patterns on a neutral syllable. Determine if the patterns were the same, different, or similar.
- Listen as two pitches are performed and then determine the quantity of the interval.
- Listen as a succession of eight pitches, ascending or descending, are performed and then determine if they form a major scale.
- Listen as three pitches are performed in either ascending or descending order and then determine if they form a major tonic triad.
- Listen as your instructor sings a known pattern on a neutral syllable and then "notate" the pattern.

VI. Symbolic Association: Diatonic Steps, Tonic Triad

Major Key Signatures

To determine the name of the major key: (a) call the sharp farthest to the right *ti* or 7, assign a tonal syllable to each line and space until *do* or 1 is reached; determine the letter name of *do* or 1; (b) call the flat farthest to the right *fa* or 4; assign a tonal syllable to each line and space until *do* or 1 is reached; determine the letter name of *do* or 1; or (c) if there are no flats or sharps, then C is *do* or 1.

- For each key signature, (a) determine the major key name and (b) notate the tonic triad.

1. <u>G</u> Major   2. __ Major   3. __ Major   4. __ Major   5. __ Major   6. __ Major   7. __ Major

8. __ Major   9. __ Major   10. __ Major   11. __ Major   12. __ Major   13. __ Major   14. __ Major

Scale Degrees Numbers and Names

- Consult the key signature, locate the tonic keynote and then write (a) the scale degree number, (b) the scale degree name, and (c) the tonal syllable for each of the notes. Sing each of the patterns using tonal syllables.

Degree #

Syllable

Name

Intervals from Tonic in the Major Scale

- Consult the key signature, locate the tonic keynote and then determine the quantity (number) of each of the following intervals. Sing each of the intervals using tonal syllables.

1. ____   2. ____   3. ____   4. ____   5. ____   6. ____   7. ____   8. ____

Tonic Triad: A triad is a group of three pitches termed tertian, built of superimposed thirds. Triads are named according to its lowest pitch or root; hence, a triad built on the tonic or first scale degree is referred to as the tonic triad. The triad's other pitches are its third and its fifth, terms that correspond to the sizes of the intervals these pitches form with the root.

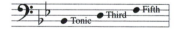

Harmonic Triad

The three tones of a triad sound simultaneously and are represented vertically on the staff.

Melodic Triad

The three tones sound separately and occur one after the other on the staff, ascending, descending, or mixed.

Inversion of Triads: When the root of a triad is the lowest-sounding pitch, the triad is in root position; when the third of the triad is the lowest-sounding pitch, the triad is in first inversion; when the fifth of the triad is the lowest-sounding pitch, the triad is in second inversion. Sing each of the patterns using tonal syllables.

Root Position

Tonic of the triad is the lowest-sounding pitch

First Inversion

Third of the triad is the lowest-sounding pitch

Second Inversion

Fifth of the triad is the lowest-sounding pitch

- Consult the key signature then (a) draw a square around the tonic keynote, (b) draw a triangle around the lowest sounding pitch, (c) circle the position or inversion of the triad, and (d) circle the type of triad: harmonic or melodic. Sing each of the triads using tonal syllables.

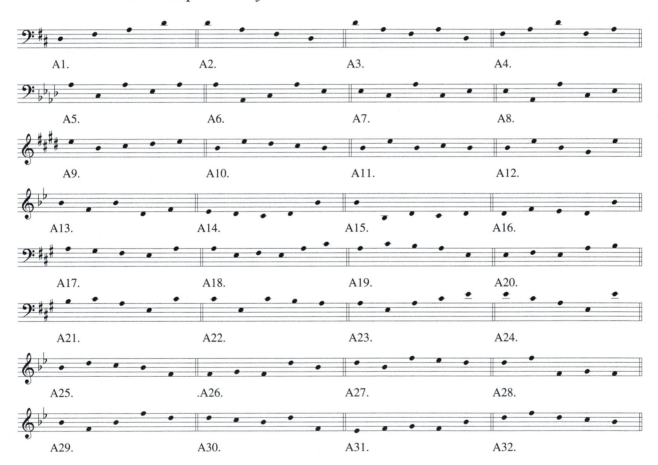

VII. Tonal and Melodic Patterns: Diatonic Steps, Tonic Triad

A. Tonal patterns: Symbolic Association

B. Melodic Patterns: Aural/Oral

Listen as your instructor sings a variety of melodic patterns; echo each pattern.[4]

---

[4]Note to instructors: The melodic patterns are found in Section VIIC of this chapter

C. Melodic Patterns: Symbolic Association

VIII. Exercises: Diatonic Steps, Tonic Triad

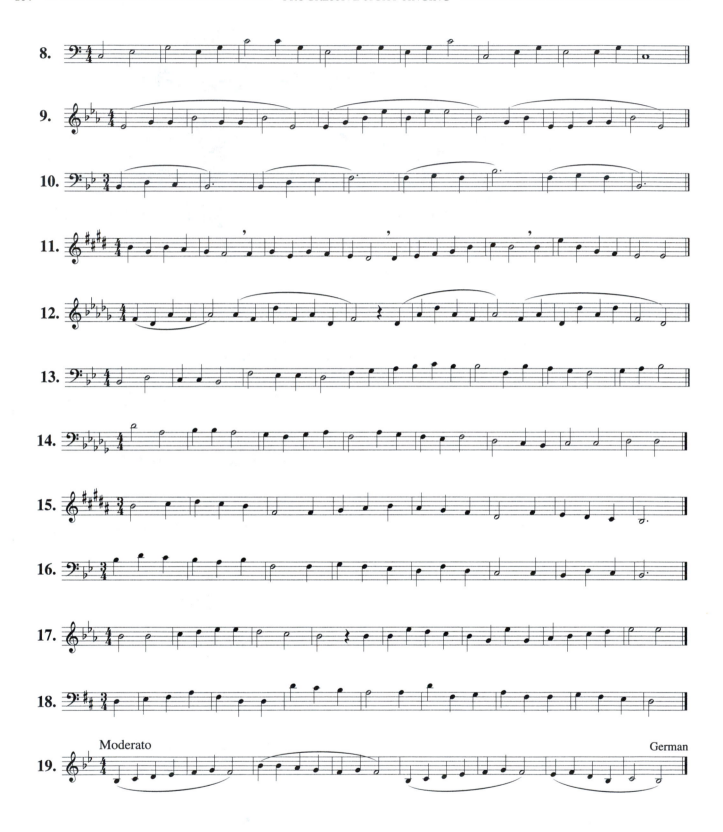

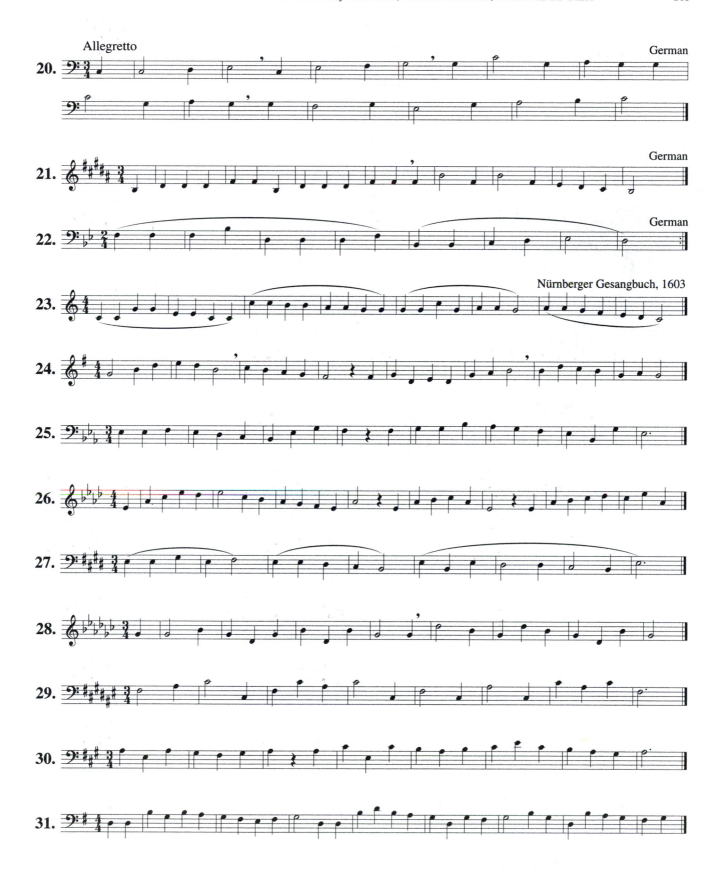

Chapter 3
Diatonic Steps and Tonic Triad in the Natural Minor Scale; Simple Meters, Undivided Beat

I. Building Aural/Oral Skills: Diatonic Steps, Tonic Triad

Reading Readiness Tonal Patterns
- Listen as your instructor sings a variety of tonal patterns; echo each pattern, use hand signs and quietly tap the beat.[1]

Vocal–Pitch Exercises: Sing each of the following drills daily using the tonal syllables designated by your instructor.[2]

Natural Minor Scale: A *natural minor scale* is an organized series of eight pitches where the whole and half step pattern is w-h-w-w-h-w-w. Unlike the major scale, the half steps fall between the 2nd and 3rd, and 5th and 6th scale degrees.

- Basic Natural Minor Scale: Sing the scale using a variety of rhythm patterns.
  - La-Based Solfège: la – ti – do – re – mi – fa – so – la' – so – fa – mi – re – do – ti – la
  - Do-Based Solfège: do – re – me – fa – so – le – te – do' – te – le – so – fa – me – re – do
  - Numbers: $1 - 2 - \flat3 - 4 - 5 - \flat6 - \flat7 - 1' - \flat7 - \flat6 - 5 - 4 - \flat3 - 2 - 1$

- Extended Natural Minor Scale: Sing the scale using a variety of rhythm patterns.
  - La-Based Solfège: la – ti – do – re – mi – fa – so – la' – ti'– la'– so – fa – mi – re – do – ti – la – so, – fa, – mi,, – fa, – so, – la
  - Do-Based Solfège: do – re – me – fa – so – le– te – do'– re'– do'– te – le – so – fa – me – re – do– te, – le, – so, – le, – te, – do
  - Numbers: $1 - 2 - \flat3 - 4 - 5 - \flat6 - \flat7 - 1' - 2' - 1' - \flat7 - \flat6 - 5 - 4 - \flat3 - 2 - 1 - \flat7, - \flat6, - 5, - \flat6, - \flat7, - 1$

- Additive Natural Minor Scale: Sing the scale using a variety of rhythm patterns.
  - La-Based Solfège: Ascending: la – ti – la; la – ti – do – ti – la; la – ti – do – re – do – ti – la; etc.

    Descending: la' – so – la'; la' – so – fa – so – la'; la' – so – fa – mi – fa – so – la'; etc.
  - Do-Based Solfège: Ascending: do – re – do; do – re – me – re – do; do – re – me – fa – me – re – do; etc.

    Descending: do' – te – do'; do' – te – le – te – do'; do' – te – le – so – le – te – do'; etc.
  - Numbers: Ascending: $1 - 2 - 1$; $1 - 2 - \flat3 - 2 - 1$; $1 - 2 - \flat3 - 4 - \flat3 - 2 - 1$; etc.

    Descending: $1' - \flat7 - 1'$; $1' - \flat7 - \flat6 - \flat7 - 1'$; $1' - \flat7 - \flat6 - 5 - \flat6 - \flat7 - 1'$; etc.

---

[1]Note to instructors: The tonal patterns are found in Section III of this chapter, and should be taught by rote using the two-step process.
[2]A description of tonal syllable systems are included in Appendix B.

- Pentachord Natural Minor Scale: Sing the scale using a variety of rhythm patterns.

Do Minor Solfège	La Minor Solfège	Numbers
te– do' – re' – me'– fa' – me'– re'– do'– te – do	so – la' – ti' – do' – re'– do'– ti'– la' – so – la	♭7 – 1'– 2' – ♭3'– 4'– ♭3'– 2'– 1'–♭7 - 1'
le – te– do' – re' – me'– re' – do' – te – le	fa – so – la' – ti' – do' – ti' – la' – so – fa	♭6 – ♭7 – 1' – 2' – ♭3' – 2' – 1' – ♭7 – ♭6
so – le – te – do' – re' – do' – te – le – so	mi – fa – so – la' – ti' – la' – so – fa – mi	5 – ♭6 – ♭7 – 1' – 2' – 1' – ♭7 – ♭6 – 5
fa – so – le – te – do' – te – le – so – fa	re – mi – fa – so – la' – so – fa – mi – re	4 – 5 – ♭6 – ♭7 – 1' – ♭7 – ♭6 – 5 – 4
me – fa – so – le – te – le – so – fa – me	do – re – mi – fa – so – fa – mi – re – do	♭3 – 4 – 5 – ♭6 – ♭7 – ♭6 – 5 – 4 – ♭3
re – me – fa – so – le – so – fa – me – re	ti – do – re – mi – fa – mi – re – do – ti	2 – ♭3 – 4 – 5 – ♭6 – 5 – 4 – ♭3 – 2
do – re – me – fa – so – fa – me – re – do	la – ti – do – re – mi – re – do – ti – la	1 – 2 – ♭3 – 4 – 5 – 4 – ♭3 – 2 – 1

(start / arrow indicating upward direction)

Tonic Triad in Minor

- Root Position and Inverted Tonic Triad: Sing each of the following as an arpeggio and as a chord.

	a. Root Position:	b. First Inversion:	c. Second Inversion:
La-Based Solfège	• la – do – mi – do – la	• do – mi – la' – mi – do	• mi – la' – do' – la' – mi
Do-Based Solfège	• do – me – so – me – do	• me – so – do' – so – me	• so – do' – me' – do' – so
Numbers	• 1 – ♭3 – 5 – ♭3 – 1	• ♭3 – 5 – 1' – 5 – ♭3	• 5 – 1' – ♭3' – 1' – 5

- Extended Arpeggio: Sing the extended arpeggio using a variety of rhythm patterns.

La-Based Solfège	la – do – mi – la' – mi – do – la – mi₁ – la
Do-Based Solfège	do – me – so – do' – so – me – do – so₁ – do
Numbers	1 – ♭3 – 5 – 1' – 5 – ♭3 – 1 – 5₁ – 1

Intervals from Tonic in the Natural Minor Scale

- Verbally label the quantity of the ascending and descending intervals from the tonic and then sing the intervals.

La-Based Solfège:

- Ascending: prime: la-la; 2nd: la-ti; 3rd: la-do; 4th: la-re; 5th: la-mi; 6th: la-fa; 7th: la-so; octave: la-la'
- Descending: prime: la'-la'; 2nd: la'-so; 3rd: la'-fa; 4th: la'-mi; 5th: la'-re; 6th: la'-do; 7th: la'-ti; octave: la'-la

Do Based Solfège:

- Ascending: prime: do-do; 2nd: do-re; 3rd: do-me; 4th: do-fa; 5th: do-so; 6th: do-le; 7th: do-te; octave: do-do'
- Descending: prime: do'-do'; 2nd: do'-te; 3rd: do'-le; 4th: do'-so; 5th: do'-fa; 6th: do'-me; 7th: do'-re; octave: do'-do

Numbers:

- Ascending: prime: 1 – 1; 2nd: 1 – 2; 3rd: 1 – ♭3; 4th: 1 – 4; 5th: 1 – 5; 6th: 1 – ♭6; 7th: 1 – ♭7; octave: 1 – 1'
- Descending: prime: 1' – 1'; 2nd: 1' – ♭7; 3rd: 1' – ♭6; 4th: 1' – 5; 5th: 1' – 4; 6th: 1' –♭3; 7th: 1' – 2; octave: 1' – 1

Intervals of a Third in the Natural Minor Scale

- Sing the ascending and descending thirds in a natural minor scale.

	Ascending	Descending
La-Based Solfège	la-do; ti-re; do-mi; re-fa; mi-so; fa-la'; so-ti'-la'	la'-fa; so-mi; fa-re; mi-do; re-ti; do-la; ti–so₁ -la
Do-Based Solfège	do-me; re-fa; me-so; fa-le; so-te; le-do'; te-re'-do'	do'-le; te-so; le-fa; so-me; fa-re; me-do; re-te₁-do
Numbers	1-♭3; 2-4; ♭3-5; 4-♭6; 5-♭7; ♭6-1'; ♭7-2'-1'	1'-♭6; ♭7-5; ♭6-4; 5-♭3; 4-2; ♭3-1; 2-♭7₁ ; 1

Intervals of a Fourth in the Natural Minor Scale

- Sing the ascending and descending fourths in a natural minor scale.

	Ascending	Descending
La-Based Solfège	la – re; ti – mi; do – fa; re – so; mi – la; fa – ti'; so – do'; la'	la' – mi; so – re; fa – do; mi – ti; re – la; do – so,; ti – fa,; la
Do-Based Solfège	do – fa; re – so; me – le; fa – te; so – do; le – re'; te – fa'; do'	do' – so; te – fa; le – me; so – re; fa – do; me – te; re – la; do
Numbers	1 – 4; 2 – 5; ♭3 – ♭6; 4 – ♭7; 5 – 1'; ♭6 – 2'; ♭7 – ♭3'; 1'	1' – 5; ♭7 – 4; ♭6 – ♭3; 5 – 2; 4 – 1; ♭3 – ♭7,; 2 – ♭6,; 1 – 5,; 1

Reading Readiness Aural Skills

- Sing the tonal syllables indicated by your instructor either via hand signs or the tonal ladder.
- Listen as two pitches are performed and then determine the quantity of the interval.
- Listen as your instructor plays or sings scales, chords, and melodies in major and minor tonalities. Determine the mode (major or minor) of each example.
- Listen as your instructor sings a known pattern on a neutral syllable and then "notate" the pattern.

II. Symbolic Association: Diatonic Steps, Tonic Triad

Minor Key Signatures

To determine minor key name: (a) call the sharp farthest to the right *ti* or 7, assign a tonal syllable to each line and space until *la* or 6 is reached; determine the letter name of *la* or 6; (b) call the flat farthest to the right *fa* or 4, assign a tonal syllable to each line and space until *la* or 6 is reached; determine the letter name of *la* or 6; (c) if there are no flats or sharps, then C is *do* or 1— find and name *la* or 6.

- For each key signature, (a) determine the minor key name and (b) notate the tonic triad.

1. e minor   2. ___minor   3. ___minor   4. ___minor   5. ___minor   6. ___minor   7. ___minor

8. ___minor 9. ___minor 10. ___minor   11. ___minor   12. ___minor   13. ___minor   14. ___minor

Natural Minor Scale: The scale degree names in the minor scale are the same as in the major scale except for the seventh scale degree. In major the seventh scale degree is a leading tone, a half step below the tonic (ti-do' or 7-1'). In the natural minor, scale degree seven is a whole step below the tonic (so-la' or ♭7-1') and is called a *subtonic*.

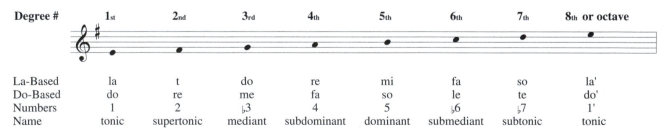

Degree #	1st	2nd	3rd	4th	5th	6th	7th	8th or octave
La-Based	la	t	do	re	mi	fa	so	la'
Do-Based	do	re	me	fa	so	le	te	do'
Numbers	1	2	♭3	4	5	♭6	♭7	1'
Name	tonic	supertonic	mediant	subdominant	dominant	submediant	subtonic	tonic

- Label the scale degree name and number prior to singing each note of the natural minor scale on tonal syllables.

- Consult the key signature and determine the tonic keynote. Write (a) the scale degree number, (b) the scale degree name, and (c) the tonal syllable for each of the notes. Sing each of the patterns using tonal syllables.

Degree #

A.

Syllable Name

Degree #

B.

Syllable Name

Intervals from Tonic in the Natural Minor Scale
- Sing each of the following intervals using tonal syllables.

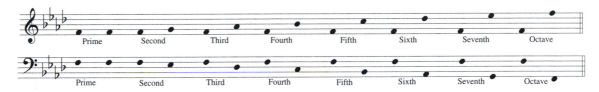

- (a) Determine the quantity (number) of each of the following intervals. Remember to count both tones and the lines and spaces spanned by the two tones. (b) Using tonal syllables sing each of the following intervals.

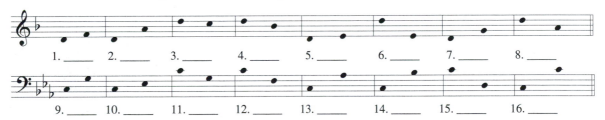

1. ____ 2. ____ 3. ____ 4. ____ 5. ____ 6. ____ 7. ____ 8. ____

9. ____ 10. ____ 11. ____ 12. ____ 13. ____ 14. ____ 15. ____ 16. ____

Tonic Triad

Harmonic Triad—three tones
sounded simultaneously

Melodic Triad—three tones
sound separately

Inversion of Triads
- Sing each of the patterns using tonal syllables.

Root Position
Tonic is lowest-sounding pitch

First Inversion
Third is lowest-sounding pitch

Second Inversion
Fifth is lowest-sounding pitch

- Consult the key signature then (a) draw a square around the tonic keynote, (b) draw a triangle around the lowest sounding pitch, (c) circle the position or inversion of the triad, and (d) circle the type of triad.

1.   Root   1st   2nd   2.   Root   1st   2nd   3.   Root   1st   2nd   4.   Root   1st   2nd

Harmonic or Melodic Triad   Harmonic or Melodic Triad   Harmonic or Melodic Triad   Harmonic or Melodic Triad

III. Tonal and Melodic Patterns: Diatonic Steps, Tonic Triad

A. Tonal Patterns: Symbolic Association

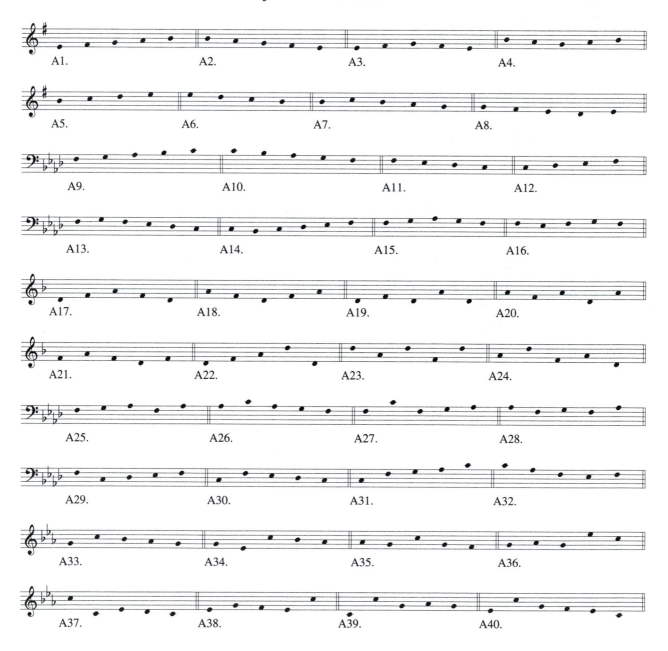

A1.   A2.   A3.   A4.

A5.   A6.   A7.   A8.

A9.   A10.   A11.   A12.

A13.   A14.   A15.   A16.

A17.   A18.   A19.   A20.

A21.   A22.   A23.   A24.

A25.   A26.   A27.   A28.

A29.   A30.   A31.   A32.

A33.   A34.   A35.   A36.

A37.   A38.   A39.   A40.

B. Melodic Patterns: Aural/Oral

1. Listen as your instructor sings a variety of melodic patterns; echo each pattern.[3]
2. Sing the extended major scale on tonal syllables and integrate the following rhythms. Use a variety of tonic pitches and remember to silently tap the beat, conduct, or use hand signs.

C. Melodic Patterns: Symbolic Association

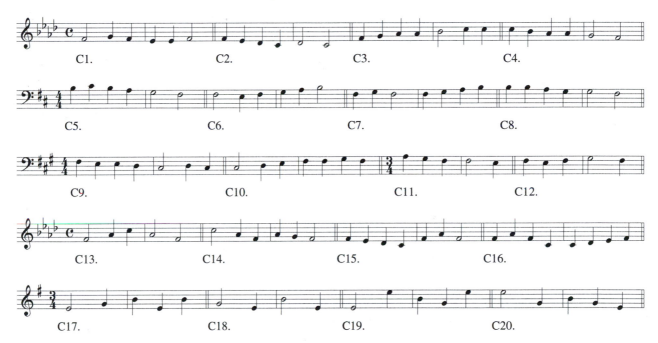

IV. Exercises: Diatonic Steps, Tonic Triad

---

[3]Note to instructors: The melodic patterns are found in Section IIIC of this chapter.

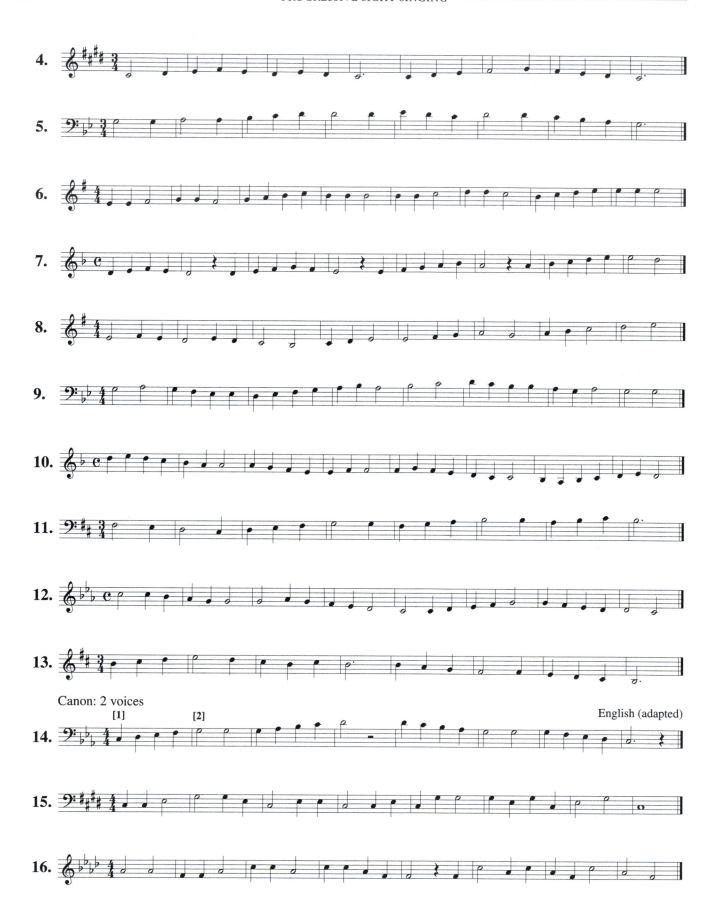

Canon: 2 voices

[1]   [2]

English (adapted)

Remember to practice your dictation skills.

Chapter 4
Diatonic Steps and Tonic Triad in the Major Scale; Simple Meters, Divided Beat

I. Integrating Rhythm and Tonal Skills: Major Mode

Reading Readiness Melodic Patterns

* Listen as your instructor sings a variety of melodic patterns; echo each pattern.[1]

Major Scale: an organized series of eight pitches (w-w-h-w-w-w-h)

* Sing the extended major scale integrating repeated eighth notes (example A) and moving eighth notes (example B).

Intervals from Tonic in the Major Scale: There are four perfect and four major/minor intervals; all of them can be located from the tonic in any major scale. Unisons (prime), fourth, fifths, and octaves belong to the group of intervals called *perfect*; seconds, thirds, sixths, and sevenths belong to the group of intervals that are major in ascending intervals from *do* or 1 (example A) and minor in descending intervals from *do'* or 1' (example B).

* Verbally label the **quality** and **quantity** of each ascending and descending interval from the tonic in a major tonality prior to singing the intervals using tonal syllables. All ascending intervals from do (1) are either major or perfect (example A) and all descending intervals from *do'* (1') are minor or perfect (example B). The differences in these qualities are not apparent from the staff notation.

Major is indicated by an upper case (M) and a lower case (m) indicates minor.

---

[1]Note to instructors: The melodic patterns are found in Section III of this chapter.

178

Vocal–Pitch Exercises: Sing each of the following drills daily.

Minor Mode	Major Mode
Natural Minor Scale	**Major Scale**
• Extended Scale	• Extended Scale
• Additive Scale	• Additive Scale
• Pentachord Scale	• Pentachord Scale
Sing each of the preceding scales integrating a variety of rhythm patterns.	Sing each of the preceding scales integrating a variety of rhythm patterns.
Tonic Chord in Minor	**Tonic Chord in Major**
• Arpeggio and Extended Arpeggio	• Arpeggio and Extended Arpeggio
• Root position, 1st inversion and 2nd inversion	• Root position, 1st inversion and 2nd inversion
Sing each of the preceding chords integrating a variety of rhythm patterns.	Sing each of the preceding chords integrating a variety of rhythm patterns.
Intervals in the Natural Minor Scale	**Intervals in the Major Scale**
• Intervals from Tonic	• Intervals from Tonic
• Intervals of a Third	• Intervals of a Third
• Intervals of a Fourth	• Intervals of a Fourth
Verbally label the quantity prior to singing each interval or sing each of the preceding intervals integrating a variety of rhythm patterns.	Verbally label the quantity prior to singing each interval or sing each of the preceding intervals integrating a variety of rhythm patterns.

Reading Readiness Aural Skills

- Listen as your instructor plays or sings scales, chords and melodies in major and minor tonalities. Determine the mode (major or minor) of each example.
- Intervals from tonic in a major scale: Listen as two pitches are performed in either ascending or descending order and then determine the quantity and quality of the interval.
- Listen as your instructor sings a known pattern on a neutral syllable and then "notate" the pattern.

II. Symbolic Association: Major Mode

Scales

- Consult the key signature and determine the tonic keynote. Write (a) the scale degree number, (b) the scale degree name, and (c) the tonal syllable for each of the notes. Remember the seventh scale degree in major is called a leading tone (half step between 7 and 1') and in minor the seventh scale degree is called subtonic (whole step between 7 and 1').

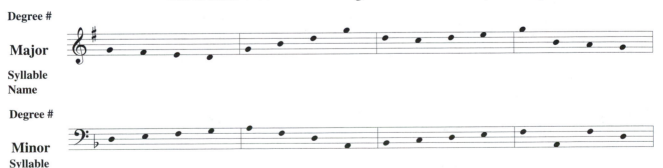

- Sing each of these patterns using tonal syllables.

Intervals from Tonic in a Minor Scale

- (a) Determine the quantity (number) of each of the following intervals. Remember to count both tones and the lines and spaces spanned by the two tones. (b) Using tonal syllables sing each of the following intervals.

Minor

1. _____   2. _____   3. _____   4. _____   5. _____   6. _____   7. _____   8. _____

Intervals from Tonic in a Major Scale

- (a) Determine the quantity and quality of each of the following intervals. Remember to count both tones and the lines and spaces spanned by the two tones. (b) Using tonal syllables sing each of the following intervals.

Major is indicated by an upper case (M) and a lower case (m) indicates minor.

Major

1. _____   2. _____   3. _____   4. _____   5. _____   6. _____   7. _____   8. _____

Tonic Triads in Major and Minor

- Consult the key signature and (a) determine the mode (major or minor), (b) draw a square around the tonic keynote, (c) draw a triangle around the lowest sounding pitch, and (d) circle the position or inversion of the triad.

1. *Major*   *Minor*   2. *Major*   *Minor*   3. *Major*   *Minor*   4. *Major*   *Minor*
    Root   1st   2nd   Root   1st   2nd   Root   1st   2nd   Root   1st   2nd

III. Melodic Patterns: Major Mode

A.

A1.   A2.   A3.   A4.

A5.   A6.   A7.   A8.

B.

B1.   B2.   B3.   B4.

B5.   B6.   B7.   B8.

IV. Exercises

Maintain a steady beat and use tonal syllables.

Canon: 2 voices
Allegro

13th Century French

Canon: 4 voices

English

Chapter 5

Diatonic Steps and Tonic Triad in the Major Scale; Simple Meters, Dotted Quarter Notes

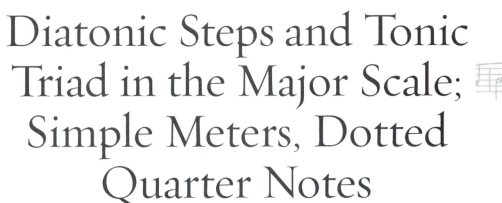

I. Integrating Rhythm and Tonal Skills: Major Mode

Reading Readiness Tonal Patterns
- Listen as your instructor sings a variety of melodic patterns; echo each pattern.[1]

Major Vocal–Pitch Exercises: Sing each of the following drills daily.
Major Scale
- Sing the extended and additive major scales integrating the dotted quarter–eighth pattern.

Intervals from Tonic in the Major Scale
- Verbally label the <u>quantity</u> and <u>quality</u> prior to singing each interval.
- Sing the intervals integrating a variety of rhythm patterns.

Intervals of Major and Minor Thirds in the Major Scale
- Verbally label the quantity and quality of each interval prior to singing each interval using tonal syllables.

  Solfège Ascending: M3: do-mi; m3: re-fa; m3: mi-so; M3: fa-la; M3: so-ti; m3: la-do';
    m3: ti-re'; do'
    Descending: m3: do'-la; M3: ti-so; M3: la-fa; m3: so-mi; m3: fa-re; M3: mi-do; m3: re-ti₁; do

  Numbers Ascending: M3: 1-3; m3: 2-4; m3: 3-5; M3: 4-6; M3: 5-7; m3: 6-1'; m3: 7-2'; 1'
    Descending: m3: 1'-6; M3: 7-5; M3: 6-4; m3: 5-3; m3: 4-2; M3: 3-1; m3: 2-7₁; 1
- Sing the ascending and descending thirds integrating a variety of rhythm patterns.

Intervals of a Fourth in the Major Scale
- Sing the ascending and descending fourths integrating a variety of rhythm patterns. All of the intervals are perfect fourths except for the tri-tone (augmented fourth) found between *fa* and *ti* (4–7).

---

[1]Note to instructors: The melodic patterns are found in Section III of this chapter.

Solfège   Ascending: P4: do-fa; P4: re-so; P4: mi-la; A4: fa-ti; P4: so- do'; P4: la-re'; P4: ti-mi'; do'

Descending: P4: do'-so; A4: ti-fa; P4: la-mi; m3: so-re; m3: fa-do; P4: mi- ti₁; P4: re-la'; do

Numbers   Ascending: P4: 1-4; P4: 2-5; P4: 3-6; A4: 4-7; P4: 5-1'; P4: 6-2'; P4: 7-3'; 1'

Descending: P4: 1'-5; A4: 7-4; P4: 6-3; P4: 5-2; P4: 4-1; P4: 3-7₁; P4: 2-6₁; 1

- Sing the ascending and descending fourths integrating a variety of rhythm patterns.

Triads Built on Each Scale Degree in the Major Scale
A triad (three notes arranged in thirds) may be formed above each degree of the major scale. Triads are named according to the lowest pitch or root. Roman numerals are used to indicate a triad's root (corresponds to the scale degree) and its quality (an upper case numeral for major; a lower case numeral for minor, and a lower case numeral followed by a degree circle for diminished).

- Verbally label the Roman numeral and quality of each triad and then sing the triad melodically using tonal syllables.

						fa¹ (4¹)
					mi¹ (3¹)	re¹ (2¹)
				re¹ (2¹)	do¹ (1¹)	
			do¹ (1¹)			do¹ (1¹)
		ti (7)		ti (7)		
	la (6)		la (6)		la (6)	
so (5)		so (5)		so (5)		ti (7)
mi (3)	fa (4)		fa (4)			
		mi (3)				
	re (2)					
do (1)						

I	ii	iii	IV	V	vi	vii°
Major	*minor*	*minor*	*Major*	*Major*	*minor*	*dim.*

- Sing the ascending and descending pentachord major scale
- Sing Variation I: ascending pentachord major scale/triads descending

Solfege	Numbers
ti – do' – re' – mi' – fa' – re' – ti – do'	7 – 1' – 2' – 3' – 4' – 2' – 7 – 1'
la – ti – do' – re' – mi' – do' – la;	6 – 7 – 1' – 2' – 3' – 1' – 6;
so – la – ti – do' – re' – ti – so;	5 – 6 – 7 – 1' – 2' – 7 – 5;
fa – so – la – ti – do' – la – fa;	4 – 5 – 6 – 7 – 1' – 6 – 4;
mi – fa – so – la – ti – so – mi;	3 – 4 – 5 – 6 – 7 – 5 – 3;
re – mi – fa – so – la – fa – re;	2 – 3 – 4 – 5 – 6 – 4 – 2;
start do – re – mi – fa – so – mi – do;	1 – 2 – 3 – 4 – 5 – 3 – 1;

- Sing Variation II: descending pentachord major scale/triads ascending

Solfège	Numbers
fa' – mi' – re' – do' – ti – re' – fa' – mi'	4' – 3' – 2' – 1' – 7 – 2' – 4' – 3'
mi' – re' – do' – ti – la – do – mi'	3' – 2' – 1' – 7 – 6 – 1' – 3;
re' – do' – ti – la – so – ti – re'	2' – 1' – 7 – 6 – 5 – 7 – 2';
do' – ti – la – so – fa – la – do'	1' – 7 – 6 – 5 – 4 – 6 – 1';
ti – la – so – fa – mi – so – ti;	7 – 6 – 5 – 4 – 3 – 5 – 7;
la – so – fa – mi – re – fa – la;	6 – 5 – 4 – 3 – 2 – 4 – 6;
start so – fa – mi – re – do – mi – so;	5 – 4 – 3 – 2 – 1 – 3 – 5;

Minor Vocal–Pitch Exercises: Sing each of the following drills daily.

Minor Mode

Natural Minor Scale	Intervals in the Natural Minor Scale
• Extended Scale	• Intervals from Tonic
• Additive Scale	• Intervals of a Third
• Pentachord Scale	• Intervals of a Fourth

Sing each of the preceding scales using a variety of rhythm patterns.	Verbally label the quantity of each interval prior to singing the interval and/or sing each of the preceding intervals integrating a variety of rhythm patterns.

Tonic Triad in Minor
• Extended Arpeggio
• Root position, 1st inversion and 2nd inversion

Sing each of the preceding integrating a variety of rhythm patterns.

Reading Readiness Aural Skills
- Listen as your instructor plays or sings scales, chords and melodies in major and minor tonalities. Determine the mode (major or minor) of each example.
- Intervals from tonic in a minor scale: Listen as two pitches are performed in either ascending or descending order and then determine the quantity of the interval.
- Intervals from tonic in a major scale: Listen as two pitches are performed in either ascending or descending order and then determine the quantity and quality of the interval.

II. Symbolic Association: Major Mode

Intervals of a Third in the Major Scale
- Verbally label the quality of each third and then sing the interval using tonal syllables. Notice that quality is not apparent from staff notation.

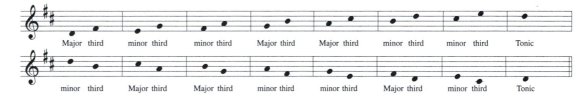

- Label the quality of each third and then sing the interval using tonal syllables.

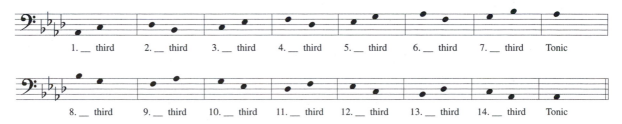

Intervals of a Fourth in the Major Scale
- Verbally label the quality of each fourth and then sing the interval. Notice that quality is not apparent from staff notation. Tritones can also be termed augmented fourths (a half step larger than a perfect fourth).

- Label the quality of each fourth and then sing the interval on tonal syllables.

Triads Built on Each Scale Degree in the Major Scale

The quality name of each triad is determined by the intervallic structure above the root and is not apparent from staff notation. Notice that triads in the position space-space-space or line-line-line are in root position.

- Major triad (I–IV–V)   = major third followed by a minor third
- Minor triad (ii–iii–vi)   = minor third followed by a major third
- Diminished triad (vii°)   = two minor thirds

- Label the Roman numeral (N) and quality (Q = M, m, or d°) of each triad and then sing the melodic triad.

Intervals from Tonic in the Major Scale

- Determine the quantity and quality of each interval and then sing the interval using tonal syllables.

Form: The smallest meaningful melodic–rhythmic entity is called a *motive*. A motive that is repeated on a higher or lower pitch level is called a *sequence*. A *phrase* is a complete musical statement or idea; it is comparable to a line in poetry. Phrases can be progressive (question) or terminal (answer) depending upon the final scale degree of the phrase. The final pitch of a phrase constitutes the *melodic cadence*. *Progressive* melodic *cadences* typically end on the 5th, 2nd or 7th scale degree; final melodic cadences typically end on the tonic or 3rd. Music that is void of repetition or variation of material is called *through-composed*.

III. Melodic Patterns: Major Mode

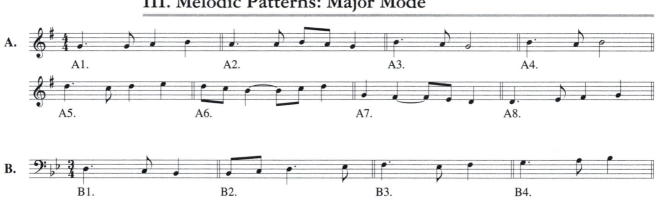

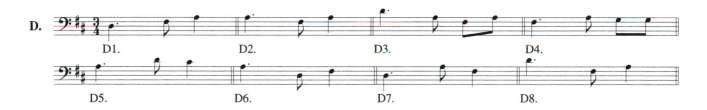

IV. Exercises: Major Mode

Do NOT write the tonal syllables in the music.

4.
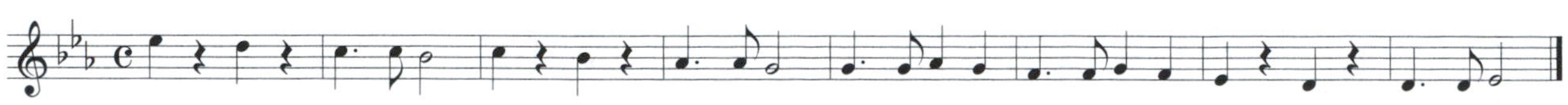

5.
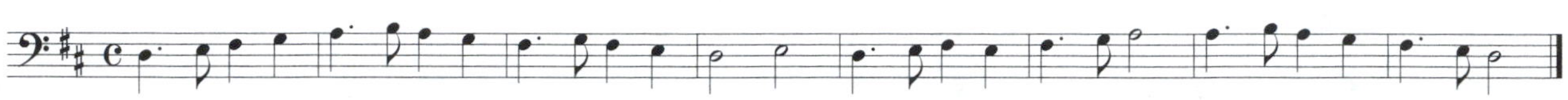

6.
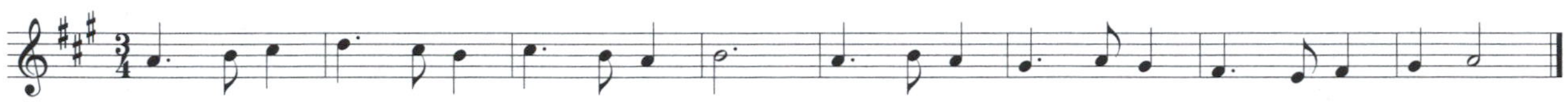

7.
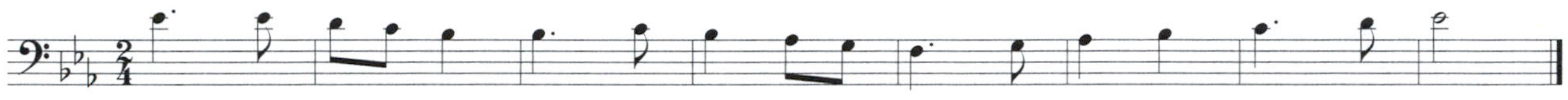

8.
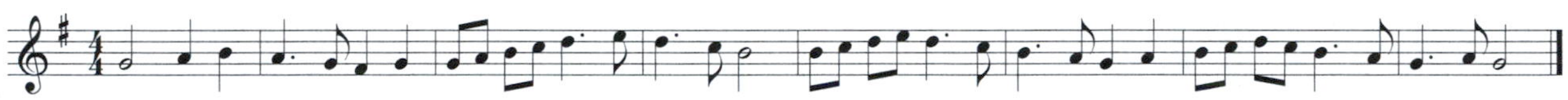

9.
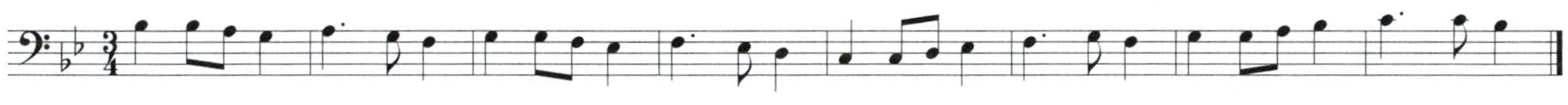

10.
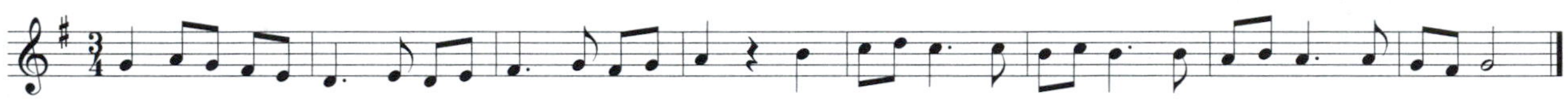

11.
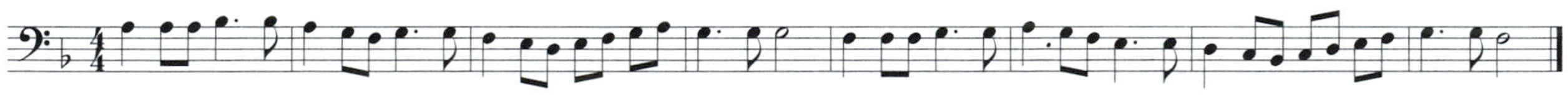

12.
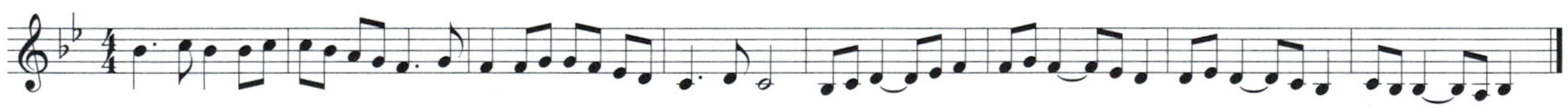

13.
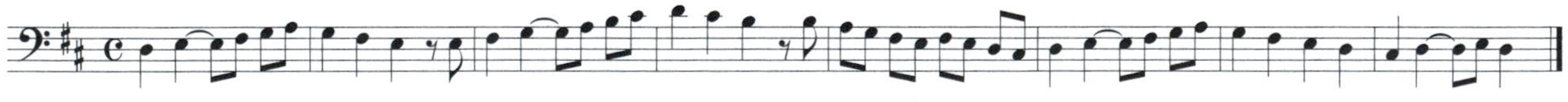

14.
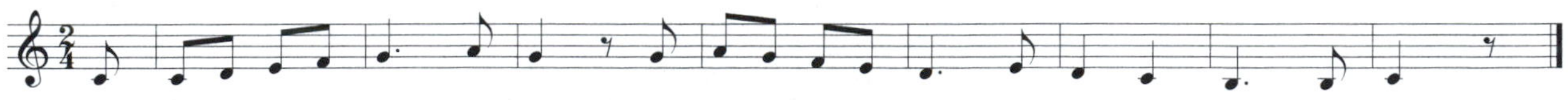

15.
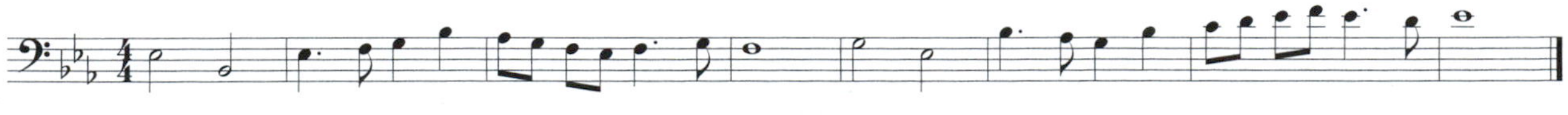

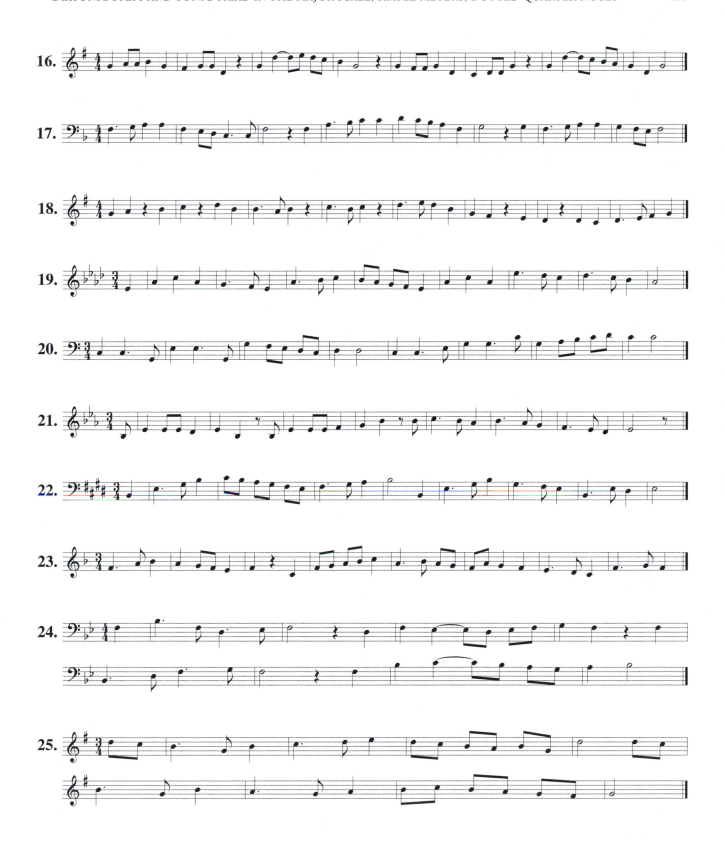

Remember to practice your dictation skills.

47. Canon: 4 voices
Vivo
Henry Purcell (1659–1695)

48. Canon: 3 voices
Getragen
German

49. Canon: 3 voices
Giocoso
Bedrich Smetana (1824–1884)

50. Canon: 2 voices
Marcia
Czech Marching Song

51. Canon: 4 voices
Vivo
Giacomo Gotifredo Ferrari (1759–1842)

52. Allegro
George Frideric Handel (1685–1759), *Judas Maccabaeus*

Chapter 6
Natural, Harmonic, and Melodic Minor Scales; Simple Meters, Eighth and Dotted Quarter Notes

I. Building Aural/Oral Skills: Natural Minor Scale

Reading Readiness Tonal Patterns

- Listen as your instructor sings a variety of tonal patterns; echo each pattern.[1]

Vocal–Pitch Exercises: Sing each of the following drills daily.

Natural Minor Scale: As described in Chapter 3, the natural minor scale has a whole step between the scale degree seven (subtonic) and the tonic (te – do, so – la or ♭7 – 1).

- Sing the natural minor scale integrating (1) repeated eighth notes, (2) moving eighth notes, and (3) the dotted quarter-eighth pattern.

Intervals from Tonic in the Natural Minor Scale

- Verbally label the **quality** (major, minor, perfect) and **quantity** of each ascending and descending intervals from the tonic prior to singing each interval on tonal syllables.

  Do-Based Minor Solfège

  Ascending: Prime: do-do; M2: do-re; m3: do-me; P4: do-fa; P5: do-so; m6: do-le; m7: do-te; P8: do-do'

  Descending: Prime: do'-do'; M2: do'-te; M3: do'-le; P4: do'-so; P5: do'-fa; M6: do'-me; m7: do'-re; P8:do'-do

  La-Based Minor Solfège

  Ascending: Prime: la-la; M2: la-ti; m3: la-do; P4: la-re; P5: la-mi; m6: la-fa; m7: la-so; P8: la-la'

  Descending: Prime: la'-la'; M2: la'-so; M3: la'-fa; P4: la'-mi; P5: la'-re; M6: la'-do; m7: la'-ti; P8:la'-la

  Numbers

  Ascending; Prime: 1-1; M2: 1-2; m3: 1-♭3; P4: 1-4; P5: 1-5; m6: 1-♭6; m7: 1-♭7; P8: 1-1'

  Descending: Prime: 1'-1'; M2: 1'-♭7; M3: 1'-♭6; P4: 1'-5; P5: 1'-4; M6: 1'-♭3; m7: 1'-2; P8: 1'-1

Intervals of a Fourth in the Natural Minor Scale

- Verbally label the quantity and quality of each interval prior to singing each interval using tonal syllables. All of the intervals are perfect fourths except for the tritone (augmented fourth) found between le – re, fa – ti, or 2-♭6.

  Do-Based Minor Solfège

  Ascending: P4: do-fa; P4: re-so; P4: me-le; P4: fa-te; P4: so-do'; A4: le-re'; P4: te-me'; do'

  Descending: P4: do'-so; P4: te-fa; P4: le-me; P4: so-re; P4: fa-do; P4: me-te₁; A4: re-le₁; P4: do-so₁-do

---

[1]Note to instructors: The tonal patterns are found in Section IIIA of this chapter.

200

La-Based Minor Solfège
 Ascending: P4: la-re; P4: ti-mi; P4: do-fa; P4: re-so; P4: mi-la'; A4: fa-ti'; P4: so-do'; la'
 Descending: P4: la'-mi; P4: so-re; P4: fa-do; P4: mi-ti; P4: re-la; P4: do-so$_1$; A4: ti-fa$_1$; P4: la-mi$_1$-la

Numbers
 Ascending; P4: 1-4; P4: 2-5; P4: ♭3-♭6; P4: 4-♭7; P4: 5-1'; A4: ♭6-2'; P4: ♭7-♭3'; 1'
 Descending: P4: 1'-5; P4: ♭7-4; P4: ♭6-♭3; P4: 5-2; P4: 4-1; P4: ♭3-♭7$_1$; A4: 2-♭6$_1$; P4: 1-5$_1$-1

Intervals of Major and Minor Thirds in the Natural Minor Scale

* Verbally label the quantity and quality of each interval prior to singing each interval using tonal syllables.

Do-Based Minor Solfège
 Ascending: m3: do-me; m3: re-fa; M3: me-so; m3: fa-le; m3: so-te; M3: le-do; M3: te-re'-do'
 Descending: M3: do'-le; m3: te-so; m3: le-fa; M3: so-me; m3: fa-re; m3: me-do; M3: re-te$_1$-do

La-Based Minor Solfège
 Ascending: m3: la-do; m3: ti-re; M3: do-mi; m3: re-fa; m3: mi-so; M3: fa-la; M3: so-ti'-la'
 Descending: M3: la'-fa; m3: so-mi; m3: fa-re; M3: mi-do; m3: re-ti; m3: do-la; M3: ti-so$_1$-la

Numbers
 Ascending: m3: 1-♭3; m3: 2-4; M3: ♭3-5; m3: 4-♭6; m3: 5-♭7; M3: ♭6-1'; M3: ♭7-2'-1'
 Descending: M3: 1'-♭6; m3: ♭7-5; m3: ♭6-4; M3: 5-♭3; m3: 4-2; m3: ♭3-1; M3: 2-♭7$_1$-1

With enough drill, each interval should be recognized via the connection between its sound and the tonal syllables.

Triads Built on Each Scale Degree in the Natural Minor Scale

A triad may be formed above each degree of the natural minor scale.

* Verbally label the Roman numeral and quality of each triad prior to singing each triad melodically using tonal syllables.

i	ii°	III	iv	v	VI	VII
so (5) mi	le (♭6) fa	te (♭7) so	do' (1') la'	re' (2') ti'	me' (♭3') do'	fa' (4') re'
me (♭3) do	fa (4) re	so (5) mi	le (♭6) fa	te (♭7) so	do' (1') la'	re' (2') ti'
do (1) la	re (2) ti	me (♭3) do	fa (4) re	so (5) mi	le (♭6) fa	te (♭7) so
i	**ii°**	**III**	**iv**	**v**	**VI**	**VII**
minor	*dim.*	*Major*	*minor*	*minor*	*Major*	*Major*

Natural Minor Pentachord Scale

* Sing the ascending and descending natural minor pentachord scale.

Do-Based Minor Solfège	*La-Based Minor Solfège*	*Numbers*
te – do' – re' – me' – fa' – me' – re' – do' – te – do'	so – la' – ti' – do' – re' – do' – ti' – la' – so – la'	♭7 – 1' – 2' – ♭3' – 4 – ♭3' – 2' – 1' – ♭7 – 1'
le – te – do' – re' – me' – re' – do' – te – le;	fa – so – la' – ti' – do' – ti' – la' – so – fa;	♭6 – ♭7 – 1' – 2' – ♭3' – 2' – 1' – ♭7 – ♭6;
so – le – te – do' – re' – do' – te – le – so;	mi – fa – so – la' – ti' – la' – so – fa – mi;	5 – ♭6 – ♭7 – 1' – 2' – 1' – ♭7 – ♭6 – 5;
fa – so – le – te – do' – te – le – so – fa;	re – mi – fa – so – la' – so – fa – mi – re;	4 – 5 – ♭6 – ♭7 – 1' – ♭7 – ♭6 – 5 – 4;
me – fa – so – le – te – le – so – fa – me;	do – re – mi – fa – so – fa – mi – re – do;	♭3 – 4 – 5 – ♭6 – ♭7 – ♭6 – 5 – 4 – ♭3;
re – me – fa – so – le – so – fa – me – re;	ti – do – re – mi – fa – mi – re – do – ti;	2 – ♭3 – 4 – 5 – ♭6 – 5 – 4 – ♭3 – 2;
start do – re – me – fa – so – fa – me – re – do;	la – ti – do – re – mi – re – do – ti – la;	1 – 2 – ♭3 – 4 – 5 – 4 – ♭3 – 2 – 1;

- Sing Variation I: ascending natural minor pentachord scale and descending triads

Do-Based Minor Solfège	*La-Based Minor Solfège*	*Numbers*
te – do' – re' – me' – fa' – re' – te – do'	so – la' – ti' – do' – re' – ti' – so – la	♭7 – 1' – 2' – ♭3' – 4' – 2' – ♭7 – 1'
le – te – do' – re' – me' – do' – le;	fa – so – la' – ti' – do' – la' – fa;	♭6 – ♭7 – 1' – 2' – ♭3' – 1' – ♭6;
so – le – te – do' – re' – te – so;	mi – fa – so – la' – ti' – so – mi;	5 – ♭6 – ♭7 – 1' – 2' – ♭7 – 5 ;
fa – so – le – te – do' – le – fa;	re – mi – fa – so – la' – fa – re;	4 – 5 – ♭6 – ♭7 – 1' – ♭6 – 4;
me – fa – so – le – te – so – me;	do – re – mi – fa – so – mi – do;	♭3 – 4 – 5 – ♭6 – ♭7 – 5 – ♭3;
re – me – fa – so – le – fa – re;	ti – do – re – mi – fa – re – ti;	2 – ♭3 – 4 – 5 – ♭6 – 4 – 2;
start do – re – me – fa – so – me – do;	la – ti – do – re – mi – do – la;	1 – 2 – ♭3 – 4 – 5 – ♭3 – 1;

- Sing Variation II: descending natural minor pentachord scale and ascending triads

Do-Based Minor Solfège	*La-Based Minor Solfège*	*Numbers*
fa' – me' – re' – do' – te – re' – fa' – me'	re' – do' – ti' – la' – so – ti' – re' – do'	4' – ♭3' – 2' – 1' – ♭7 – 2' – 4' – ♭3'
me' – re' – do' – te – le – do' – me';	do' – ti' – la' – so – fa – la' – do';	♭3' – 2' – 1' – ♭7 – ♭6 – 1' – ♭3';
re' – do' – te – le – so – te – re';	ti' – la' – so – fa – mi – so – ti';	2' – 1' – ♭7 – ♭6 – 5 – ♭7 – 2';
do' – te – le – so – fa – le – do';	la' – so – fa – mi – re – fa – la';	1' – ♭7 – ♭6 – 5 – 4 – ♭6 – 1';
te – le – so – fa – me – so – te;	so – fa – mi – re – do – mi – so;	♭7 – ♭6 – 5 – 4 – ♭3 – 5 – ♭7;
le – so – fa – me – re – fa – le;	fa – mi – re – do – ti – re – fa;	♭6 – 5 – 4 – ♭3 – 2 – 4 – ♭6;
start so – fa – me – re – do – me – so;	mi – re – do – ti – la – do – mi;	5 – 4 – ♭3 – 2 – 1 – ♭3 – 5;

With enough drill, each triad should be recognized via the connection between the sound and the tonal syllables.

Reading Readiness Aural Activities

- Listen as your instructor plays or sings a phrase. Determine the type of melodic cadence.
- Listen as your instructor plays or sings scales, chords, and melodies in major and minor tonalities. Determine the mode (major or minor) of each example.
- Listen as two pitches are performed in either ascending or descending order and then determine the quantity and quality of the interval. Remember: Major is indicated by an upper case (M) and a lower case (m) indicates minor.

II. Symbolic Association: Natural Minor Scale

Natural Minor Scale

- Consult the key signature and determine the tonic keynote. Verbally label the scale degree name prior to singing each pitch using tonal syllables.

Intervals from Tonic in the Natural Minor Scale

- Verbally label the quantity and quality of each interval prior to singing the interval using tonal syllables. Staff notation only indicates quantity; the differences in qualities are not apparent from the staff notation.

Prime   Major second   minor third   Perfect fourth   Perfect fifth   minor sixth   minor seventh   Perfect eighth

Prime   Major second   Major third   Perfect fourth   Perfect fifth   Major sixth   minor seventh   Perfect eighth

- Determine the quantity and quality of each interval and then sing the interval on tonal syllables.

1. ____   2. _____   3. _____   4. ____   5. _____   6. _____   7. _____   8. _____

Intervals of Major and Minor Thirds in the Natural Minor Scale

- Verbally label the quality of each third prior to singing the interval using tonal syllables. Notice that staff notation only indicates quantity; the differences in qualities are not apparent from the staff notation.

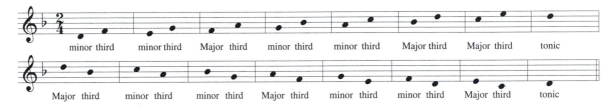

minor third   minor third   Major third   minor third   minor third   Major third   Major third   tonic

Major third   minor third   minor third   Major third   minor third   minor third   Major third   tonic

- Determine the quality of each third, and then verbally label it prior to singing the interval using tonal syllables.

1. __ third   2. __ third   3. __ third   4. __ third   5. __ third   6. __ third   7. __ third   8. __ third

Intervals of a Fourth in the Natural Minor Scale

- Verbally label the quality of each fourth prior to singing the interval using tonal syllables. Remember the quality name of each interval is not apparent from staff notation.

Perfect fourth   Perfect fourth   Perfect fourth   Perfect fourth   Perfect fourth   Tritone (Aug)   Perfect fourth   Tonic

Perfect fourth   Perfect fourth   Perfect fourth   Perfect fourth   Perfect fourth   Perfect fourth   Tritone (Aug)   Tonic

- Determine the quality of each fourth, and then verbally label it prior to singing the interval using tonal syllables.

1. __ fourth   2. __ fourth   3. __ fourth   4. __ fourth   5. __ fourth   6. __ fourth   7. __ fourth   8. __ fourth

Triads Formed on Each Scale Degree in the Natural Minor Scale

Major triad (III—VI—VII)	=	major third and a minor third
Minor triad (i—iv—v)	=	minor third and a major third
Diminished triad (ii°)	=	two minor thirds

- Verbally label the Roman numeral and quality of each triad and then sing the triad melodically on tonal syllables.

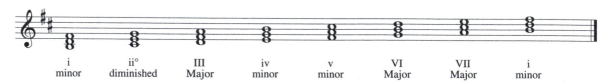

i	ii°	III	iv	v	VI	VII	i
minor	diminished	Major	minor	minor	Major	Major	minor

- Determine the Roman numeral (N) and quality (Q=M, m or d°) of each triad and then sing each triad.

1. N___ Q___   2. N___ Q___   3. N___ Q___   4. N___ Q___   5. N___ Q___   6. N___ Q___   7. N___ Q___

III. Tonal and Melodic Patterns: Natural Minor Scale

A. Tonal Patterns: Symbolic Association

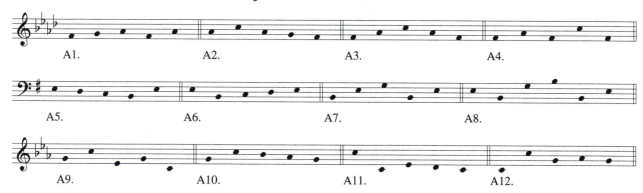

B. Melodic Patterns: Aural/Oral

1. Listen as your instructor sings a variety of melodic patterns; echo each pattern.[2]
2. Sing the extended natural minor scale using tonal syllables by rote and integrate the following rhythm.

C. Melodic Patterns: Symbolic Association

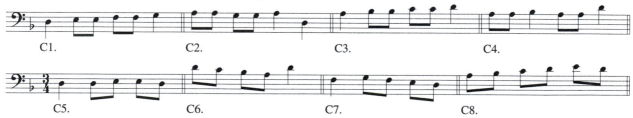

[2]Note to instructors: The melodic patterns are found in Section III of this chapter.

IV. Exercises: Natural Minor Scale

Remember to practice your dictation skills.

V. Building Aural/Oral Skills: Harmonic Minor Scale

Reading Readiness Tonal Patterns

- Listen as your instructor sings a variety of tonal patterns; echo each pattern.[3]

Vocal–Pitch Exercises: Sing each of the following drills daily.

Harmonic Minor Scale

In the *harmonic minor scale*, scale degree seven (te/so/♭7) is raised a half step (*ti/si/♮7*), giving the scale a leading tone that strengthens the feeling of tonic. Listen for the <u>augmented</u> second, one-half step larger than a major second, that appears between the sixth and seventh scale degrees (*le to ti, fa to si,* or ♭6 to 7).

- Sing the ascending and descending harmonic minor scale.
  Do-Based Minor Solfège: do – re – me – fa – so– le – ti – do' – ti – le – so – fa – me – re – do
  La-Based Minor Solfège: la – ti – do – re – mi – fa – si – la' – si – fa – mi – re – do – ti – la
  Numbers: 1 – 2 – ♭3 – 4 – 5 – ♭6 – ♮7 – 1₁ – 7 – ♭6 – 5 – 4 – ♭3 – 2 – 1
- Integrate (a) repeated eighth notes, (b) moving eighth notes, and (c) the dotted quarter-eighth pattern.

Harmonic Minor Pentachord Scale

- Sing the ascending and descending harmonic minor pentachord scale.

Do-Based Minor Solfège	La-Based Minor Solfège	Numbers
ti – do' – re' – me' – fa' – me' – re' – do' – ti – do'	si – la' – ti' – do' – re' – do' – ti' – la' – si – la'	7 – 1' – 2' – ♭3' – 4 – ♭3' – 2' – 1' – 7 – 1'
le – ti – do' – re' – me' – re' – do' – ti – le;	fa – si – la' – ti' – do' – ti' – la' – si – fa;	♭6 – 7 – 1' – 2' – ♭3' – 2' – 1' – 7 – ♭6;
so – le – ti – do' – re' – do' – ti – le – so;	mi – fa – si – la' – ti' – la' – si – fa – mi;	5 – ♭6 – 7 – 1' – 2' – 1' – 7 – ♭6 – 5;
fa – so – le – ti – do' – ti – le – so – fa;	re – mi – fa – si – la' – si – fa – mi – re;	4 – 5 – ♭6 – 7 – 1' – 7 – ♭6 – 5 – 4;
me – fa – so – le – ti – le – so – fa – me;	do – re – mi – fa – si – fa – mi – re – do;	♭3 – 4 – 5 – ♭6 – 7 – ♭6 – 5 – 4 – ♭3;
re – me – fa – so – le – so – fa – me – re;	ti – do – re – mi – fa – mi – re – do – ti;	2 – ♭3 – 4 – 5 – ♭6 – 5 – 4 – ♭3 – 2;
start do – re – me – fa – so – fa – me – re – do;	la – ti – do – re – mi – re – do – ti – la;	1 – 2 – ♭3 – 4 – 5 – 4 – ♭3 – 2 – 1;

- Sing Variation I: ascending harmonic minor pentachord scale and descending triads.

Do-Based Minor Solfège	La-Based Minor Solfège	Numbers
ti – do' – re' – me' – fa' – re' – ti – do'	si – la' – ti' – do' – re' – ti' – si – la'	7 – 1' – 2' – ♭3' – 4' – 2' – 7 – 1'
le – te – do' – re' – me' – do' – le;	fa – so – la' – ti' – do' – la' – fa;	♭6 – ♭7 – 1' – 2' – ♭3' – 1' – ♭6;
so – le – ti – do' – re' – ti – so;	mi – fa – si – la' – ti' – si – mi;	5 – ♭6 – 7 – 1' – 2' – 7 – 5;
fa – so – le – te – do' – le – fa;	re – mi – fa – so – la' – fa – re;	4 – 5 – ♭6 – ♭7 – 1' – ♭6 – 4;
me – fa – so – le – ti – so – me;	do – re – mi – fa – si – mi – do;	♭3 – 4 – 5 – ♭6 – 7 – 5 – ♭3;
re – me – fa – so – le – fa – re;	ti – do – re – mi – fa – re – ti;	2 – ♭3 – 4 – 5 – ♭6 – 4 – 2;
start do – re – me – fa – so – me – do;	la – ti – do – re – mi – do – la;	1 – 2 – ♭3 – 4 - 5 – ♭3 – 1;

- Sing Variation II: descending harmonic minor pentachord scale and ascending triads.

Do-Based Minor Solfège	La-Based Minor Solfège	Numbers
fa' – me' – re' – do' – ti – re' – fa' – me'	re' – do' – ti' – la' – si – ti' – re' – do'	4' – ♭3' – 2' – 1' – 7 – 2' – 4' – ♭3'
me' – re' – do' – te – le – do' – me';	do' – ti' – la' – so – fa – la' – do';	♭3' – 2' – 1' – ♭7 – ♭6 – 1' – ♭3';
re' – do' – ti – le – so – ti – re';	ti' – la' – si – fa – mi – si – ti';	2' – 1' – 7 – ♭6 – 5 – 7 – 2';
do' – te – le – so – fa – le – do';	la' – so – fa – mi – re – fa – la';	1' – ♭7 – ♭6 – 5 – 4 – ♭6 – 1';
ti – le – so – fa – me – so – ti;	si – fa – mi – re – do – mi – si;	7 – ♭6 – 5 – 4 – ♭3 – 5 – 7;
le – so – fa – me – re – fa – le;	fa – mi – re – do – ti – re – fa;	♭6 – 5 – 4 – ♭3 – 2 – 4 – ♭6;
start so – fa – me – re – do – me – so;	mi – re – do – ti – la – do – mi;	5 – 4 – ♭3 – 2 – 1 – ♭3 – 5;

---

[3]Note to instructors: The melodic patterns are found in Section VII A of this chapter.

Intervals from Tonic in the Harmonic Minor Scale
- Verbally label the quality and quantity of each ascending and descending intervals from the tonic prior to singing each interval using tonal syllables.

  Do-Based Minor Solfège

  Ascending: Prime: do – do; M2: do – re; m3: do – me; P4: do – fa; P5: do – so; m6: do – le; M7: do – ti; P8: do – do'

  Descending: Prime: do' – do'; m2: do' – ti; M3: do' – le; P4: do' – so; P5: do' – fa; M6: do' – me; m7: do' – re; P8: do' – do

  La–Based Minor Solfège

  Ascending: Prime: la – la; M2: la – ti; m3: la – do; P4: la – re; P5: la – mi; m6: la – fa; M7: la – si; P8: la – la'

  Descending: Prime: la' – la'; m2: la' – si; M3: la' – fa; P4: la' – mi; P5: la' – re; M6: la' – do; m7: la' – ti; P8: la' – la

  Numbers

  Ascending; Prime: 1 – 1; M2: 1 – 2; m3: 1 – ♭3; P4: 1 – 4; P5: 1 – 5; m6: 1 – ♭6; M7: 1 – 7; P8: 1 – 1'

  Descending: Prime: 1' – 1'; m2: 1' – 7; M3: 1' – ♭6; P4: 1' – 5; P5: 1' – 4; M6: 1' – ♭3; m7: 1' – 2; P8: 1' – 1

Intervals of Major and Minor Thirds in the Harmonic Minor Scale
- Verbally label the quality and quantity of each third prior to singing the intervals using tonal syllables.

  Do-Based Solfège

  Ascending: m3: do – me; m3: re – fa; M3: me – so; m3: fa – le; M3: so – ti; M3: le – do; m3: ti – re' – do'

  Descending: M3: do' – le; M3: ti – so; m3: le – fa; M3: so – me; m3: fa – re; m3: me – do; m3: re – ti₁ – do

  La-Based Solfège

  Ascending: m3: la – do; m3: ti – re; M3: do – mi; M3: re – fa; M3: mi – si; M3: fa – la; m3: si – ti – la'

  Descending: M3: la' – fa; M3: si – mi; m3: fa – re; M3: mi – do; m3: re – ti; m3: do – la; m3: ti – si₁ – la

  Numbers

  Ascending: m3: 1 – ♭3; m3: 2 – 4; M3: ♭3 – 5; m3: 4 – ♭6; M3: 5 – 7; M3: ♭6 – 1'; m3: 7 – 2' – 1'

  Descending: M3: 1' – ♭6; M3: 7 – 5; m3: ♭6 – 4; M3: 5 – ♭3; m3: 4 – 2; m3: ♭3 – 1; m3: 2 – 7₁ – 1

Intervals of a Fourth in the Harmonic Minor Scale

Verbally label the quality and quantity of each fourth prior to singing the intervals using tonal syllables. (Augmented is a half step larger; diminished is a half step smaller.)

  Do-Based Minor Solfège

  Ascending: P4: do – fa; P4: re – so; P4: me – le; A4: fa – ti; P4: so – do'; A4: le – re'; d4: ti – me'; do'

  Descending: P4: do' – so; A4: ti – fa; P4: le – me; P4: so – re; P4: fa – do; d4: me – ti₁; A4: re – le₁; P4: do – so₁ – do

  La-Based Minor Solfège

  Ascending: P4: la – re; P4: ti – mi; P4: do – fa; A4: re – si; P4: mi – la'; A4: fa – ti'; d4: si – do'; la'

  Descending: P4: la' – mi; A4: si – re; P4: fa – do; P4: mi – ti; P4: re – la; d4: do – si₁; A4: ti – fa₁; P4: la – mi₁ – la

  Numbers

  Ascending: P4: 1 – 4; P4: 2 – 5; P4: ♭3 – ♭6; A4: 4 – 7; P4: 5 – 1'; A4: ♭6 – 2'; d4: 7 – ♭3'; 1'

  Descending: P4: 1' – 5; A4: 7 – 4; P4: ♭6 – ♭3; P4: 5 – 2; P4: 4 – 1; d4: ♭3 – 7₁; A4: 2 – ♭6₁; P4: 1 – 5₁ – 1

Triads Built on Each Scale Degree in the Harmonic Minor Scale

- Verbally label the Roman numeral and quality of each triad prior to singing the triad melodically.

i	ii°	III⁺	iv	V	VI	vii°
minor	*dim.*	*Aug.*	*minor*	*Major*	*Major*	*dim.*
so (5) mi me (♭3) do do (1) la	le (♭6) fa fa (4) re re (2) ti	ti (7) si so (5) mi me (♭3) do	do′ (1′) la′ le (♭6) fa fa (4) re	re′ (2′) ti′ ti (7) si so (5) mi	me′ (♭3′) do′ do′ (1′) la′ le (♭6) fa	fa′ (4′) re′ re′ (2′) ti′ ti (7) si

With enough drill, each chord, interval and scale should be recognized via the connection between its sound and the tonal syllables.

Reading Readiness Aural Skills

- Listen as your instructor plays or sings a phrase. Determine the type of melodic cadence.
- Listen as your instructor plays or sings scales, chords, and melodies in major and minor tonalities. Determine the mode (major or minor) of each example.
- Listen as two pitches are performed in either ascending or descending order and then determine the quantity and quality of the interval.

VI. Symbolic Association: Harmonic Minor Scale

Harmonic Minor Scale

In the harmonic minor scale, one of the pitches is raised. Since this pitch is not part of the diatonic scale, an *accidental* must be inserted before the notehead. In some keys the note is raised by using a sharp (example A) and in other keys, the note is raised using a natural (example B), a symbol that cancels the effect of the key signature. Accidentals affect their assigned note for the entire measure.

In the harmonic minor scale, scale degree seven is raised a half step, giving the scale a leading tone that strengthens the feeling of tonic.

- Consult the key signature and determine the tonic keynote. Verbally label the name of the scale degree prior to singing each pitch using tonal syllables.

Intervals from Tonic in the Harmonic Minor Scale
- Verbally label the quanity and quality of each interval prior to singing the intervals using tonal syllables. Staff notation only indicates quantity; the differences in qualities are not apparent from the staff notation.

Prime · Major second · minor third · Perfect fourth · Perfect fifth · minor sixth · Major seventh · Perfect eighth

Prime · minor second · Major third · Perfect fourth · Perfect fifth · Major sixth · minor seventh · Perfect eighth

- Determine the quantity and quality of each interval and then sing the interval using tonal syllables.

1. ____ 2. ____ 3. ____ 4. ____ 5. ____ 6. ____ 7. ____ 8. ____

Intervals of Major and Minor Thirds in the Harmonic Minor Scale
- Verbally label the quality of each third prior to singing the interval using tonal syllables. The quality name of each interval is not apparent from staff notation.

minor third · minor third · Major third · minor third · Major third · Major third · minor third · tonic

Major third · Major third · minor third · Major third · minor third · minor third · minor third · tonic

- Determine the quality of each third and then sing the interval using tonal syllables.

1. ____ 2. ____ 3. ____ 4. ____ 5. ____ 6. ____ 7. ____ 8. ____

Intervals of a Fourth in the Harmonic Minor Scale
- Verbally label the quality of each fourth prior to singing the interval using tonal syllables. Remember the quality name of each interval is not apparent from staff notation.

Perfect fourth · Perfect fourth · Perfect fourth · Tritone (Aug.) · Perfect fourth · Tritone (Aug.) · Diminished fourth · Tonic

Perfect fourth · Tritone (Aug.) · Perfect fourth · Perfect fourth · Perfect fourth · Diminished fourth · Tritone (Aug.) · Tonic

- Determine the quality of each fourth and then sing the interval using tonal syllables.

1. ____ 2. ____ 3. ____ 4. ____ 5. ____ 6. ____ 7. ____ 8. ____

Triads Formed on Each Scale Degree in the Harmonic Minor Scale

Major triad (V–VI)	=	major third and a minor third
Augmented triad (III+)	=	two major thirds
Minor triad (i–iv)	=	minor third and a major third
Diminished triad (ii°–vii°)	=	two minor thirds

- Verbally label the Roman numeral and quality of each triad and then sing the triad melodically on tonal syllables.

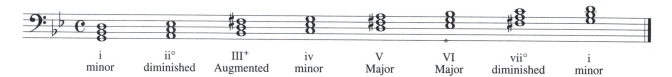

i	ii°	III⁺	iv	V	VI	vii°	i
minor	diminished	Augmented	minor	Major	Major	diminished	minor

- Determine the Roman numeral (N) and quality (Q=M, A+, m, or d°) of each triad and then sing each triad using tonal syllables.

1. N ___ Q ___   2. N ___ Q ___   3. N ___ Q ___   4. N ___ Q ___   5. N ___ Q ___   6. N ___ Q ___   7. N ___ Q ___

VII. Tonal and Melodic Patterns: Harmonic Minor Scale

A. Tonal Patterns: Symbolic Association

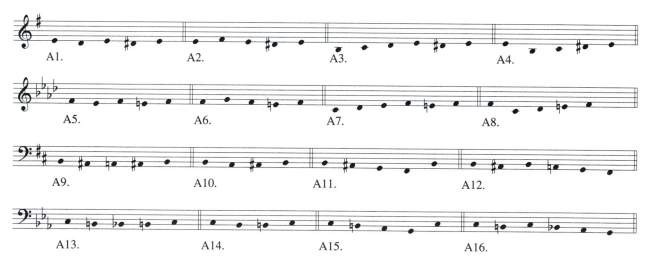

B. Melodic Patterns: Aural/Oral

1. Listen as your instructor sings a variety of melodic patterns; echo each pattern.[4]

2. Sing the extended harmonic minor scale using tonal syllables and integrate the following rhythm.

[4]Note to Instructors: The melodic patterns are found in Section VIIC of this chapter.

C. Melodic Patterns: Aural/Oral

C1. C2. C3. C4.

C5. C6. C7. C8.

C9. C10. C11. C12.

C13. C14. C15. C16.

C17. C18. C19. C20.

C21. C22. C23. C24.

VIII. Exercises: Harmonic Minor Scale

1.

2.

3.

Canon: 3 voices

[1] [2] [3] English

4.

Canon: 4 voices

Thomas Ravenscroft (c. 1582–c. 1635); *Pammelia,* 1609

[1] [2] [3] [4]

5.

24. Geshwind — German

25.

26.

27.

28. Canon: 5 voices — Thomas Ravenscroft (c. 1582–c. 1635); *Pammelia,* 1609
[1] [2] [3] [4] [5]

29. Adagio — English
mp *p* *mp* *mf*

The following exercises include the augmented second for pedagogical reasons.

30.

31.

32.

33.

IX. Building Aural/Oral Skills: Melodic Minor Scale

Reading Readiness Tonal Patterns

- Listen as your instructor sings a variety of tonal patterns; echo each pattern.[5]

Vocal–Pitch Exercises: Sing each of the following drills daily.

Melodic Minor Scale

In the *melodic minor scale* the sixth and seventh scale degrees are raised a half step as the scale ascends and lowered as the scale descends (reverts to the natural minor scale).

- Sing the ascending and descending melodic minor scale.

  Do-Based Minor Solfège: do – re – me – fa – so – la – ti – do' – te – le – so – fa – me – re – do

  La-Based Minor Solfège: la – ti – do – re – mi – fi – si – la' – so – fa – mi – re – do – ti – la

  Numbers: 1 – 2 – ♭3 – 4 – 5 – 6 – 7 – 1' – ♭7 – ♭6 – 5 – 4 – ♭3 – 2 – 1

Melodic Minor Pentachord Scale

- Sing the ascending and descending melodic minor pentachord scale.

Do-Based Minor Solfège	*La-Based Minor Solfège*	*Numbers*
ti – do' – re' – me' – fa' – me' – re' – do' – te – do'	si – la' – ti' – do' – re' – do' – ti' – la' – so – la'	7 – 1' – 2' – ♭3' – 4 – ♭3' – 2' – 1' – ♭7-1'
la – ti – do' – re' – me' – re' – do' – te – le;	fi – si – la' – ti' – do' – ti' – la' – so – fa;	6 – 7 – 1' – 2' – ♭3' – 2' – 1' – ♭7 – ♭6;
so – la – ti – do' – re' – do' – te – le – so;	mi – fi – si – la' – ti' – la' – so – fa – mi;	5 – 6 – 7 – 1' – 2' – 1' – ♭7 – ♭6 – 5;
fa – so – la – ti – do' – te – le – so – fa;	re – mi – fi – si – la' – so – fa – mi – re;	4 – 5 – 6 – 7 – 1' – ♭7 – ♭6 – 5 – 4;
me – fa – so – la – ti – le – so – fa – me;	do – re – mi – fi – si – fa – mi – re – do;	♭3 – 4 – 5 – 6 – 7 – ♭6 – 5 – 4 – ♭3;
re – me – fa – so – la – so – fa – me – re;	ti – do – re – mi – fi – mi – re – do – ti;	2 – ♭3 – 4 – 5 – 6 – 5 – 4 – ♭3 – 2;
do – re – me – fa – so – fa – me – re – do;	la – ti – do – re – mi – re – do – ti – la;	1 – 2 – ♭3 – 4 – 5 – 4 – ♭3 – 2 – 1;

start

- Sing Variation I: ascending melodic minor pentachord scale and descending triads.

Do-Based Minor Solfège	*La-Based Minor Solfège*	*Numbers*
ti – do' – re' – me' – fa' – re' – te – do'	si – la' – ti' – do' – re' – ti' – so – la	7 – 1' – 2' – ♭3' – 4' – 2' – ♭7 - 1'
la – ti – do' – re' – me' – do' – le;	fi – si – la' – ti' – do' – la' – fa;	6 – 7 – 1' – 2' – ♭3' – 1' – ♭6;
so – la – ti – do' – re' – te – so;	mi – fi – si – la' – ti' – so – mi;	5 – 6 – 7 – 1' – 2' – ♭7 – 5 ;
fa – so – la – ti – do' – le – fa;	re – mi – fi – si – la' – fa – re;	4 – 5 – 6 – 7 – 1' – ♭6 – 4;
me – fa – so – la – ti – so – me;	do – re – mi – fi – si – mi – do;	♭3 – 4 – 5 – 6 – 7 – 5 – ♭3;
re – me – fa – so – la – fa – re;	ti – do – re – mi – fi – re – ti;	2 – ♭3 – 4 – 5 – 6 – 4 – 2;
do – re – me – fa – so – me – do;	la – ti – do – re – mi – do – la;	1 – 2 – ♭3 – 4 - 5 – ♭3 – 1;

start

- Sing Variation II: descending melodic minor pentachord scale and ascending triads.

Do-Based Minor Solfège	*La-Based Minor Solfège*	*Numbers*
fa' – me' – re' – do' – te – re' – fa' – me'	re' – do' – ti' – la' – so – ti' – re' – do'	4' – ♭3' – 2' – 1' – ♭7 – 2' – 4' – ♭3'
me' – re' – do' – te – le – do' – me';	do' – ti' – la' – so – fa – la' – do';	♭3' – 2' – 1' – ♭7 – ♭6 – 1' – ♭3';
re' – do' – te – le – so – ti – re';	ti' – la' – so – fa – mi – si – ti';	2' – 1' – ♭7 – ♭6 – 5 – 7 – 2';
do' – te – le – so – fa – la – do';	la' – so – fa – mi – re – fi – la';	1' – ♭7 – ♭6 – 5 – 4 – 6 – 1';
te – le – so – fa – me – so – ti;	so – fa – mi – re – do – mi – si;	♭7 – ♭6 – 5 – 4 – ♭3 – 5 – 7;
le – so – fa – me – re – fa – la;	fa – mi – re – do – ti – re – fi;	♭6 – 5 – 4 – ♭3 – 2 – 4 – 6;
so – fa – me – re – do – me – so;	mi – re – do – ti – la – do – mi;	5 – 4 – ♭3 – 2 – 1 – ♭3 – 5;

start

---

[5]Note to instructors: The melodic patterns are found in Section XIA of this chapter.

Intervals from Tonic in the Melodic Minor Scale

- Verbally label the quality and quantity of each ascending and descending interval from the tonic.

  Do-Based Minor Solfège

  > Ascending: Prime: do – do; M2: do – re; m3: do – me; P4: do – fa; P5: do – so; M6: do – la; M7: do – ti; P8: do – do'
  >
  > Descending: Prime: do' – do'; M2: do' – te; M3: do' – le; P4: do' – so; P5: do' – fa; M6: do' – me; m7: do' – re; P8: do' – do

  La-Based Minor Solfège

  > Ascending: Prime: la – la; M2: la – ti; m3: la – do; P4: la – re; P5: la – mi; M6: la – fi; M7: la – si; P8: la – la'
  >
  > Descending: Prime: la' – la'; M2: la' – so; M3: la' – fa; P4: la' – mi; P5: la' – re; M6: la' – do; m7: la' – ti; P8: la' – la

  Numbers

  > Ascending; Prime: 1 – 1; M2: 1 – 2; m3: 1 – ♭3; P4: 1 – 4; P5: 1 – 5; M6: 1 – 6; M7: 1 – 7; P8: 1 – 1'
  >
  > Descending: Prime: 1' – 1'; M2: 1' – ♭7; M3: 1' – ♭6; P4: 1' – 5; P5: 1' – 4; M6: 1' – ♭3; m7th: 1' – 2; P8: 1' – 1

Intervals of Major and Minor Thirds in the Melodic Minor Scale

- Verbally label the quality of each third prior to singing the intervals using tonal syllables.

  Do-Based Minor Solfège

  > Ascending: m3: do – me; m3: re – fa; M3: me – so; M3: fa – la; M3: so – ti; m3: la – do; m3: ti – re' – do'
  >
  > Descending: M3: do' – le; m3: te – so; m3: le – fa; M3: so – me; m3: fa – re; m3: me – do; M3: re – te, – do

  La-Based Minor Solfège

  > Ascending: m3: la – do; m3: ti – re; M3: do – mi; M3: re – fi; M3: mi – si; m3: fi – la; m3: si – ti' – la'
  >
  > Descending: M3: la' – fa; m3: so – mi; m3: fa – re; M3: mi – do; m3: re – ti; m3: do – la; M3: ti – so, – la

  Numbers

  > Ascending: m3: 1 – ♭3; m3: 2 – 4; M3: ♭3 – 5; M3: 4 – 6; M3: 5 – 7; m3: 6 – 1'; m3: 7 – 2' – 1'
  >
  > Descending: M3: 1' – ♭6; m3: ♭7 – 5; m3: ♭6 – 4; M3: 5 – ♭3; m3: 4 – 2; m3: ♭3 – 1; M3: 2 – ♭7, – 1

Intervals of a Fourth in the Melodic Minor Scale

- Verbally label the quality of each fourth prior to singing the intervals on tonal syllables.

  Do-Based Minor Solfège

  > Ascending: P4: do – fa; P4: re – so; A4: me – la; A4: fa – ti; P4: so – do'; P4: la – re'; d4: ti – me' – do'
  >
  > Descending: P4: do' – so; P4: te – fa; P4: le – me; P4: so – re; P4: fa – do; P4: me – te,; A4: re – le, – ti, – do

  La-Based Minor Solfège

  > Ascending: P4: la – re; P4: ti – mi; A4: do – fi; A4: re – si; P4: mi – la'; P4: fi – ti'; d4: si – do'; la'
  >
  > Descending: P4: la' – mi; P4: so – re; P4: fa – do; P4: mi – ti; P4: re – la; P4: do – so,; A4: ti – fa, – si, – la

  Numbers

  > Ascending: P4: 1 – 4; P4: 2 – 5; A4: ♭3 – 6; A4: 4 – 7; P4: 5 – 1'; P4: 6 – 2'; d4: 7 – ♭3'; 1'
  >
  > Descending: P4: 1' – 5; P4: ♭7 – 4; P4: ♭6 – ♭3; P4: 5 – 2; P4: 4 – 1; P4: ♭3 – ♭7,; P4: 2 – ♭6, – 7, – 1

With enough drill, each triad, interval, and scale will be recognized via the connection between its sound and its tonal syllables.

Reading Readiness Aural Skills
- Listen as your instructor plays minor scales. Determine the type of minor scale.
- Listen as two pitches are performed in either ascending or descending order and then determine the interval.

X. Symbolic Association: Melodic Minor Scale

Melodic Minor Scales

In the melodic minor scale the 6th and 7th scale degrees are raised a half step (*la* and *ti*, *fi* and *si* or 6 and 7) as the scale ascends and lowered (*le* and *te*, *fa* and *so* or ♭6 and ♭7) as the scale descends (reverts to the natural minor scale).

- Consult the key signature and determine the tonic keynote. Verbally label the scale degree name prior to singing each pitch using tonal syllables.

Intervals in the Melodic Minor Scale

- Verbally label the quality and quality of each interval prior to singing the intervals on tonal syllables.[6]

- Determine the quantity and quality of each interval and then sing the interval using tonal syllables.

1. _____ 2. _____ 3. _____ 4. _____ 5. _____ 6. _____ 7. _____ 8. _____

Intervals of Major and Minor Thirds in the Melodic Minor Scale

- Verbally label the quality of each third prior to singing the interval on tonal syllables.

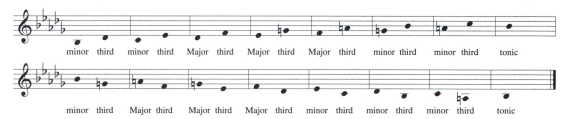

---

[6]Frequently composers will use the ascending form of the melodic minor scale in descending passages. Consequently the ascending and descending intervals formed by the raised 6th and 7th scale degrees to the tonic must be drilled.

- Determine the quality of each third and then sing the interval using tonal syllables.

1. ____ 2. ____ 3. ____ 4. ____ 5. ____ 6. ____ 7. ____ 8. ____

- Verbally label the quality of each fourth prior to singing the interval on tonal syllables.

Perfect fourth   Perfect fourth   Tritone (Aug.)   Tritone (Aug.)   Perfect fourth   Perfect fourth   Diminished fourth   Tonic

Perfect fourth   Tritone (Aug.)   Tritone (Aug.)   Perfect fourth   Perfect fourth   Diminished fourth   Perfect fourth   Tonic

Intervals of a Fourth in the Melodic Minor Scale

- Determine the quality of each fourth and then sing the interval using tonal syllables.

1. ____ 2. ____ 3. ____ 4. ____ 5. ____ 6. ____ 7. ____ 8. ____

XI. Tonal and Melodic Patterns: Melodic Minor Scale

A. Tonal Patterns: Symbolic Association

A1.   A2.

A3.   A4.

A5.   A6.   A7.   A8.

A9.   A10.   A11.   A12.

B. Melodic Patterns: Aural/Oral

1. Listen as your instructor sings a variety of melodic patterns; echo each pattern.[7]
2. Sing the extended harmonic minor scale using tonal syllables and integrate the following rhythm.

[7]Note to instructors: The melodic patterns are found in Section XIC of this chapter.

C. Melodic Patterns: Symbolic Association

XII. Exercises: Melodic Minor Scale

XIII. Exercises: Interval in Tonic Triad (i) and the Relative Major Triad (III)

The following exercises include the intervals from the tonic triad (i) and the relative major triad (III)

Chapter 7
Major and Minor Modes;
Compound Meters
Dotted Quarter = Beat Unit

I. Integrating Rhythm and Tonal Skills: Major Mode

Reading Readiness Melodic Patterns
- Listen as your instructor sings a variety of melodic patterns in major; echo each pattern.[1]

Vocal–Pitch Exercises: Sing each of the following drills daily.
Major Scale
- Sing the extended major scale integrating rhythm patterns A and B (see p. 228).
- Sing the pentachord major scales integrating the indicated rhythm pattern.
  Basic pentachord scale: Pattern E and F   Variation I: Pattern G   Variation II: Pattern H

Intervals in the Major Scale
Intervals from the Tonic
- Verbally label the quality and quantity of each ascending and descending interval from the tonic prior to singing each interval using tonal syllables.
- Sing the intervals integrating rhythm patterns I and J.

Intervals of a Third
- Verbally label the quality and quantity of each interval prior to singing the interval using tonal syllables.
- Sing the intervals integrating rhythm patterns K and L.

Intervals of a Fourth
- Sing the intervals of a fourth integrating rhythm pattern K and L.

Triads
Tonic Chord in the Major Scale
- Sing the tonic chord as an arpeggio integrating rhythm patterns I and J.
- Sing the tonic chord in root position, 1st inversion and 2nd inversion while integrating rhythm patterns C and D.

Triads Built on Each Scale Degree of the Major Scale.
- Verbally label the Roman numeral and quality of each triad prior to singing the triad melodically using tonal syllables.
- Sing each triad as a melodic triad integrating rhythm patterns C and D.

---

[1]Note to instructors: Review Chapter 5 in Part I—Rhythmic Reading. The melodic patterns are found in Section III of this chapter.

Rhythm Patterns

II. Symbolic Association: Major Mode

Major Key Signatures

- For each key signature, (a) determine major key name and (b) notate the harmonic tonic triad.

1. <u>D</u> Major 2. __ Major 3. __ Major 4. __ Major 5. __ Major 6. __ Major 7. __ Major

8. __ Major 9. __ Major 10. __ Major 11. __ Major 12. __ Major 13. __ Major 14. __ Major

Intervals in the Major Scale

- Determine the quantity and quality of each of the following intervals and then sing each using tonal syllables.

1. _____ 2. _____ 3. _____ 4. _____ 5. _____ 6. _____ 7. _____ 8. _____

- Determine the quality of each third and then sing the interval on tonal syllables.

1. __ third 2. __ third 3. __ third 4. __ third 5. __ third 6. __ third 7. __ third 8. __ third

- Determine the quality of each fourth and then sing the interval using tonal syllables.

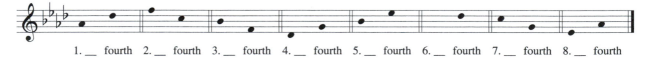

1. __ fourth 2. __ fourth 3. __ fourth 4. __ fourth 5. __ fourth 6. __ fourth 7. __ fourth 8. __ fourth

Triads Built on Each Scale Degree of the Major Scale

- Using tonal syllables, sing each melodic triad and then determine its Roman numeral (N) and quality (Q = M, m, or d°).

1. N __ Q __ 2. N __ Q __ 3. N __ Q __ 4. N __ Q __ 5. N __ Q __ 6. N __ Q __ 7. N __ Q __

III. Melodic Patterns: Major Mode

IV. Exercises: Major Mode

9. Andante cantabile   Polish Lullaby

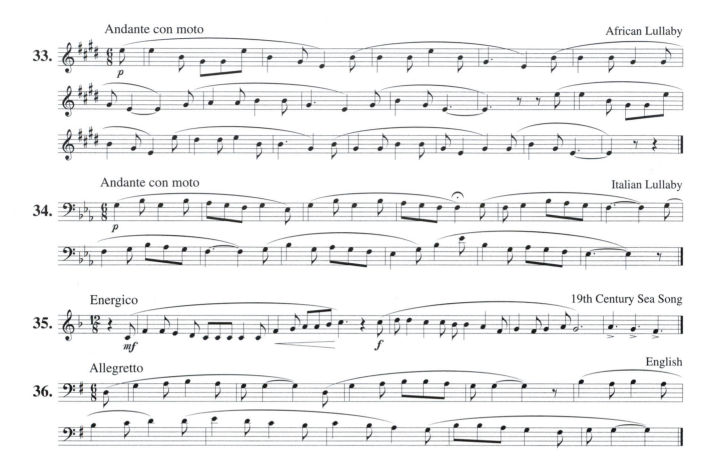

V. Integrating Rhythm and Tonal Skills: Minor Mode

Reading Readiness Melodic Patterns

- Listen as your instructor sings a variety of melodic patterns in minor; echo each pattern.[2]

Vocal—Pitch Exercises: Sing each of the following drills daily.
Minor Scales

- Sing the additive natural, harmonic, and melodic minor scales.
- Sing the natural, harmonic, and melodic minor scales integrating rhythm patterns A and B.
- Sing the pentachord natural, harmonic, and melodic scales integrating the indicated rhythm pattern.
- Basic pentachord scale: Pattern E   Variation I: Pattern F   Variation II: Pattern G

Intervals in the Natural, Harmonic, and Melodic Minor Scales
Intervals from the tonic in each of the three forms of the minor scale

- Verbally label the **quality** and **quantity** of each ascending and descending interval from the tonic prior to singing each interval using tonal syllables.
- Sing the intervals integrating rhythm patterns I and J.

Major and minor thirds in each of the three forms of the minor scale

- Verbally label the **quality** and **quantity** of each interval prior to singing the interval using tonal syllables.

---

[2]Note to Instructors: The melodic patterns are found in Section VII of this chapter.

- Sing the intervals integrating rhythm patterns K and L.

Fourths in each of the three forms of the minor scale
- Sing the intervals of a fourth integrating rhythm pattern H.

Triads
Tonic triad in the minor scales
- Sing the tonic chord as an arpeggio integrating rhythm patterns I and J.
- Sing the tonic chord in root position, 1st inversion, and 2nd inversion while integrating rhythm patterns C and D.

Triads built on each degree of the natural and harmonic minor scales
- Verbally label the Roman numeral and quality of each triad prior to singing the triad melodically using tonal syllables.
- Sing each triad as a melodic triad integrating rhythm patterns C and D.

Rhythm Patterns

VI. Symbolic Association: Minor Mode

Natural, Harmonic, and Melodic Minor Scales
- Sing each of the following scales using tonal syllables and then determine the form.

Minor Key Signatures

- For each key signature, (a) determine the minor key name and (b) notate the harmonic tonic triad.

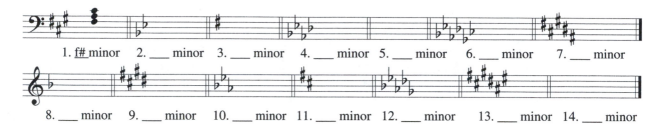

1. f# minor 2. ___ minor 3. ___ minor 4. ___ minor 5. ___ minor 6. ___ minor 7. ___ minor

8. ___ minor 9. ___ minor 10. ___ minor 11. ___ minor 12. ___ minor 13. ___ minor 14. ___ minor

Intervals from Tonic in the Natural, Harmonic, and Melodic Minor Scales

- Determine the quantity and quality of each of the following intervals and then sing each using tonal syllables.

1. _____ 2. _____ 3. _____ 4. _____ 5. _____ 6. _____ 7. _____ 8. _____

Intervals of a Third in the Natural, Harmonic, and Melodic Minor Scales

- Determine the quality of each of the following intervals and then sing each using tonal syllables.

1. __third 2. __third 3. __third 4. __third 5. __third 6. __third 7. __third 8. __third

Intervals of a Fourth in the Natural, Harmonic, and Melodic Minor Scales

- Determine the quality of each of the following intervals and then sing each using tonal syllables.

1. __fourth 2. __fourth 3. __fourth 4. __fourth 5. __fourth 6. __fourth 7. __fourth 8. __fourth

Triads Formed on each of the Scale Degrees in the Natural and Harmonic Minor Scales

- Using tonal syllables, perform the melodic triads indicated and then name its Roman numeral (N) and quality (Q = M, A+, m, or d°).

1. N __ Q __ 2. N __ Q __ 3. N __ Q __ 4. N __ Q __ 5. N __ Q __ 6. N __ Q __ 7. N __ Q __

VII. Melodic Patterns: Minor Mode

VIII. Exercises: Minor Mode

The following exercises contain the tonic triad (i) and the relative major (iii).

Canon: 3 voices

John Frederick Lampe (1703–1751)

Chapter 8

I and V₇ in Major Mode; Simple and Compound Meters

I. Building Aural/Oral Skills: Dominant Triad, Major Mode

Reading Readiness Tonal Patterns

* Listen as your instructor sings a variety of tonal patterns in major; echo each pattern.[1]

Vocal–Pitch Exercises

Chromatic Scale: A chromatic scale includes all twelve pitches contained in an octave; twelve half-steps.

* Sing the ascending and descending chromatic scale (12 half steps) using tonal syllables.

  Solfège: do, di, re, ri, mi, fa, fi, so, si, la, li, ti, do'; do', ti, te, la, le, so, se, fa, mi, me, re, ra, do

  Numbers: 1, #1, 2, #2, 3, 4, #4, 5, #5, 6, #6, 7, 1'; 1', 7, ♭7, 6, ♭6, 5, ♭5, 4, 3, ♭3, 2, ♭2, 1

Ascending and Descending Intervals Moving Out from the Tonic in the Major Scale

* Verbally label the quality and quantity of each interval prior to singing each interval on tonal syllables.

  Solfège: Prime: do – do; M2: do – re; m2: do – ti₁; M3: do – mi; m3: do – la₁; P4: do – fa; P4: do – so₁; P5: do – so; P5: do – fa₁; M6: do – la; m6: do – mi₁; M7: do – ti; m7: do – re₁: P8: do – do' – do – do₁ – do

  Numbers: Prime: 1 – 1; M2: 1 – 2; m2: 1 – 7₁; M3: 1 – 3; m3: 1 – 6₁; P4: 1 – 4; P4: 1 – 5₁; P5: 1 – 5; P5: 1 – 4₁; M6: 1 – 6; m6: 1 – 3₁; M7: 1 – 7; m7: 1 – 2₁: P8: 1 – 1' – 1 – 1₁ – 1

* Using tonal syllables, sing the intervals integrating a variety of rhythm patterns.

Dominant Triad (V): The tonic (I) and dominant (V) triads have the strongest ability to establish a feeling for key.

* Sing the following tonic-dominant triads using tonal syllables as melodic triads.
* Using tonal syllables, sing each triad progression integrating a variety of rhythm patterns.

Root Position			*1st Inversion*			*2nd Inversion*		
							ti (7)	
so (5)			so (5)	so (5)		so (5)	so (5)	
mi (3)			mi (3)			mi (3)		
	re (2)			re (2)			re (2)	
do (1)		do (1)	do (1)		do (1)	do (1)		do (1)
	ti₁ (7₁)			ti₁ (7₁)				
	so₁ (5₁)							
I	**V**	**I**	**I**	**V₆**	**I**	**I**	**V₆₄**	**I**

---

[1]Note to instructors: Review Chapter 5 in Part I—Rhythmic Reading. The tonal patterns are found in Section III in this chapter.

First Inversion Triads Built on Each Degree of the Major Scale
- Verbally label the Roman numeral and quality of each triad prior to singing the triad melodically using tonal syllables.
- Using tonal syllables, sing each triad integrating a variety of rhythm patterns.

						ti¹ (7¹)
					la¹ (6¹)	
				so¹ (5¹)		
			fa¹ (4¹)			fa¹ (4¹)
		mi¹ (3¹)			mi¹ (3¹)	
	re¹ (2¹)			re¹ (2¹)		re¹ (2¹)
do¹ (1¹)			do¹ (1¹)		do¹ (1¹)		do¹ (1¹)
		ti (7)		ti (7)		
	la (6)		la (6)			
so (5)		so (5)				
	fa (4)					
mi (3)						

I₆	ii₆	iii₆	IV₆	V₆	vi₆	vii₆°
Major	*minor*	*minor*	*Major*	*Major*	*minor*	*dim.*

II. Symbolic Association: Dominant Triad, Major Mode

Dominant Triad (V)

The root of the dominant triad is a stable tone (dominant—5th scale degree) but the third (leading tone—7th scale degree), and fifth (supertonic-2nd scale degree) are active tones. Notice that the third (*ti*/7) or fifth (*re*/2) of the dominant triad is a scale step below or above the tonic tone (*do*/1).

- Sing each of the melodic triads using tonal syllables.

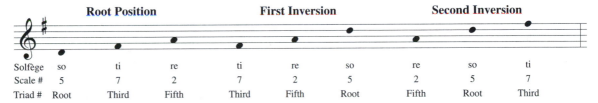

	Root Position			**First Inversion**			**Second Inversion**		
Solfège	so	ti	re	ti	re	so	re	so	ti
Scale #	5	7	2	7	2	5	2	5	7
Triad #	Root	Third	Fifth	Third	Fifth	Root	Fifth	Root	Third

Melodies contain *chord tones* and nonharmonic tones. The most common types of nonharmonic tones are *passing tones* (connects two different chord tones by step) and *neighbor tones* (connects two chord tones of the same pitch by step.

- Label chord (CT), neighbor (NT), and passing (PT) tones in the following melodies and then sing each melody using tonal syllables.

The melodic-harmonic pattern that occurs at the end of a phrase is called a cadence. Cadences are either terminal (ends on the tonic chord—very stable) or progressive (ends on the dominant chord—instability, implies continuation). A harmonic cadence that moves from V to I is called an authentic cadence and a cadence that ends on V is called a half cadence.

- Label the type(s) of cadences in each of the melodies (A. and B.).

First Inversion Triads Built on Each Scale Degree of the Major Scale

- Verbally label the Roman numeral and quality of each triad prior to singing each melodic triad on tonal syllables.

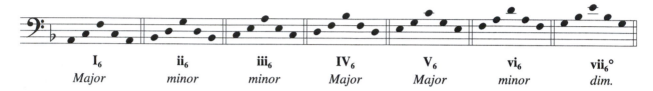

Determine the Roman numeral (N) and quality (Q=M, A+, m, or d°) of each triad and then sing the triads.

III. Tonal Patterns: Dominant Triad, Major Mode

A. Dominant Chord Tones (Root Position)

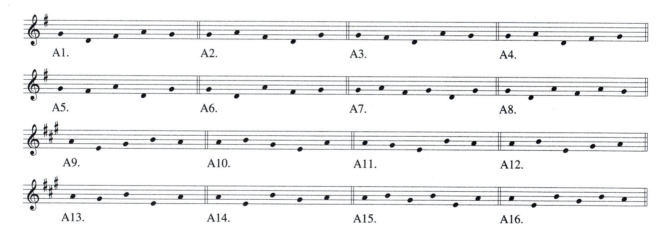

B. Tonic—Dominant (Root)

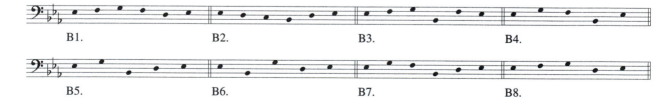

C. Dominant Chord Tones (First Inversion)

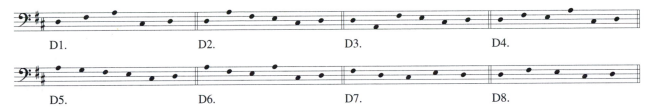

D. Tonic—Dominant (First Inversion)

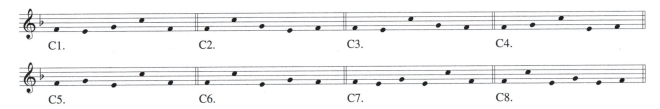

E. Dominant Chord Tones (Second Inversion)

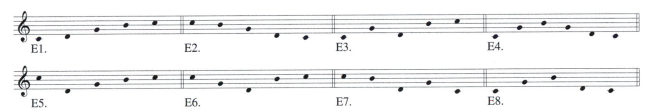

F. Tonic—Dominant (Second Inversion)

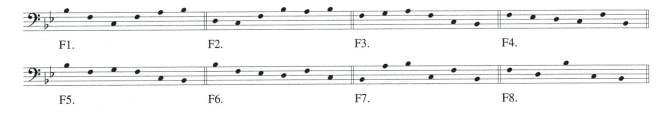

IV. Exercises: Dominant Triad, Major Mode, Simple Meters

V. Building Aural/Oral Skills: Dominant Seventh Chord, Major Mode

Reading Readiness Tonal Patterns

- Listen as your instructor sings a variety of tonal patterns in major; echo each pattern.[2]

Vocal–Pitch Exercises
Chromatic Scale

- Sing the ascending and descending chromatic scale (12 half steps) using tonal syllables.

Ascending and Descending Intervals Moving out from the Tonic in the Major Scale

- Verbally label the quality and quantity of each interval prior to singing each interval using tonal syllables.

- Sing the intervals integrating a variety of rhythm patterns.

Dominant Seventh Chord (V₇)

When the fourth scale degree (*fa*/4) is added to the dominant triad, an interval of a seventh is formed above the tonic of the dominant chord, hence the name, dominant seventh. By adding the fourth scale degree (subdominant) an active tone, to the already active dominant triad, the dominant seventh chord has additional impetus to move to the tonic. Notice that this four-note chord contains both the V and vii° triads.

- Sing the tonic–dominant seventh triads as melodic triads.
- Using tonal syllables, sing each I–V₇ progression integrating a variety of rhythm patterns.

Root Position			First Inversion			Second Inversion			Third Inversion		
										re′ (2′)	
							ti (7)			ti (7)	
so (5)			so (5)	so (5)		so (5)	so (5)		so (5)	so (5)	
	fa (4)			fa (4)			fa (4)			fa (4)	
mi (3)			mi (3)			mi (3)			mi (3)		
	re (2)			re (2)			re (2)				
do (1)		do (1)	do (1)		do (1)	do (1)		do (1)	do (1)		do (1)
	ti, (7,)			ti, (7,)							
	so, (5,)										
I	$\mathbf{V_7}$	**I**	**I**	$\mathbf{V^6_5}$	**I**	**I**	$\mathbf{V^4_3}$	**I**	**I**	$\mathbf{V^4_2}$	**I**

Second Inversion Triads Built on each Degree of the Major Scale

- Verbally label the Roman numeral and quality of each triad prior to singing the triad melodically on tonal syllables.
- Using tonal syllables, sing each triad integrating a variety of rhythm patterns.

---

[2]Note to instructors: The tonal patterns are found in Section VII of this chapter.

I_4^6	ii_4^6	iii_4^6	IV_4^6	V_4^6	vi_4^6	vii_4^{o6}
						re^l (2^l)
					do^l (1^l)	do^l (1^l)
				ti (7)		ti (7)
			la (6)		la (6)	
		so (5)		so (5)		
	fa (4)		fa (4)			fa (4)
mi (3)		mi (3)			mi (3)	
	re (2)			re (2)		
do (1)			do (1)			
		ti₁ (7₁)				
	la₁ (6₁)					
so₁ (5₁)						
Major	*minor*	*minor*	*Major*	*Major*	*minor*	*dim.*

VI. Symbolic Association: Dominant Seventh Chord, Major Mode

Dominant Seventh Chord (V₇)

The dominant seventh chord is a four-note chord built on the dominant of the scale. Notice that the chord is a major triad plus a minor third (a major third plus two minor thirds).

- Sing each of the arpeggios using tonal syllables.

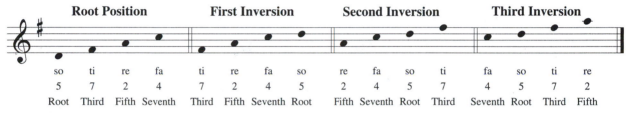

Root Position				First Inversion				Second Inversion				Third Inversion			
so	ti	re	fa	ti	re	fa	so	re	fa	so	ti	fa	so	ti	re
5	7	2	4	7	2	4	5	2	4	5	7	4	5	7	2
Root	Third	Fifth	Seventh	Third	Fifth	Seventh	Root	Fifth	Seventh	Root	Third	Seventh	Root	Third	Fifth

- Label chord (CT), neighbor (NT), and passing (PT) tones in the following melodies and then sing each one using tonal syllables.

A.

B.

- Label the type(s) of cadences in each of the melodies given.

Second Inversion Triads Built on each Degree of the Major Scale

- Verbally label the Roman numeral and quality of each triad prior to singing each melodic triad using tonal syllables.

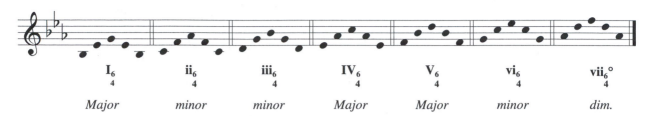

I_6 ii_6 iii_6 IV_6 V_6 vi_6 $vii_6°$
$_4$ $_4$ $_4$ $_4$ $_4$ $_4$ $_4$

Major   *minor*   *minor*   *Major*   *Major*   *minor*   *dim.*

- Determine the Roman numeral (N) and quality (Q = M, A⁺, m, or d°) of each triad and then sing each triad.

1. N__ Q__   2. N__ Q__   3. N__ Q__   4. N__ Q__   5. N__ Q__   6. N__ Q__   7. N__ Q__

VII. Tonal Patterns: Dominant Seventh Chord, Major Mode

A. Dominant Seventh (Root Position)

A1.   A2.   A3.   A4.

B. Dominant Seventh (First Inversion)

B1.   B2.   B3.   B4.

C. Dominant Seventh (Second Inversion)

C1.   C2.   C3.   C4.

D. Dominant Seventh (Third Inversion)

D1.   D2.   D3.   D4.

E. Tonic—Dominant Seventh

E1.   E2.   E3.   E4.

E5.   E6.   E7.   E8.

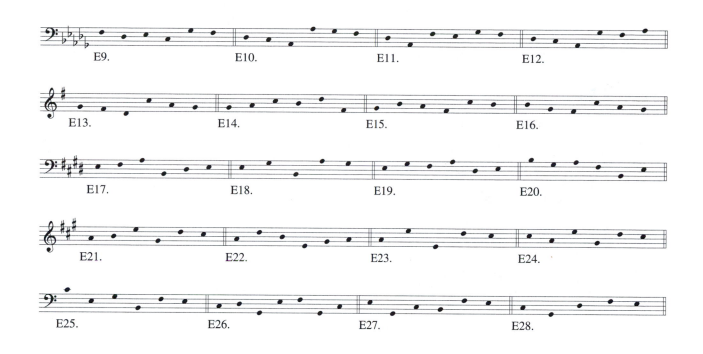

E9. E10. E11. E12.

E13. E14. E15. E16.

E17. E18. E19. E20.

E21. E22. E23. E24.

E25. E26. E27. E28.

VIII. Exercises: Dominant Seventh Chord, Major Mode, Simple Meters

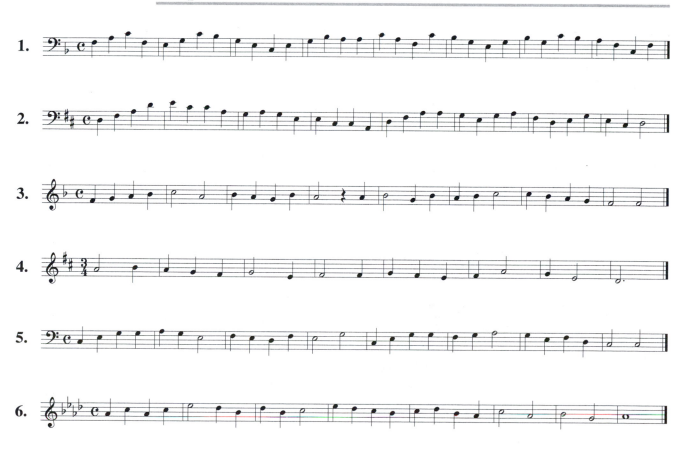

1.

2.

3.

4.

5.

6.

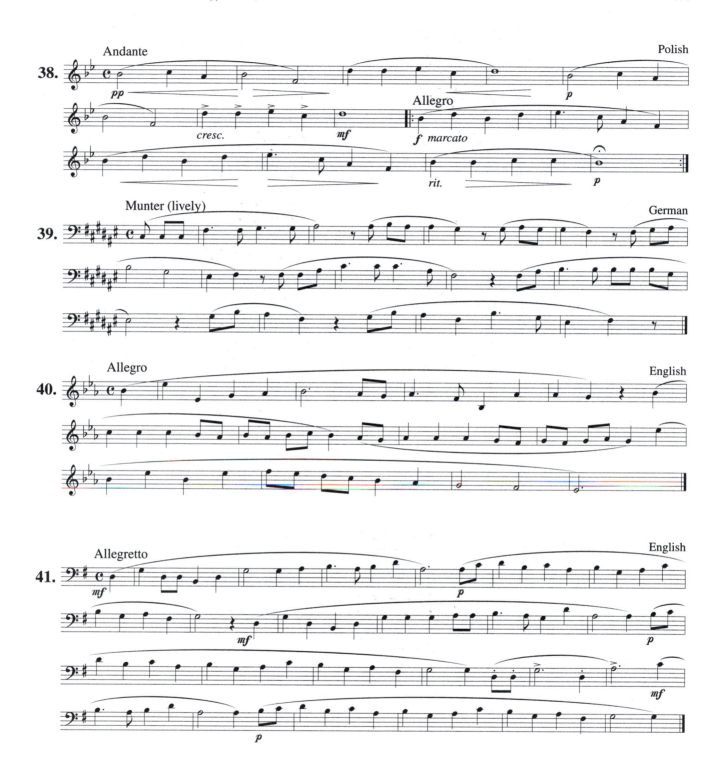

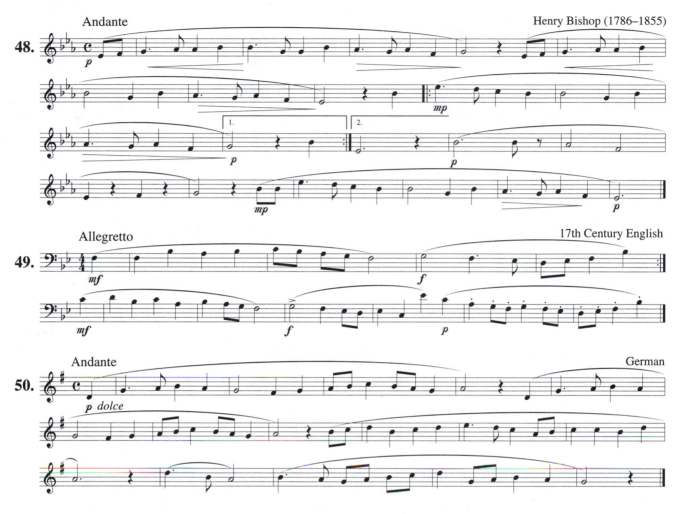

IX. Exercises: Dominant and Dominant Seventh, Major Mode, Compound Meters

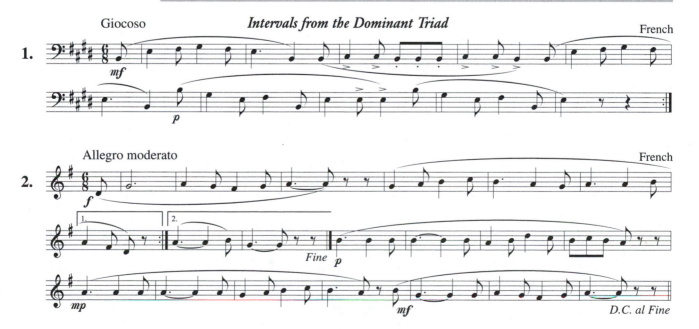

Intervals from the Dominant Seventh Chord

Chapter 9
i and V₇ in Minor Mode; Simple and Compound Meters

I. Building Aural/Oral Skills: Dominant Triad, Minor Mode

Reading Readiness Tonal Patterns
- Listen as your instructor sings a variety of tonal patterns in minor; echo each pattern.[1]

Vocal–Pitch Exercises
Chromatic Scale
- Sing the ascending and descending chromatic scale (12 half steps) using tonal syllables.

Ascending and Descending Intervals Moving out from the Tonic in the Natural Minor Scale
- Verbally label the quality and quantity of each interval prior to singing each interval on tonal syllables.

    Do-Based Minor Solfège: Prime: do – do; M2: do – re; M2: do – te₁; m3: do – me; M3: do – le₁; P4: do – fa; P4: do – so₁; P5: do – so; P5: do – fa₁; m6: do – le; M6: do – me₁; m7: do – te; m7: do – re₁; P8: do – do¹ – do – do₁ – do

    La-Based Minor Solfège: Prime: la – la; M2: la – ti; M2: la – so₁; m3: la – do; M3: la – fa₁; P4: la – re; P4: la – mi₁; P5: la – mi; P5: la – re₁; m6: la – fa; M6: la – mi₁; m7: la – so; m7: la – ti₁; P8: la – la¹ – la – la₁ – la

    Number: Prime: 1 – 1; M2: 1 – 2; M2: 1 – ♭7₁; m3: 1 – ♭3; M3: 1 – ♭6₁; P4: 1 – 4; P4: 1 – 5₁; P5: 1 – 5; P5: 1 – 4₁; m6: 1 – ♭6; M6: 1 – ♭3₁; m7: 1 – ♭7; m7: 1 – 2₁; P8: 1 – 1' – 1 – 1₁ – 1

- Using tonal syllables, sing the intervals integrating a variety of rhythm patterns.

Dominant Triad (V): The tonic (i) and dominant (V) triads have the strongest ability to establish a feeling for key.
- Using tonal syllables, sing the tonic and dominant triads as melodic triads using tonal sillables.
- Using tonal syllables, sing each triad progression integrating a variety of rhythm patterns.

Root Position		1st Inversion		2nd Inversion

	Root Position			1st Inversion				2nd Inversion ti (7) si	

```
        Root Position                    1st Inversion                          2nd Inversion
                                                                                 ti (7) si
so (5) mi                        so (5) mi   so (5₁) mi                so (5) mi   so (5) mi

me (♭3) do                       me (♭3) do                           me (♭3) do

              re (2) ti                      re (2) ti                           re (2) ti
do (1) la                do (1) la   do (1) la          do (1) la   do (1) la          do (1) la
              ti (7₁) si                     ti (7₁) si

              so (5₁) mi

    i         V         i        i        V₆        i        i        V⁶₄        i
```

First Inversion Triads Built on Each Scale Degree of the Minor Scales
- Verbally label the Roman numeral and quality of each triad prior to singing the triad melodically on tonal syllables.
- Using tonal syllables, sing each triad integrating a variety of rhythm patterns.

---

[1]Note to instructors: Review Chapter 5 in Part I—Rhythmic Reading. The melodic patterns are found in Section III of this chapter.

te'(♭7')so'   ti'(7') si'

le'(♭6') fa'

so'(5')mi'   so'(5')mi'   fa'(4')re'   fa'(4') re'

fa'(4') re'   me'(♭3')do'

me'(♭3')do'   me'(♭3')do'   me'(♭3')do'

re'(2')ti'   re'(2')ti'   re'(2')ti'   re'(2')ti'   re'(2') ti'

do'(1')la'   do'(1')la'   do'(1')la'   do'(1')la'

te(♭7)so   ti(7)si   te(♭7)so   ti(7) si

le(♭6)fa   le(♭6) fa

so(5)mi   so(5)mi   so(5)mi

fa(4)re

me(♭3)do

i_6	ii°_6	III_6	III^+_6	iv_6	v_6	V_6	VI_6	VII_6	vii°_6
minor	dim.	Major	Aug.	minor	minor	Major	Major	Major	dim.

II. Symbolic Association: Dominant Triad, Minor Mode

Dominant Triad (V)

The root of the dominant triad is a stable tone (dominant—5th scale degree) but the third (leading tone—7th scale degree,) and fifth (supertonic—2nd scale degree) are active tones. Notice that the third and fifth of the dominant triad are a scale step below or above the tonic, respectively.

- Sing each of the melodic triads using tonal syllables.

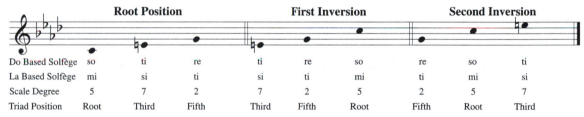

	Root Position			**First Inversion**			**Second Inversion**		
Do Based Solfège	so	ti	re	ti	re	so	re	so	ti
La Based Solfège	mi	si	ti	si	ti	mi	ti	mi	si
Scale Degree	5	7	2	7	2	5	2	5	7
Triad Position	Root	Third	Fifth	Third	Fifth	Root	Fifth	Root	Third

- Label chord (CT), neighbor (NT), and passing (PT) tones and type(s) of cadences in the following melody and then sing the melody using tonal syllables.

First Inversion Triads Built on Each Scale Degree of the Harmonic Minor Scale

- Verbally label the Roman numeral and quality of each triad and then sing the melodic triads using tonal syllables.

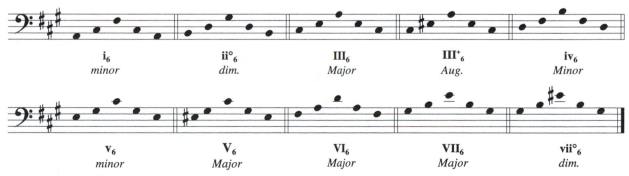

i_6	ii°_6	III_6	III^+_6	iv_6
minor	dim.	Major	Aug.	Minor

v_6	V_6	VI_6	VII_6	vii°_6
minor	Major	Major	Major	dim.

- Determine the Roman numeral (N) and quality (Q = M, A⁺, m, or d°) of each triad and then sing the triads using tonal syllables.

1. N ___ Q ___ 2. N ___ Q ___ 3. N ___ Q ___ 4. N ___ Q ___ 5. N ___ Q ___

6. N ___ Q ___ 7. N ___ Q ___ 8. N ___ Q ___ 9. N ___ Q ___ 10. N ___ Q ___

III. Tonal Patterns: Dominant Triad, Minor Mode

A. Dominant Chord Tones (Root Position)

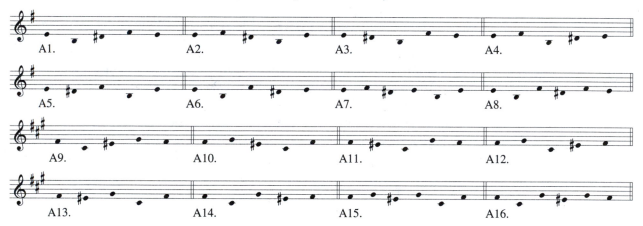

A1.   A2.   A3.   A4.

A5.   A6.   A7.   A8.

A9.   A10.   A11.   A12.

A13.   A14.   A15.   A16.

B. Tonic—Dominant (Root)

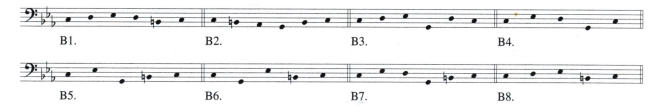

B1.   B2.   B3.   B4.

B5.   B6.   B7.   B8.

C. Dominant Chord Tones (First Inversion)

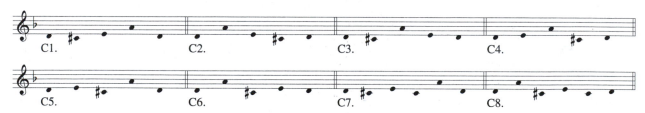

C1.   C2.   C3.   C4.

C5.   C6.   C7.   C8.

D. Tonic—Dominant (First Inversion)

E. Dominant Chord Tones (Second Inversion)

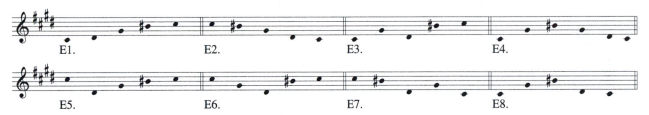

F. Tonic—Dominant (Second Inversion)

IV. Exercises: Dominant Triad, Minor Mode, Simple Meters

V. Building Aural/Oral Skills: Dominant Seventh Chord, Minor Mode

Readiness Tonal Patterns

- Listen as your instructor sings a variety of tonal patterns in minor; echo each pattern.[2]

Vocal–Pitch Exercises
Chromatic Scale

- Sing the ascending and descending chromatic scale (12 half steps) using tonal syllables.

Ascending and Descending Intervals Moving Out From the Tonic in the Minor Scale

- Verbally label the quality and quantity of each interval prior to singing each interval using tonal syllables.
- Using tonal syllables, sing the intervals integrating a variety of rhythm patterns.

Dominant Seventh Chord (V₇)

When the fourth scale degree (fa/4/re) is added to the dominant triad, an interval of a seventh is formed above the tonic of the dominant chord, hence the name, dominant seventh. By adding the fourth scale degree (subdominant) an active tone, to the already active dominant triad, the dominant seventh chord has additional impetus to move to the tonic. Notice that this four-note chord contains both the V and vii° triads.

- Sing the tonic—dominant seventh triads as melodic triads using tonal syllables.
- Using tonal syllables, sing each i – V7 progression integrating a variety of rhythm patterns.

Root Position		First Inversion		Second Inversion		Third Inversion	Root
						re¹ (2¹) ti¹	
				ti (7) si		ti (7) si	
so (5) mi		so (5) mi	so (5) mi	so (5) mi	so (5) mi	so (5) mi	so (5) mi
	fa (4) re		fa (4) re		fa (4) re		fa (4) re
me (♭3) do		me (♭3) do		me (♭3) do		me (♭3) do	me (♭3) do
	re (2) ti			re (2) ti			
do (1) la		do (1) la	re (2) ti	do (1) la		do (1) la	do (1) la
	ti₍ (7₎) si₍		do (1) la				
			ti₍ (7₎) si₍				
	so₍ (5₎) mi₍						
i	**V₇**	**i**	**V$_5^6$**	**i**	**V$_3^4$**	**i**	**V$_2^4$**	**i**

---

[2]Note to instructors: The tonal patterns are found in Section VII of this chapter.

Second Inversion Triads Built on Each Degree of the Major Scale

- Verbally label the Roman numeral and quality of each triad prior to singing the triad melodically on tonal syllables.
- Using tonal syllables, sing each triad integrating a variety of rhythm patterns.

```
                                                        re¹(2¹)ti¹    re¹(2¹)ti¹
                                   do¹(1¹)la¹                                       do¹(1¹)la¹
               te(♭7)so  ti(7)si                 te(♭7)so   ti(7)si
      le(♭6)fa                         le(♭6)fa
   so(5)mi  so(5)mi          so(5)mi  so(5)mi                    fa(4)re   fa(4)re
 fa(4)re                fa(4)re                       me(♭3)do
me(♭3)do  me(♭3)do  me(♭3)do
           re(2)ti                     re(2)ti   re(2)ti
 do(1)la                    do(1)la
           te₁(♭7₁)so₁  ti₁(7₁)si₁
   le(♭6₁)fa₁
so₁(5₁)mi₁
```

i^6_4	$ii^{\circ 6}_4$	III^6_4	III^{+6}_4	iv^6_4	v^6_4	V^6_4	VI^6_4	VII^6_4	$vii^{\circ 6}_4$
minor	*dim.*	*Major*	*Aug.*	*minor*	*minor*	*Major*	*Major*	*Major*	*dim.*

VI. Symbolic Association: Dominant Seventh Chord, Minor Mode

Dominant Seventh Chord (V_7)

The dominant seventh chord is a four-note chord built on the dominant of the scale. Notice that the chord is a major triad plus a minor third (a major third plus two minor thirds).

- Sing each of the arpeggios using tonal syllables.

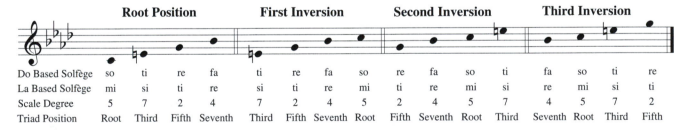

	Root Position				First Inversion				Second Inversion				Third Inversion			
Do Based Solfège	so	ti	re	fa	ti	re	fa	so	re	fa	so	ti	fa	so	ti	re
La Based Solfège	mi	si	ti	re	si	ti	re	mi	ti	re	mi	si	re	mi	si	ti
Scale Degree	5	7	2	4	7	2	4	5	2	4	5	7	4	5	7	2
Triad Position	Root	Third	Fifth	Seventh	Third	Fifth	Seventh	Root	Fifth	Seventh	Root	Third	Seventh	Root	Third	Fifth

- Label chord (CT), neighbor (NT), and passing tones (PT) in the following melodies and then sing each one using tonal syllables.

- Label the type(s) of cadences in each of the melodies given.

Second Inversion Triads Built on Each Degree of the Minor Scale

- Verbally label the Roman numeral and quality of each triad prior to singing each melodic triad using tonal syllables.

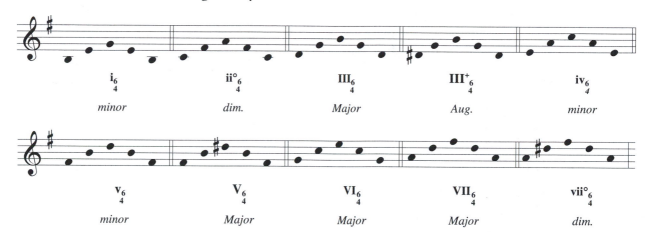

i_6^4	$ii°_6^4$	III_6^4	$III^+_6{}_4$	iv_6^4
minor	*dim.*	*Major*	*Aug.*	*minor*

v_6^4	V_6^4	VI_6^4	VII_6^4	$vii°_6^4$
minor	*Major*	*Major*	*Major*	*dim.*

- Determine the Roman numeral (N) and quality (Q = M, A⁺, m, or d°) of each triad and then sing each triad using tonal syllables.

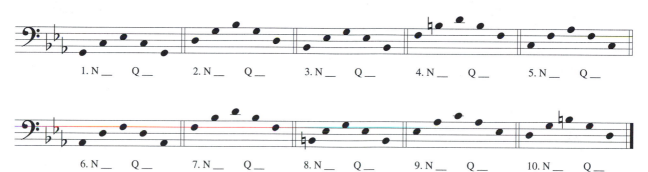

1. N __ Q __   2. N __ Q __   3. N __ Q __   4. N __ Q __   5. N __ Q __

6. N __ Q __   7. N __ Q __   8. N __ Q __   9. N __ Q __   10. N __ Q __

VII. Tonal Patterns: Dominant Seventh Chord, Minor Mode

A. Dominant Seventh (Root Position)

A1.   A2.   A3.   A4.

B. Dominant Seventh (First Inversion)

B1.   B2.   B3.   B4.

C. Dominant Seventh (Second Inversion)

C1.   C2.   C3.   C4.

D. Dominant Seventh (Third Inversion)

E. Tonic—Dominant Seventh

VIII. Exercises: Dominant Seventh Chord, Minor Mode, Simple Meters

Intervals from the Relative Major

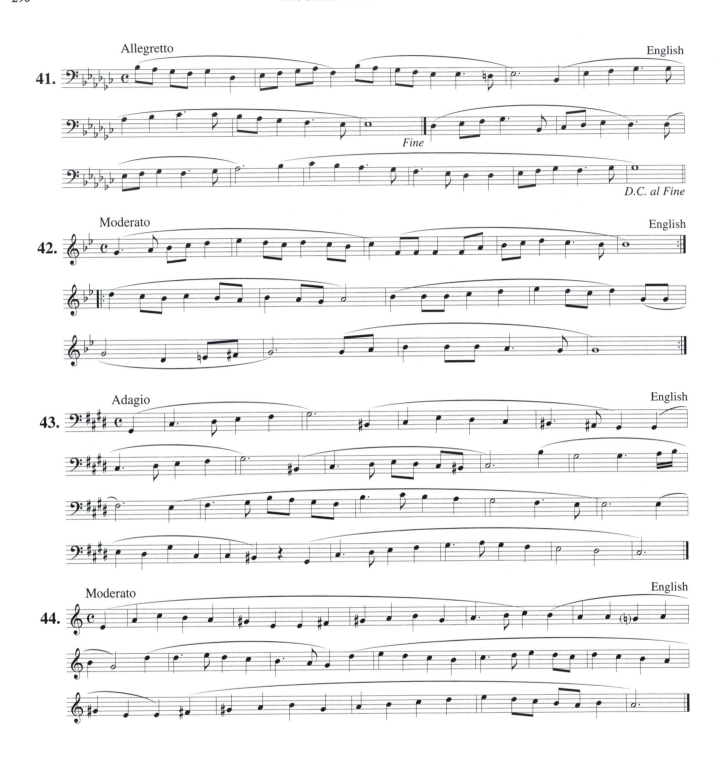

IX. Exercises: Dominant and Dominant Seventh, Minor Mode, Compound Meters

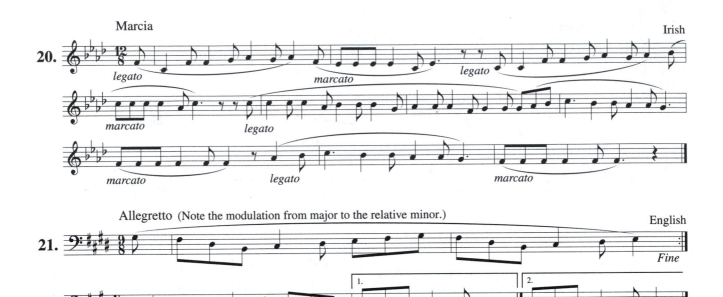

Chapter 10
I and V₇ in Major Mode; Other Rhythms in Simple Meters

I. Integrating Rhythm Tonal Skills: Major Mode

Reading Readiness Melodic Patterns

- Listen as your instructor sings a variety of melodic patterns in major; echo each pattern.[1]

Vocal–Pitch Exercises

Sing each of the following drills daily integrating a variety of rhythm patterns. Select from the rhythm patterns below or create your own.

Rhythm Patterns

Major Scale

- Sing the extended, additive, and pentachord major scales integrating a variety of rhythm patterns.

Intervals in the Major Scale

- Using tonal syllables, sing the ascending and descending intervals from tonic integrating a variety of rhythm patterns.
- Using tonal syllables, sing the intervals moving out from tonic integrating a variety of rhythm patterns.
- Using tonal syllables, sing the intervals of a third integrating a variety of rhythm patterns.
- Using tonal syllables, sing the intervals of a fourth integrating a variety of rhythm patterns.

Root and Inverted Triads Built on Each Scale Degree of the Major Scale

- Using tonal syllables, sing the root position, 1st inversion and 2nd inversion triads integrating a variety of rhythm patterns.

Harmony

- Using tonal syllables, sing the I–V₇ chord progressions integrating a variety of rhythm patterns.

---

[1]Note to instructors: The melodic patterns are found in Section IIIA–triplets, IVA–syncopation, and VA–sixteenth notes.

Chromatic Intervals

- Verbally label the quantity and quality of each ascending and descending chromatic interval prior to singing each interval on tonal syllables.

    Solfège

    Ascending: Prime: do – do; A1: do – di; M2: do – re; A2: do – ri; M3: do – mi; P4: do – fa; A4: do – fi; P5: do – so; A5: do – si; M6: do – la; A6: do – li; M7: do – ti; P8: do – do'

    Descending: Prime: do' – do'; m2: do' – ti; M2: do' – te; m3: do' – la; M3: do' – le; P4: do' – so; A4: do' – se; P5: do' – fa; m6: do' – mi; M6: do' – me; m7: do' – re; M7: do' – ra; P8: do' – do

    Numbers:

    Ascending: Prime: 1 – 1; A1: 1 – #1; M2: 1 – 2; A2: 1 – #2; M3: 1 – 3; P4: 1 – 4; A4: 1 – #4; P5: 1 – 5; A5: 1 – #5; M6: 1 – 6; A6: 1 – #6; M7: 1 – 7; P8: 1 – 1'

    Descending: Prime: 1' – 1'; m2: 1' – 7; M2: 1 – ♭7; m3: 1' – 6; M3: 1' – ♭6; P4: 1' – 5; A4: 1' – ♭5; P5: 1' – 4; m6: 1' – 3; M6: 1' – ♭3; m7: 1' – 2; M7: 1' – ♭2 ; P8: 1' – 1

II. Symbolic Association

Chromatic Intervals

- Verbally label the quantity and quality of each interval and then sing the interval using tonal syllables.

Ascending Intervals

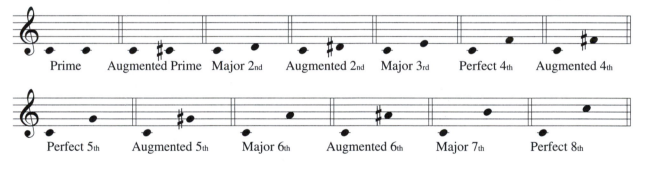

Descending Intervals

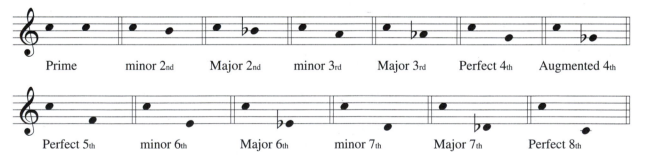

- Determine the quantity and quality of each interval and then sing the interval using tonal syllables.

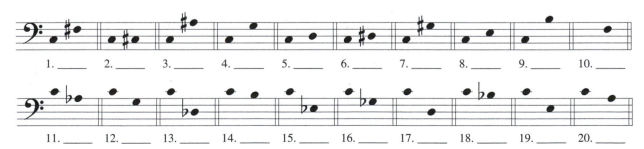

Root and Inverted Triads

- Determine the Roman numeral, quality, and inversion of each melodic triad and then sing the triad using tonal syllables.

Dominant and Dominant Seventh Chords

- Determine the missing Roman numeral, quality, and inversion and then sing the succession of pitches using tonal syllables.

III. Melodic Patterns and Exercises: Triplets, Tonic Only

A. Melodic Patterns

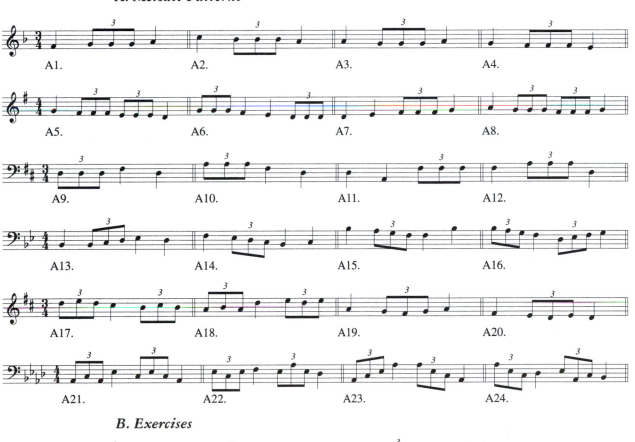

B. Exercises

Canon: 3 voices   Traditional (adapted)

18.

Moderato (Note the la-mi interval.)   Swiss

19.

Remember to practice your dictation skills.

IV. Melodic Patterns and Exercises: Syncopation, Tonic Only

A. Melodic Patterns

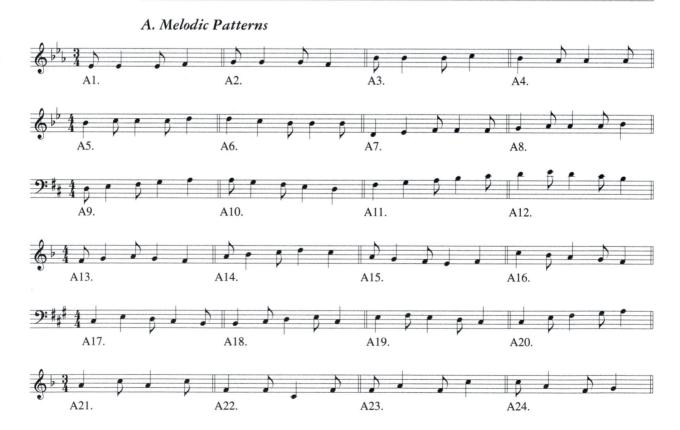

A1.   A2.   A3.   A4.

A5.   A6.   A7.   A8.

A9.   A10.   A11.   A12.

A13.   A14.   A15.   A16.

A17.   A18.   A19.   A20.

A21.   A22.   A23.   A24.

B. Exercises

7.

8.

9.

10.

11.

12.

Canon: 2 voices

13. [1] [2]

Canon: 4 voices

Thomas Ravenscroft (c. 1582–c. 1635); *Deuteromelia*, 1609

14. [1] [2] [3] [4]

Keep a steady beat and use tonal syllables.

Canon: 3 voices

Traditional

15.

Moderato

Polish

16.

Moderato

English

17.

Allegro

African-American Spiritual

18.

V. Melodic Patterns and Exercises: Subdvided Beat, Tonic Only

A. Melodic Patterns

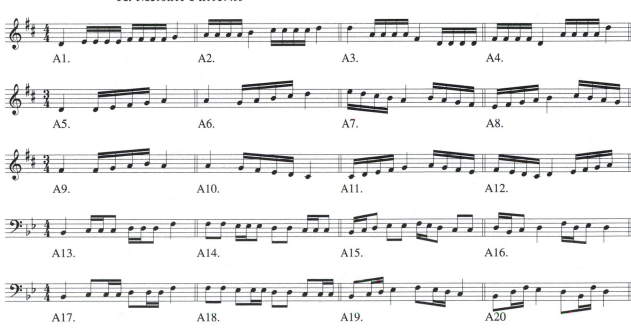

A1.   A2.   A3.   A4.

A5.   A6.   A7.   A8.

A9.   A10.   A11.   A12.

A13.   A14.   A15.   A16.

A17.   A18.   A19.   A20

(Continued)

A21.   A22.   A23.   A24.

A25.   A26.   A27.   A28.

A29.   A30.   A31.   A32.

B. Exercises

1.

Canon: 4 voices

English

2.

Allegro commodo

Flemish

3.

Allegretto (Note the mi–la interval.)

English

4.

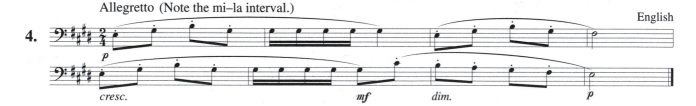

5.

6.

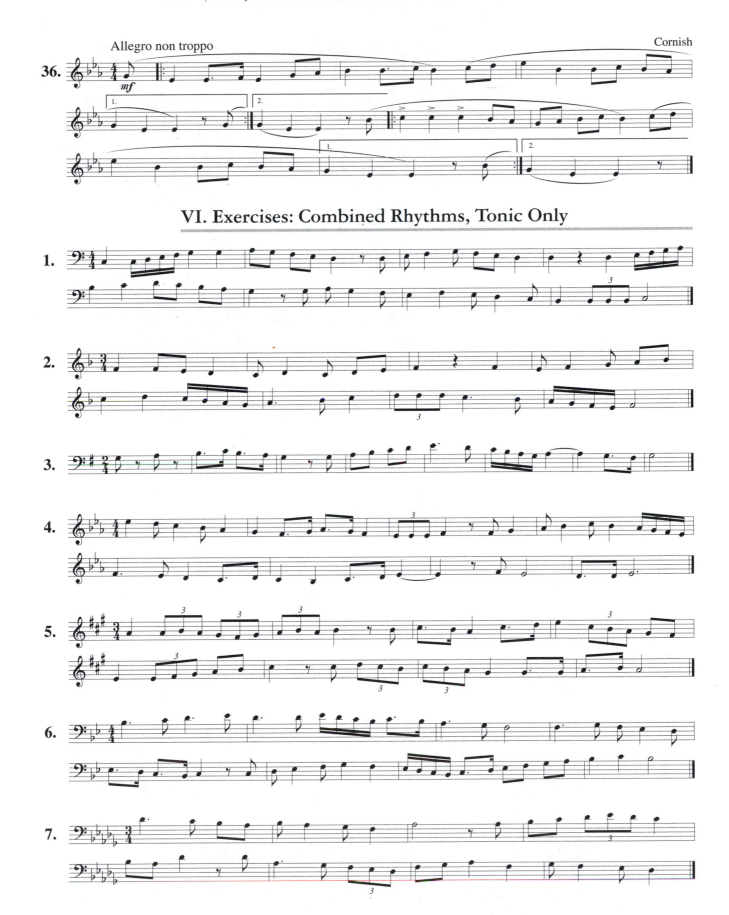

VI. Exercises: Combined Rhythms, Tonic Only

VII. Exercises: Combined Rhythms, Tonic and Dominant

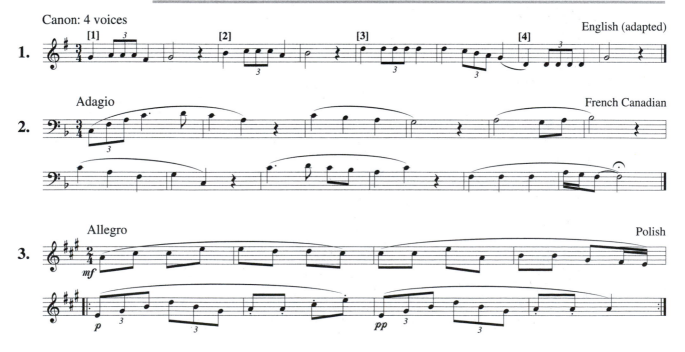

Remember to practice your dictation skills.

25. Allegro non troppo (Note the la–do–mi intervals.) William Boyce (1710-1779)

26. Moderato (Note the la–do–mi intervals.) Dutch

27. Canon: 5 voices Latin Canon; *Pammelia*, 1609

28. Andante Greek

29. Con spirito (Note the la–mi interval.) English

Chapter 11

i and V₇ in Minor Mode; Other Rhythms in Simple Meters

I. Integrating Rhythm and Tonal Skills: Minor Modes

Reading Readiness Melodic Patterns

* Listen as your instructor sings a variety of melodic patterns in minor; echo each pattern[1].

Vocal–Pitch Exercises

Sing each of the following drills daily integrating a variety of rhythm patterns; select from the rhythm patterns below or create your own.

Rhythm Patterns

A.

B.

C.

D.

E.

F.

Natural, Harmonic, and Melodic Minor Scales

* Using tonal syllables, sing the extended, additive, and pentachord scales in each of the three forms of the minor scales integrating a variety of rhythm patterns.

Intervals in Three Forms of the Minor Scales

* Using tonal syllables, sing the ascending and descending intervals from tonic and the intervals moving out from tonic in each of the three forms of the minor scales integrating a variety of rhythm patterns.
* Using tonal syllables, sing the intervals of a third in each of the three forms of the minor scales integrating a variety of rhythm patterns.
* Using tonal syllables, sing the intervals of a fourth in each of the three forms of the minor scales integrating a variety of rhythm patterns.

Root and Inverted Triads Built on each Scale Degree of the Minor Scales

* Using tonal syllables, sing the root position, 1st inversion and 2nd inversion triads as melodic triads in each of the three forms of the minor scales. Repeat integrating a variety of rhythm patterns.

Harmony

* Using tonal syllables, sing the succession of pitches in the i–V₇ chord progressions integrating a variety of rhythm patterns.

---

[1]Note to instructors: The melodic patterns are found in Section IIIA–triplets, IVA–syncopation, and VA–sixteenth notes.

Chromatic Intervals
- Verbally label the quantity and quality of each ascending and descending chromatic interval prior to singing the interval on tonal syllables.
- Using tonal syllables, sing the chromatic intervals integrating a variety of rhythm patterns.

II. Symbolic Association

Chromatic Intervals
- Determine the quantity and quality of each interval and then sing the interval.

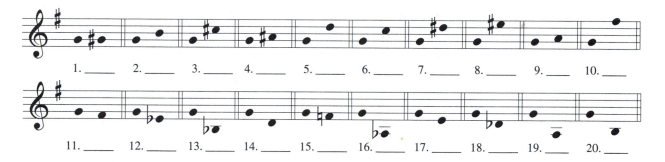

1. ____ 2. ____ 3. ____ 4. ____ 5. ____ 6. ____ 7. ____ 8. ____ 9. ____ 10. ____

11. ____ 12. ____ 13. ____ 14. ____ 15. ____ 16. ____ 17. ____ 18. ____ 19. ____ 20. ____

Minor Scales
- Determine the form (Natural, Harmonic, Melodic) of each scale and then sing the scales.

1. _____ Scale

2. _____ Scale

3. _____ Scale

Root and Inverted Triads Built on each Scale Degree of the Minor Scales
- Determine the Roman numeral, quality, and inversion of each melodic triad and then sing the triads.

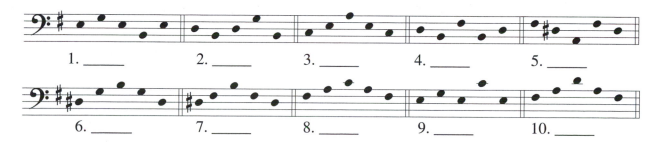

1. ____   2. ____   3. ____   4. ____   5. ____

6. ____   7. ____   8. ____   9. ____   10. ____

Dominant and Dominant Seventh Chords

- Determine the missing Roman numerals, quality, and inversions and then sing the succession of pitches.

1. ____ 2. ____ 3. ____ 4. ____ 5. ____ 6. ____ 7. ____

III. Melodic Patterns and Exercises: Triplets, Tonic Only

A. Melodic Patterns

B. Exercises

Do NOT write tonal or rhythm syllables in the music.

IV. Melodic Patterns and Exercises: Syncopation, Tonic Only

A. Melodic Patterns

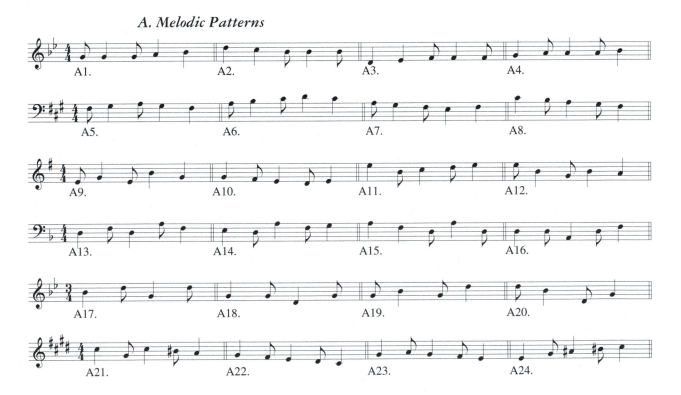

B. Exercises

V. Melodic Patterns and Exercises: Subdivided Beat, Tonic Only

A. Melodic Patterns

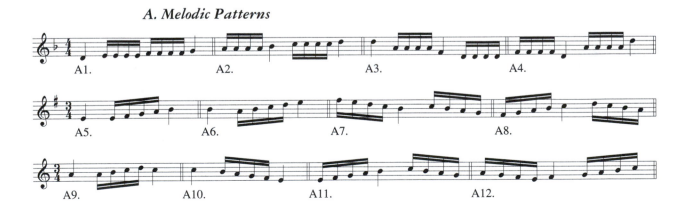

B. Exercises

VI. Exercises: Combined Rhythms, Tonic Only

VII. Exercises: Combined Rhythms, Tonic And Dominant

Chapter 12
I and V₇ in Major and Minor Modes; Half Note = Beat Unit

I. Integrating Rhythm and Tonal Skills: Major and Minor Modes

Reading Readiness Melodic Patterns
Listen as your instructor sings a variety of melodic patterns in major or minor modes; echo each pattern.

Vocal–Pitch Exercises
Sing each of the following drills daily integrating a variety of rhythm patterns; select from the rhythm patterns that follow or create your own.

Rhythm Patterns

Notice that while the notation will look different, the sound will be the same as when the beat is represented by the quarter note.

Scales
- Sing the basic and additive chromatic, major, and minor scales integrating a variety of rhythm patterns.

Intervals
- Sing each of the following intervals using tonal syllables. Prior to singing each interval, verbally label the quantity and quality of each interval.

Major Scale
- Ascending and descending intervals from tonic
- Intervals moving out from tonic
- Intervals of a third
- Intervals of a fourth

Three Forms of Minor Scale
- Ascending and descending intervals from tonic
- Intervals moving out from tonic
- Intervals of a third
- Intervals of a fourth

---

[1]Note to instructors: The melodic patterns are found in Section IIIA–major and VA–minor.

- Using tonal syllables, sing each of the preceding intervals integrating a variety of rhythm patterns.
- Sing the ascending and descending chromatic intervals using tonal syllables. Prior to singing each interval, verbally label the quality and quantity of each interval.
- Using tonal syllables, sing each of the preceding intervals integrating a variety of rhythm patterns.

Root and Inverted Triads

- Using tonal syllables, sing the root position, 1st inversion and 2nd inversion triads as melodic triads in the major scale and each of the three forms of the minor scales. Repeat integrating a variety of rhythm patterns.

Harmony

- Using tonal syllables, sing the tonic - dominant seventh chord progressions in major and minor. Repeat integrating a variety of rhythm patterns.

II. Symbolic Association

- Sing the extended major and minor scales by rote integrating each of the following rhythm exercises.

III. Melodic Patterns and Exercises: Major Mode, Tonic Only

A. Melodic Patterns

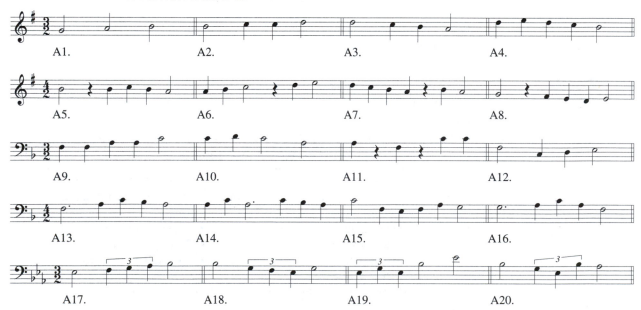

A21.   A22.   A23.   A24.

B. Exercises

Canon: 4 voices
Adagio   Alfred Edward Moffat (1866–1950)

Canon: 3 voices
Traditional

Canon: 9 voices

Thomas Ravenscroft (c. 1582–c. 1635); *Pammelia*, 1609

Canon: 4 voices

English

IV. Exercises: Major Mode, Tonic and Dominant

Moderato

Henry Purcell (c. 1659–1695); Excerpts from "An Evening Hymn"

16.

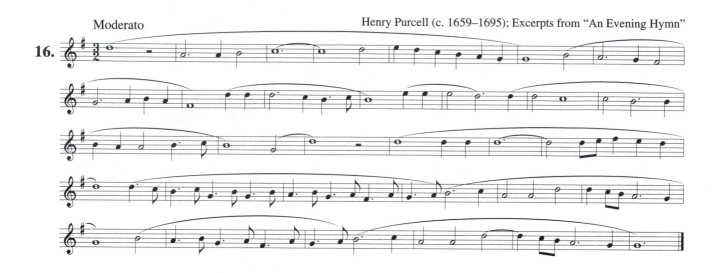

V. Melodic Patterns and Exercises: Minor Mode, Tonic Only

A. Melodic Patterns

A1.   A2.   A3.   A4.

A5.   A6.   A7.   A8.

A9.   A10.   A11.   A12.

B. Exercises

1.

2.

3.

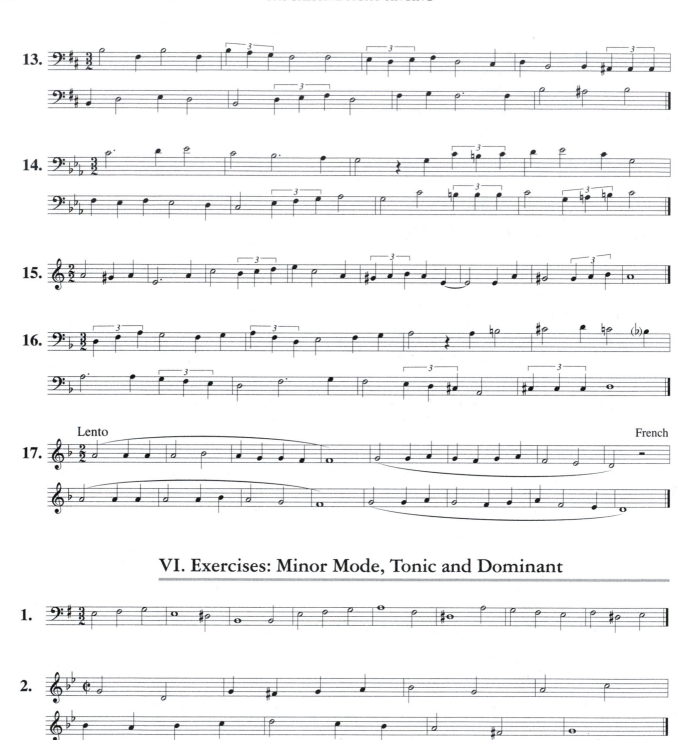

VI. Exercises: Minor Mode, Tonic and Dominant

Chapter 13

I and V₇ in Major and Minor Modes; Eighth Note = Beat Unit

I. Integrating Rhythm and Tonal Skills: Major and Minor Modes

Reading Readiness Melodic Patterns

Listen as your instructor sings a variety of melodic patterns in major or minor modes; echo each pattern.[1]

Vocal–Pitch Exercises

Sing each of the following drills daily integrating a variety of rhythm patterns; select from the rhythm patterns that follow or create your own.

Rhythm Patterns

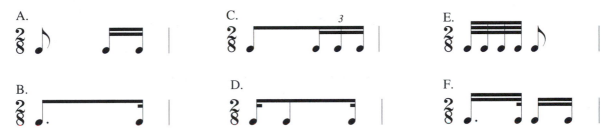

Notice that while the notation will look different, the sound will be the same as when the beat is represented by the quarter note.

Scales

- Sing the basic and additive chromatic, major, and minor scales integrating a variety of rhythm patterns.

Chromatic Intervals

- Verbally label the quality and quantity of the ascending and descending intervals in the chromatic scale prior to singing the interval on tonal syllables. Repeat integrating a variety of rhythm patterns.

- Verbally label the quality and quantity of the ascending and descending intervals moving out from the tonic in the chromatic scale prior to singing the interval on tonal syllables. Repeat integrating a variety of rhythm patterns.

Solfège
   Prime: do – do; A1: do – di; m2: do – ti₁; M2: do – re; M2: do – te₁; A2: do – ri; m3: do – la₁;
   M3: do – mi; M3: do – le₁; P4: do – fa; P4: do – so₁; A4: do – fi; A4: do – se₁; P5: do – so; P5:
   do – fa₁; A5: do – si; m6: do – mi₁; M6: do – la; M6: do – me₁; A6: do – li; m7: do – re₁; M7:
   do – ti; M7: do – ra₁; P8: do – do¹ – do – do₁ – do

Numbers
   Prime: 1 – 1; A1: 1 – #1; m2: 1 – 7₁; M2: 1 – 2; M2: 1 – ♭7₁; A2: 1 – #2; m3: 1 – 6₁;
   M3: 1 – 3; M3: 1 – ♭6₁; P4: 1 – 4; P4: 1 – 5₁; A4: 1 – #4; A4: 1 – ♭5₁; P5: 1 – 5; P5: 1 –
   4₁; A5: 1 – #5; m6: 1 – 3₁; M6: do – la; M6: 1 – ♭3₁; A6: 1 – #6; m7: 1 – 2₁; M7: 1 – 7;
   M7: 1 – ♭2₁; P8: 1 – 1¹ – 1 – 1₁ – 1

---

[1]Note to instructors: The melodic patterns are found in Section IIIA–major and VA–minor.

Root and Inverted Triads

- Using tonal syllables, sing the root position, 1st inversion, and 2nd inversion triads in the major scale and each of the three forms of the minor scales as melodic triads, integrating a variety of rhythm patterns.

Harmony

- Sing the tonic–dominant seventh chord progressions in major and minor integrating a variety of rhythm patterns.

II. Symbolic Association

- Sing the extended major and minor scales by rote integrating each of the following rhythm exercises.

III. Melodic Patterns and Exercises: Major Mode, Tonic Only

A. Melodic Patterns

B. Exercises

IV. Exercises: Major Mode, Tonic and Dominant

V. Melodic Patterns and Exercises: Minor Mode, Tonic Only

A. Melodic Patterns

B. Exercises

1.

2.

3.

VI. Exercises: Minor Mode, Tonic and Dominant

Canon: 3 voices

Melville Collection, 1612

Chapter 14

I and V₇ in Major and Minor; Compound Meters More Rhythms

I. Integrating Rhythm and Tonal Skills: Major and Minor Modes

Reading Readiness Melodic Patterns
- Listen as your instructor sings a variety of melodic patterns in major or minor modes; echo each pattern.[1]

Vocal–Pitch Exercises
Sing each of the following drills daily integrating a variety of rhythm patterns; select from the patterns that follow.

Rhythm Patterns

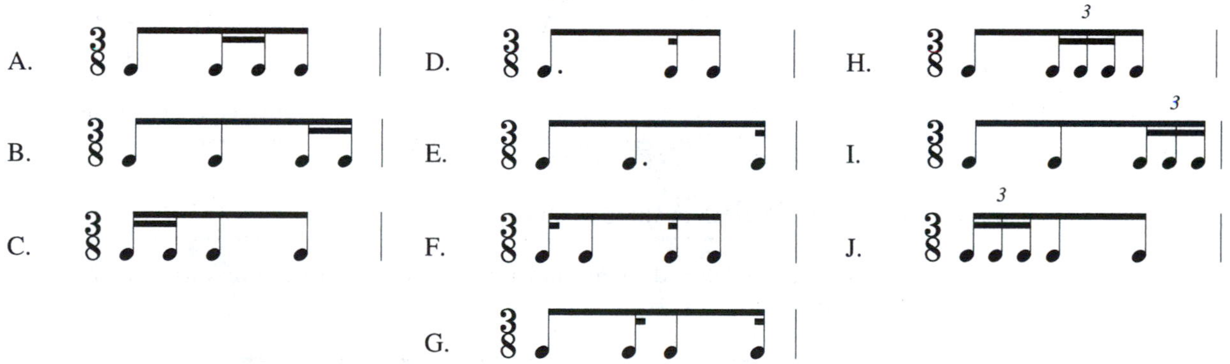

Scales
- Using tonal syllables, sing the basic and additive chromatic, major, and minor scales integrating a variety of rhythm patterns.

Intervals
- Using tonal syllables, sing each of the following intervals integrating a variety of rhythm patterns.
  - Ascending and descending intervals from the tonic in the major and minor scales.
  - Intervals moving out from tonic in the major and minor scales.
  - Intervals of a third and fourth in the major and minor scales.
  - Ascending and descending intervals in the chromatic scale.
  - Intervals moving out from tonic in the chromatic scale.

---

[1]Note the Instructors: The melodic patterns are found in Section IIIA—major and VA—minor.

357

Triads

- Using tonal syllables, sing the root position, 1st inversion and 2nd inversion triads built on each scale degree in the major and minor scales integrating a variety of rhythm patterns.
- Using tonal syllables sing each of the four types of triads (Major, minor, Augmented, and diminished) built on the tonic triad in root position, 1st inversion and 2nd inversion.

Root Position				*1st Inversion*				*2nd Inversion*			
								mi'-3'	mi'-3'	me'-♭3'	me'-♭3'
				do'-1'	do'-1'	do'-1'	do'-1'	do'-1'	do'-1'	do'-1'	do'-1'
so-5	si-#5	so-5	se-♭5	so-5	si-#5	so-5	se-♭5	so-5	si-#5	so-5	se-♭5
mi-3	mi-3	me-♭3	me-♭3	mi-3	mi-3	me-♭3	me-♭3				
do-1	do-1	do-1	do-1								
M	**A⁺**	**m**	**d°**	**M₆**	**A₆⁺**	**m₆**	**d₆°**	**M₆⁴**	**A₆⁴⁺**	**m₆⁴**	**d₆⁴°**

- Practice building the Major, minor, Augmented and diminished triads on each scale degree of the major scale.

    Examples:

    Triads Built on the Second Scale Degree
    Solfège   m: re – fa – la; M: re – fi – la; A+: re – fi – li; d°: re – fa – le
    Numbers   m: 2 – 4 – 6; M: 2 – #4 – 6; A+: 2 – #4 –# 6; d°: 2 – 4 – ♭6

    Triads Built on the Fifth Scale Degree
    Solfège   M: so – ti - re; A+: so – ti – ri; m: so – te - re; d°: so – te - ra
    Numbers   M: 5 – 7 – 2; A+: 5 – 7 – #2; m: 5 – ♭7 – 2; d°: 5 – ♭7 – ♭2

Harmony

- Using tonal syllables, sing the tonic—dominant seventh chord progressions in major and minor modes. Repeat integrating a variety of rhythm patterns.

II. Symbolic Association

- Sing the extended major and minor scales by rote integrating each of the following rhythm exercises.

Major, Minor, Augmented, and Diminished Triads

- Verbally label the Roman numeral and quality of each triad prior to singing the triad melodically using tonal syllables.

• Determine the quality and position of each triad and then sing the triad using tonal syllables.

1. _____ 2. _____ 3. _____ 4. _____

5. _____ 6. _____ 7. _____ 8. _____

9. _____ 10. _____ 11. _____ 12. _____

III. Melodic Patterns and Exercises: Major Mode, Tonic Only

A. Melodic Patterns

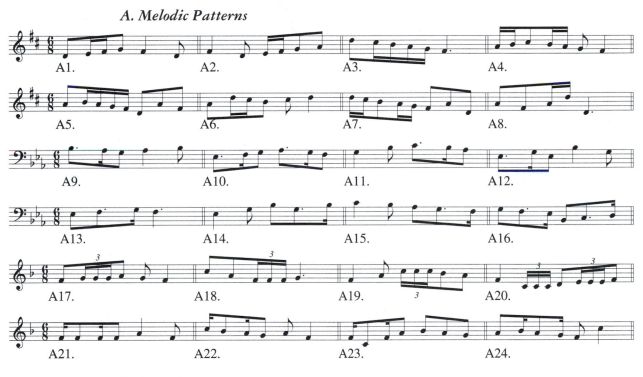

A1. A2. A3. A4.

A5. A6. A7. A8.

A9. A10. A11. A12.

A13. A14. A15. A16.

A17. A18. A19. A20.

A21. A22. A23. A24.

B. Exercises

1.

2.

35. Vivo (Note the do–la interval.)   Sea Chanty

36. Bewegt (Note the do–la interval.)   Heinrich Werner (1800–1833)

IV. Exercises: Major Mode, Tonic and Dominant

Allegretto (Note the intervals in the vi chord.)

19th Century English

30.

V. Melodic Patterns and Exercises: Minor Mode, Tonic Only

A. Melodic Patterns

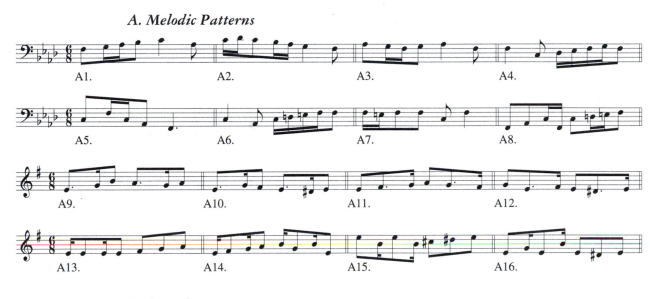

A1.   A2.   A3.   A4.

A5.   A6.   A7.   A8.

A9.   A10.   A11.   A12.

A13.   A14.   A15.   A16.

B. Exercises

1.

2.

Allegretto

English

3.

VI. Exercises: Minor Mode, Tonic and Dominant

Chapter 15

I, ii, IV, and V$_7$ in Major Mode; Simple and Compound Meters

I. Building Aural/Oral Skills: Subdomiant Triad, Major Mode

Reading Readiness Tonal Patterns
- Listen as your instructor sings a variety of tonal patterns in major; echo each pattern.[1]

Vocal–Pitch Exercises
Scales
- Using tonal syllables, sing the basic and additive chromatic, major, and minor scales integrating a variety of rhythm patterns.

Intervals
- Using tonal syllables, sing each of the following intervals integrating a variety of rhythm patterns.
  - Ascending and descending intervals from the tonic in the major and minor scales.
  - Intervals moving out from tonic in the major and minor scales.
  - Intervals of a third and fourth in the major and minor scales.
  - Ascending and descending intervals in the chromatic scale.
  - Intervals moving out from tonic in the chromatic scale.

Major, Minor, Augmented, and Diminished Triads
- Sing each of the four types of triads in root position, 1st inversion, and 2nd inversion. Build the triads on various scale degrees.

Harmony
The subdominant triad (IV) lies between the stability of the tonic triad and the momentum of the dominant triad. Since you already know where *mi*/3 and *so*/5 are, *fa*/4 and *la*/6 are right next door.

- Using tonal syllables, sing the succession of pitches in the following chord progressions integrating a variety of rhythm patterns.

Root Position

	I	IV	V	I
	so (5)			
	mi (3)			
			re (2)	
	do (1)	do (1)		do (1)
		ti₍ (7₍)		
		la₍ (6₍)	so₍ (5₍)	
		fa₍ (4₍)		

1st Inversion

	I	IV₆	V₆	I
	so (5)		so (5)	
		fa (4)		
	mi (3)			
			re (2)	
	do (1)	do (1)		do (1)
			ti₍ (7₍)	
		la₍ (6₍)		

2nd Inversion

	I	IV₆₄	V₆₄	I
			ti (7)	
		la (6)		
	so (5)		so (5)	
		fa (4)		
	mi (3)			
			re (2)	
	do (1)	do (1)		do (1)

[1]Note to instructors: The tonal patterns are found in Section IIIA–subdominant and VIA–supertonic.

II. Symbolic Association

Subdominant Triad (IV)

- The root (subdominant) and third (submediant) of the subdominant triad are active tones but the fifth (tonic) is a stable tone. Sing each of the melodic triads using tonal syllables.

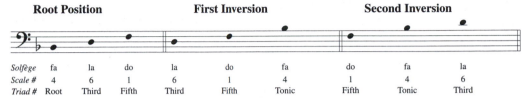

	Root Position			First Inversion			Second Inversion		
Solfège	fa	la	do	la	do	fa	do	fa	la
Scale #	4	6	1	6	1	4	1	4	6
Triad #	Root	Third	Fifth	Third	Fifth	Tonic	Fifth	Tonic	Third

- Melodically *do* (1) and *mi* (3) represent a tonic function, *fa* (4) and *la* (6) represent the subdominant function (dominant preparation) and *re* (2), *so* (5), and *ti* (7) represent the dominant function.

Solfège	do	mi	fa	la	re	so	ti
Scale #	1	3	4	6	2	5	7
Function	Tonic		Subdominant		Dominant		

- Examine the melodies that follow and label (a) chord (CT), neighbor (NT) and passing (PT) tones; (b) I, IV, and V chords; and (c) types of cadences—authentic, half, or plagal (IV-I). Sing each melody using tonal syllables.

Major, Minor, Augmented, and Diminished Triads

- Determine the quality and position of each triad and then sing the triad using tonal syllables.

III. Tonal Patterns: Subdominant Triad, Major Mode

A. Tonic—Subdominant Chord Tones (Root Position)

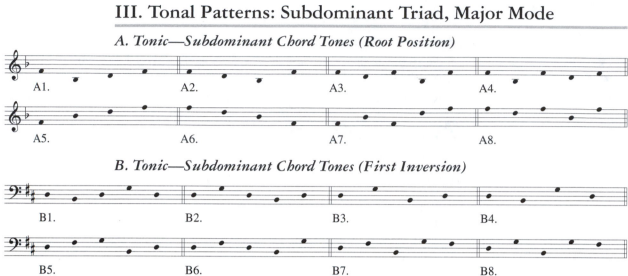

B. Tonic—Subdominant Chord Tones (First Inversion)

C. Tonic—Subdominant Chord Tones (Second Inversion)

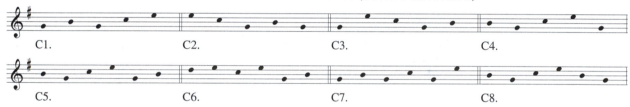

D. Tonic—Subdominant—Dominant Chord Tones

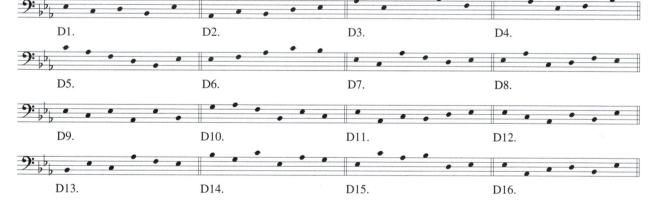

IV. Exercises: I, IV, V$_7$, Major Mode, Simple Meter

A. Simple Rhythms

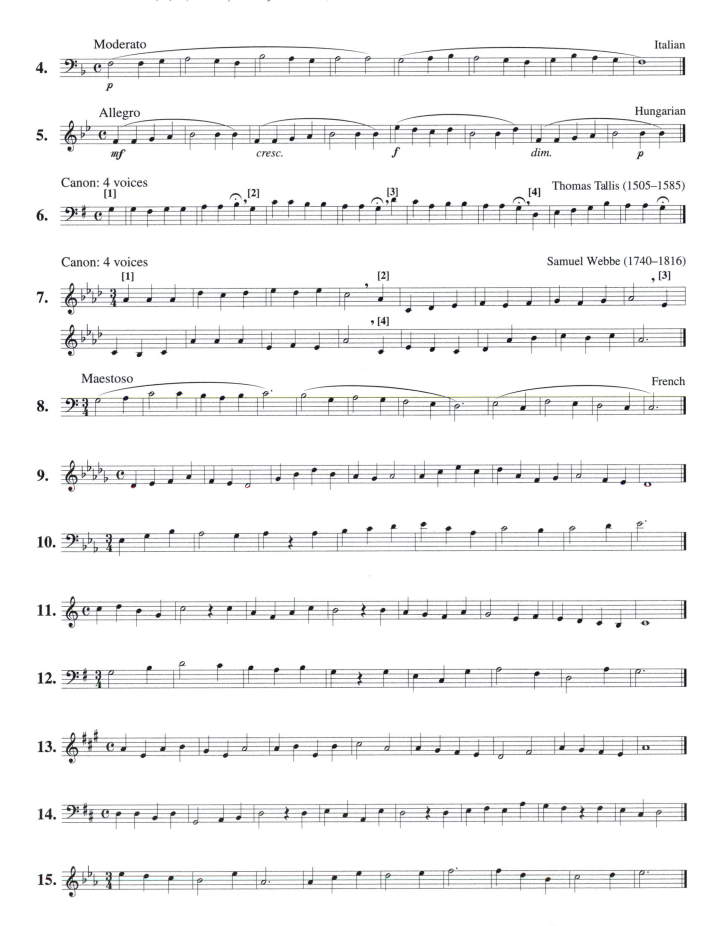

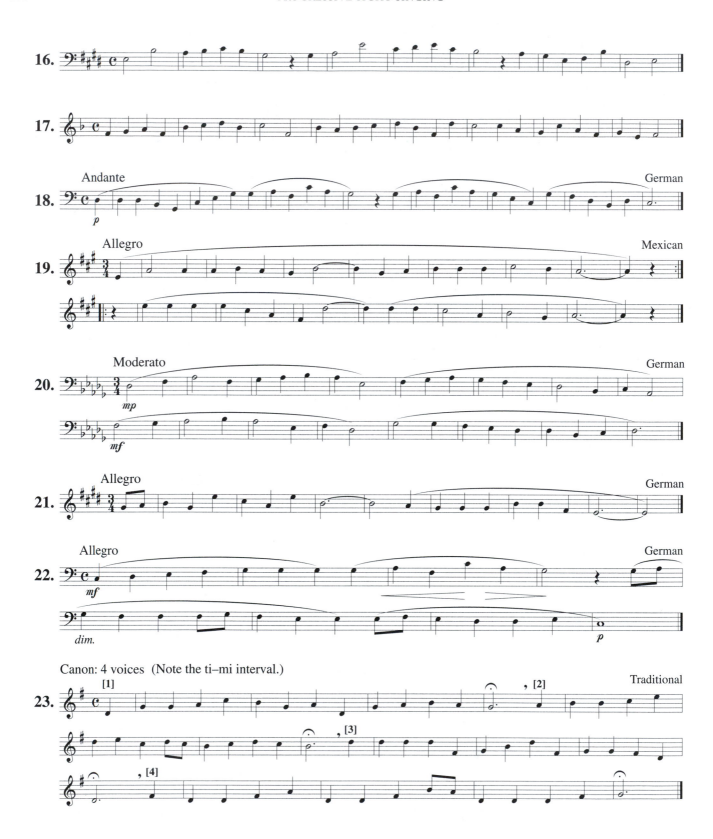

B. Complex Rhythms

C. Simple Meter, Half Note = Beat Unit

21. Canon: 3 voices

Thomas Ravenscroft (c. 1582–c. 1635); *Pammelia,* 1609

22. Leonhard Lechner (1553–1606)

V. Exercises: I, IV, V₇, Major Mode, Compound Meters

A. Simple Rhythms

3. Allegro   Dutch

B. Complex Rhythms

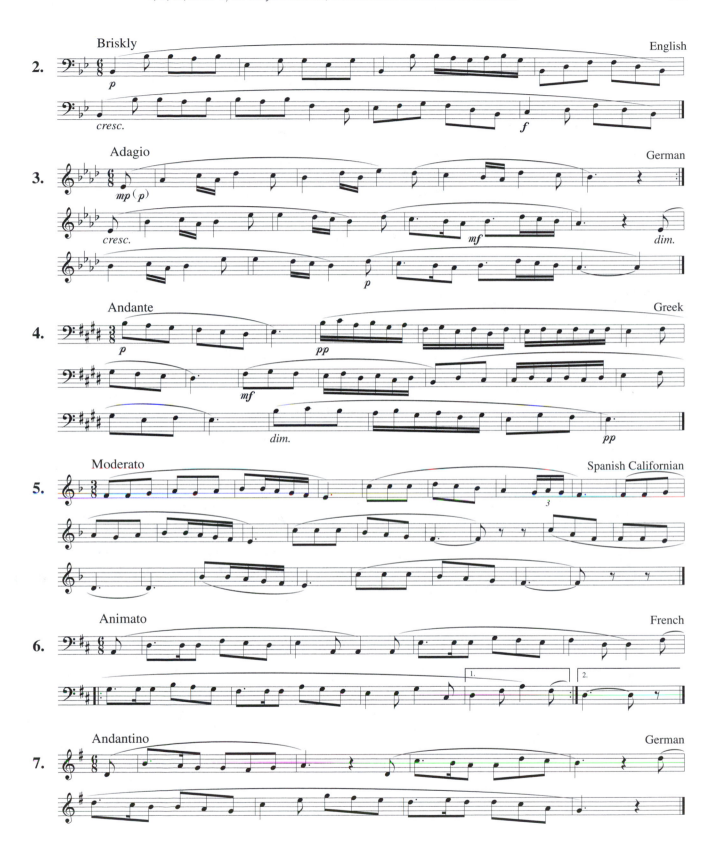

VI. Melodic Patterns and Exercises: Supertonic Triad, Simple and Compound Meters

A. Tonal Patterns

Supertonic Chord Tones—Root Position

A1.   A2.   A3.   A4.

Supertonic Chord Tones—First Inversion

A5.   A6.   A7.   A8.

Supertonic Chord Tones—Second Inversion

A9.   A10.   A11.   A12.

B. Exercises

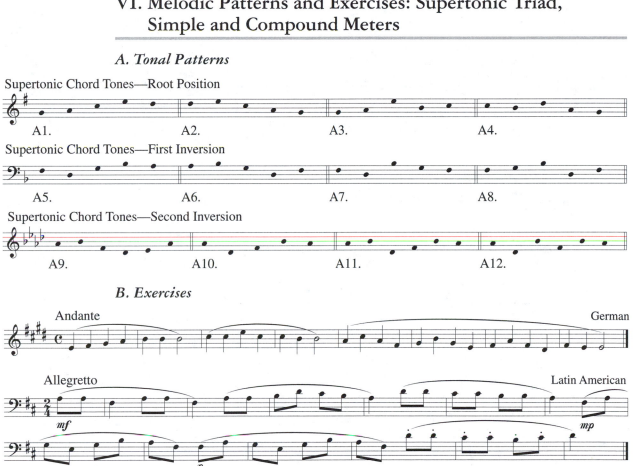

Chapter 16

i, iv and V_7 in Minor Mode; Simple and Compound Meters

I. Building Aural/Oral Skills: Subdominant Triad, Minor Mode

Reading Readiness Tonal Patterns
- Listen as your instructor sings a variety of tonal patterns in minor; echo each pattern.[1]

Vocal–Pitch Exercises
Scales
- Using tonal syllables, sing the basic and additive chromatic, major and minor scales integrating a variety of rhythm patterns.

Intervals
- Using tonal syllables, sing each of the following intervals integrating a variety of rhythm patterns.
  - Ascending and descending intervals from the tonic in the major and minor scales.
  - Intervals moving out from tonic in the major and minor scales.
  - Intervals of a third and fourth in the major and minor scales.
  - Ascending and descending intervals in the chromatic scale.
  - Intervals moving out from tonic in the chromatic scale.

Harmony
The subdominant triad (iv) lies between the stability of the tonic triad and the momentum of the dominant triad. Notice that the root and third of the subdominant chord are right next door to the third and fifth of the tonic chord.

- Using tonal syllables sing the succession of pitches in the tonic—subdominant chord progressions. Repeat integrating a variety of rhythm patterns.

Root Position		*1st Inversion*		*2nd Inversion*		
					le (♭6) fa	
so (5) mi		so (5) mi		so (5) mi		
			fa (4) re		fa (4) re	
me (♭3) do		me (♭3) do		me (♭3) do		
do (1)la	do (1)la	do (1)la	do (1)la	do (1)la	do (1)la	do (1)la
	le͵ (♭6͵) fa͵		le͵ (♭6͵) fa͵			
	fa͵ (4͵) re͵					
i	**iv**	**i**	**iv₆**	**i**	**iv₆₄**	**i**

---

[1]Note to instructors: The patterns are found in Section III of this chapter.

- Using tonal syllables sing the succession of pitches in the following tonic—subdominant—dominant chord progressions. Repeat integrating a variety of rhythm patterns.

Root Position

```
so (5) mi
me(♭3) do
do (1) la   do (1) la    re (2) ti
            le₁ (♭6₁) fa₁   ti₁ (7₁) si₁
            fa₁ (4₁) re₁    so₁ (5₁) mi₁
   i         iv            V
```

$$i \qquad iv \qquad V$$

1st Inversion

```
so (5) mi                  so (5) mi
            fa (4) re
me (♭3) do
            do (1) la       re (2) ti
do (1) la                   ti₁ (7₁) si₁
            le₁ (♭6₁) fa₁
   i         iv₆            V₆
```

$$i \qquad iv_6 \qquad V_6$$

2nd Inversion

```
                ti (7) si
      le (♭6) fa
so (5) mi                so (5) mi
                fa (4) re
me (♭3) do
      do (1) la    re (2) ti
do (1) la                do (1) la
   i      iv₆/₄   V₆/₄     i
```

$$i \qquad iv_6^4 \qquad V_6^4 \qquad i$$

II. Symbolic Association

Subdominant Triad (iv)

- The root (subdominant) and third (submediant) of the subdominant triad are active tones but the fifth (tonic) is a stable tone. Sing each of the following melodic triads on tonal syllables.

	Root Position			First Inversion			Second Inversion		
Do Based Solfège	fa	le	do	le	do	fa	do	fa	le
La Based Solfège	re	fa	la	fa	la	re	la	re	fa
Numbers	4	♭6	1	♭6	1	4	1	4	♭6

- The subdominant triad (sixth scale degree is the 3rd of the triad) is most often minor although it can be major (raised sixth scale degree in melodic minor). Sing each of the triads melodically using tonal syllables.

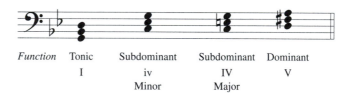

Function	Tonic	Subdominant	Subdominant	Dominant
	I	iv	IV	V
		Minor	Major	

- Melodically *do* (1) *la* and *me* (♭3) *do* represent a tonic function, *fa* (4) *re* and *le* (♭6) *fa* represent the subdominant function (dominant preparation) and *re* (2) *ti*, *so* (5) *mi,* and *ti* (7) si represent the dominant function.

	Tonic Function		Subdominant Function		Dominant Function		
Do-Based Solfège	do	me	fa	le	re	so	ti
La-Based Solfège	la	do	re	a	ti	mi	si
Numbers	1	♭3	4	♭6	2	5	#7

- Examine the melodies that follow and label (a) chord (CT), neighbor (NT), and passing (PT) tones; (b) i, iv, and V chords; and (c) types of cadences—authentic, half, or plagal (iv-i). Sing each melody using tonal syllables.

German (adapted)

A.

American

B.

III. Tonal Patterns: Subdominant Triad, Minor Mode

A. Tonic—Subdominant Chord Tones (Root Position)

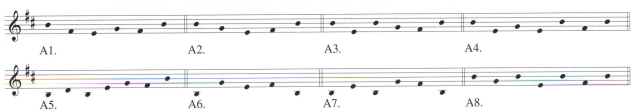

B. Tonic—Subdominant Chord Tones (First Inversion)

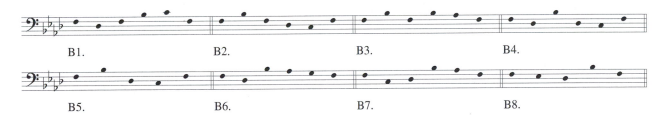

C. Tonic—Subdominant Chord Tones (Second Inversion)

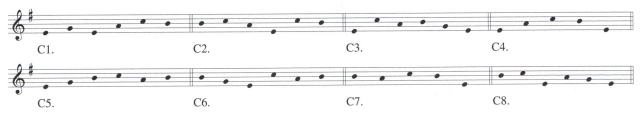

D. Tonic—Subdominant—Dominant Chord Tones

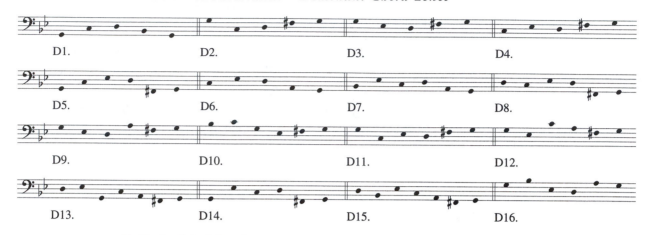

E. Raised Subdominant—Major IV

IV. Exercises: i, iv, IV, and V₇, Minor Mode, Simple Meters

A. Simple Rhythms

Canon: 5 voices

Thomas Ravenscroft (c. 1582–c. 1635); *Pammelia*, 1609

C. Simple Meter, Half Note = Beat Unit

Moderato

Russian

Nicht schnell

Anton Bruckner (1824–1896)

Canon: 3 voices
Thomas Brewer (1611–c. 1660–70)

V. Exercises i, iv, IV, and V₇ Minor Mode, Compound Meters

Chapter 17
Chromatic Alterations; Simple and Compound Meters

I. Building Aural/Oral Skills

Reading Readiness Tonal Patterns
- Listen as your instructor sings a variety of tonal patterns; echo each pattern.[1]

Vocal–Pitch Exercises
Scale
- Sing the basic and additive chromatic scales integrating a variety of rhythm patterns.

Chromatic Intervals
- Exercise 1:

  Solfège:

  Ascending: do, ti♭, do; re, di, re; mi, ri, mi; fa, mi, fa; so, fi, so; la, si, la; ti, li, ti, do⌐

  Descending: do⌐, ra⌐, do⌐; ti, do⌐, ti; la, te, la; so, le, so; fa, se, fa; mi, fa, mi; re, me, re; do, ra, do, ti♭, do

  Numbers:

  Ascending: 1, 7♭, 1, 2, #1, 2; 3, #2, 3; 4, 3, 4; 5; #4, 5, 6, #5, 6; 7, #6, 7, 1⌐

  Descending: 1⌐, ♭2⌐, 1⌐; 7, 1⌐, 7; 6, ♭7, 6; 5, ♭6, 5; 4, ♭5, 4; 3, 4, 3; 2, ♭3, 2; 1, ♭2, 1, 7♭, 1

- Exercise 2:

  Solfège:

  Ascending: do, ti♭, ti, di, re; re, di, ri mi; mi, ri, fa, fi; fa, mi, fi, so; so, fi, si, la; la, si, li, ti; ti, li, di⌐, do⌐, ti, do⌐

  Descending: do⌐, te, ti; ti, le, la; la, se, so; so, mi, fa; fa, me, mi; mi, ra, re; re, ti♭, do

  Numbers:

  Ascending: 1, 7♭, #1, 2; 2, #1, #2, 3; 3, #2, 4, #4; 4, 3, #4, 5; 5, #4, #5, 6; 6, #5, #6, 7; 7, #6, #1⌐, 1⌐, 7, 1⌐

  Descending: 1⌐, ♭7, 7; 7, ♭6, 6; 6, ♭5, 5; 5, 3, 4; 4, ♭3, 3; 3, ♭2, 2; 2, 7♭, 1

II. Symbolic Association

- Chromatically altered tones may be used as nonharmonic tones–neighbor (CNT) or passing (CPT) tones.

---

[1]Note to instructors: The tonal patterns are found at the beginning of each section of this chapter.

- Chromatically altered chord tones may imply tonicization—any major or minor diatonic triad other than the tonic heard temporarily as a new tonic (secondary dominant). The following are the most common tonicized triads.

- Chromatically altered chord tones may indicate a borrowed chord—a change of mode from major to parallel minor or the reverse.

III. Tonal Patterns and Exercises: Raised Fourth Scale Degree, Major Mode

A. Tonal Patterns

B. Exercises

IV. Tonal Patterns and Exercises: Raised Fourth Scale Degree, Minor Mode

A. Tonal Patterns

B. Exercises

Canon: 3 voices
[1]   Anonymous

13.

V. Tonal Patterns and Exercises: Lowered Seventh Scale Degree, Major Mode

A. Tonal Patterns

A1.   A2.   A3.   A4.

A5.   A6.   A7.   A8.

A9.   A10.   A11.   A12.

B. Exercises

1.

Allegro   English

2.

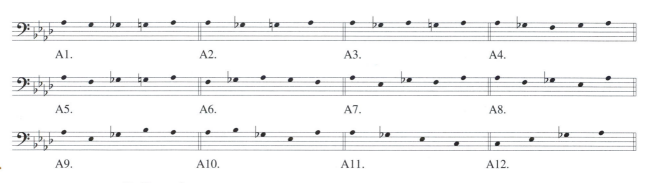

Allegro   British

3.

p   *cresc.*

dim.   *p*

Allegretto   German

4.

VI. Tonal Patterns and Exercises: Raised Tonic, Major Mode

A. Tonal Patterns

B. Exercises

8. Moderato — Hungarian

9. Andantino — Friedrich Kücken (1810–1882)

10. Andante — Spanish

11. Allegro — 19th Century English

12. Allegro — British

VII. Tonal Patterns and Exercises: Raised Second Scale, Major Mode

A. Reading Readiness Tonal Patterns

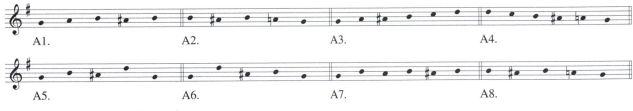

A1.   A2.   A3.   A4.

A5.   A6.   A7.   A8.

B. Exercises

1.

2.

3.

4.

5.

6.

Franz Schubert (1797–1828); Mass in E Flat

15.

Canon: 3 voices

Anonymous

16.

[1]   [2]   [3]

mf   mp   cresc.   f

Canon: 4 voices

Franz Joseph Haydn (1732-1809)

17.

[1]

[2]

[3]

[4]

Chapter 18

Modes

I. Symbolic Association: Diatonic Seven Tone Scales

A. For many centuries before the development of the major-minor tonal system in the seventeenth century, most Western music was based on *modes*, diatonic seven-tone scales known variously as the *medieval modes* or *church modes*. Notice the arrangements of the whole and half steps; most of these scales feature a subtonic rather than a leading tone.

1. The modes can be found by playing a white-note scale starting on each of the white keys on the keyboard. Sing each of the modes.

a. Ionian (w-w-h-w-w-w-h) Major scale

b. Dorian (w-h-w-w-w-h-w)

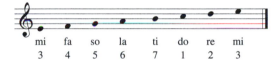

c. Phrygian (h-w-w-w-h-w-w)

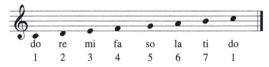

d. Lydian (w-w-w-h-w-w-h)

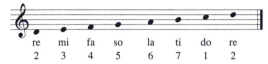

e. Mixolydian (w-w-h-w-w-h-w)

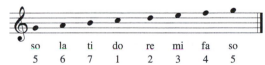

f. Aeolian (w-h-w-w-h-w-w) Natural minor scale

g. Locrian (h-w-w-h-w-w-w) Rarely used

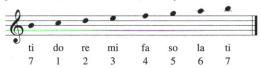

2. Modes can be transposed to begin on any pitch. Notice the relation of the tonic of the mode to the key signature. Sing each of the modes starting on C.

a. Ionian

b. Dorian

c. Phrygian

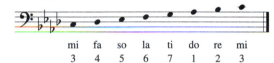

d. Lydian

e. Mixolydian

f. Aeolian

g. Locrian

B. Modes are classified as either major or minor, based on the interval formed by the first and third pitches of the mode. Compare each of the major modes and minor modes.[1]

Major Modes

1. Notice the difference between the major scale (Ionian Mode) and the Lydian and Mixolydian modes. Like the major scale, the Lydian mode has a leading tone, while the Mixolydian mode has a subtonic. Sing each mode.

Minor Modes

2. Notice the difference between the natural minor scale (Aeolian Mode) and the Dorian and Phrygian modes. Like the natural minor scale, the minor modes have a subtonic. Sing each mode.

a. Ionian—Major Scale

do	re	mi	fa	so	la	ti	do
1	2	3	4	5	6	7	1

a. Aeolian—Natural Minor Scale

"la" based	la	ti	do	re	mi	fa	so	la
Numbers	1	2	♭3	4	5	♭6	♭7	1
"do" based	do	re	me	fa	so	le	te	do

b. Lydian—Major Scale with Raised Fourth Scale Degree

do	re	mi	fi	so	la	ti	do
1	2	3	♯4	5	6	7	1

b. Dorian—Natural Minor Scale with a Raised Sixth Scale Degree

"la" based	la	ti	do	re	mi	fi	so	la
Numbers	1	2	♭3	4	5	6	♭7	1
"do" based	do	re	me	fa	so	la	te	do

c. Mixolydian—Major Scale with Lowered Seventh Scale Degree

do	re	mi	fa	so	la	te	do
1	2	3	4	5	6	♭7	1

c. Phrygian—Natural Minor Scale with a Lowered Second Scale Degree

"la" based	la	te	do	re	mi	fa	so	la
Numbers	1	♭2	♭3	4	5	♭6	♭7	1
"do" based	do	ra	me	fa	so	le	te	do

C. Building Aural/Oral Skills

1. *Minor Scales and Minor Modes:* Listen as your instructor plays or sings minor scales and minor modes.
   Determine the type of scale or mode.

a. Natural Minor (Aeolian)	Harmonic Minor	Melodic Minor	Dorian	Phrygian
b. Natural Minor (Aeolian)	Harmonic Minor	Melodic Minor	Dorian	Phrygian
c. Natural Minor (Aeolian)	Harmonic Minor	Melodic Minor	Dorian	Phrygian
d. Natural Minor (Aeolian)	Harmonic Minor	Melodic Minor	Dorian	Phrygian

2. *Major Scale and Major Modes*: Listen as your instructor plays or sings a major scale and major modes.
   Determine the type of scale or mode.

a. Major (Ionian)	Lydian	Mixolydian		c. Major (Ionian)	Lydian	Mixolydian
b. Major (Ionian)	Lydian	Mixolydian		d. Major (Ionian)	Lydian	Mixolydian

---

[1]Remember the Locrian mode is rarely used; consequently, it will not be addressed in this text.

II. Exercises

1. Yankee Doodle in Seven Modes

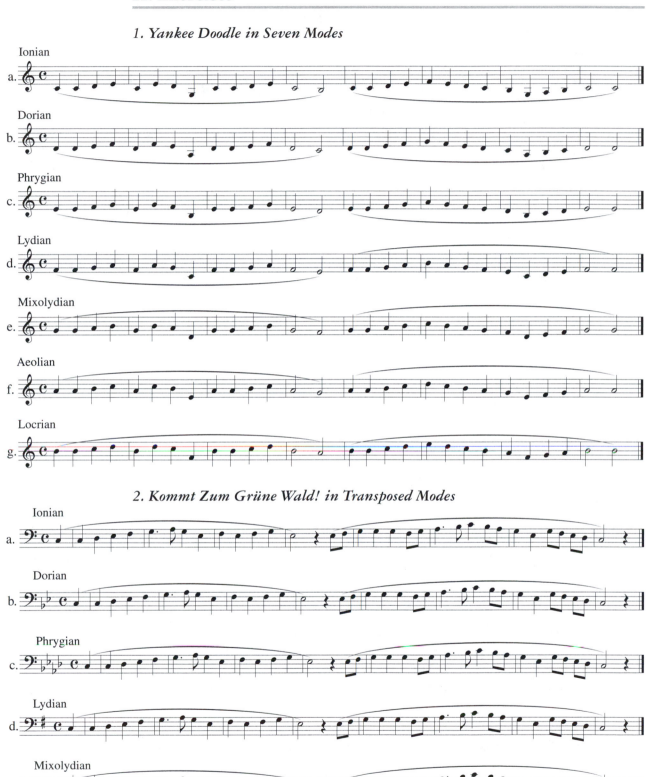

2. Kommt Zum Grüne Wald! in Transposed Modes

3. Joy to the World in Major Modes

4. Joy to the World in Minor Modes

Remember to use these exercises as dictation examples.

Rhythm Reading Systems

Numerous rhythm syllable systems are available to aid in the study of rhythm.[1] Depending upon the system, syllables are based on beat functions, time values of notes, position of notes in a measure, or a combination of these. The syllables provide a link between aural/oral vocalization and visual identification.

Regardless of the system used, the macro beat should be monitored by (a) silently tapping the thighs with one or both hands, using large arm movements that start from the shoulder(s); (b) silently tapping the macro beat in one hand and the micro beat in the other hand; (c) walking in place to the macro beat while silently tapping the micro beat; or (d) conducting.

Gordon Rhythm Syllables[2]

Developed by Edwin Gordon, James Froseth, and Albert Blaser, the system is based on beat function: a different syllable is assigned at the beat (du) and division level (simple meter—du, de; compound meter—du, da, di). Notice that this is not true at the subdivision level, the same syllable (ta) occurs in more than one location within a beat (See Figure 1). Within simple or compound meters, the same syllables are used regardless of notation. Specific syllables for common rhythm patterns are shown in Chart A. Note that the originating syllable is sustained for notes of more than one pulse or notes elongated by a tie or extension dot.

Figure 1. Overview of Gordon Rhythm Syllables

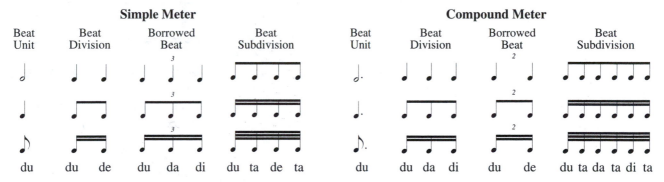

The Gordon system does distinguish between usual meters and unusual meters (See Figure 2) by substituting the consonant "b" for the consonant "d" at the division level. The subdivision level still uses "ta" in more than one location within a beat. Note that in unusual meters, one must switch from one division type (du-be) to another (du-ba-bi) and vice versa.

---

[1] A history of rhythm systems can be found in Edwin E. Gordon's *Learning Sequences in Music* (Chicago: GIA Publications, 1997), 69–83.

[2] Eric Bluestine, *The Ways Children Learn Music* (Chicago: GIA Publications, 1995), 97–101; Gordon, 82–83.

Figure 2. Gordon Syllables for Unusual Meters

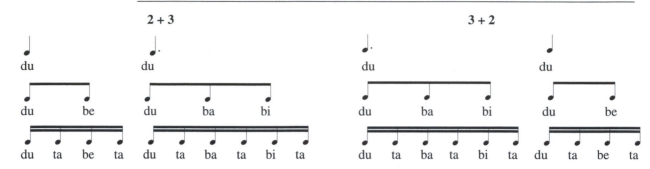

Takadimi Rhythm Syllables[3]

Richard Hoffman, William Pelto, and John White developed the Takadimi Rhythm System to teach basic rhythm skills to college-level students who lack the requisite skills. Specific syllables are assigned to a location within a beat (See Figure 3). In simple meters, "ta" is used for any attack on the beat, the division of the beat is "ta-di," and the subdivision of beat is "ta-ka-di-mi." In compound meters, the attack on the beat is, once again "ta," the beat division is "ta-ki-da," and the beat subdivision is "ta-va-ki-di-da-ma." Note that within an individual beat division the initial consonant changes but the vowel sound remains the same (Simple Meter: ta-ka, di-mi; Compound Meter: ta-va, ki-di, da-ma). Note that syllables are also provided for irregular divisions within the two types of meter.

Figure 3. Overview of Takadimi Rhythm Syllables

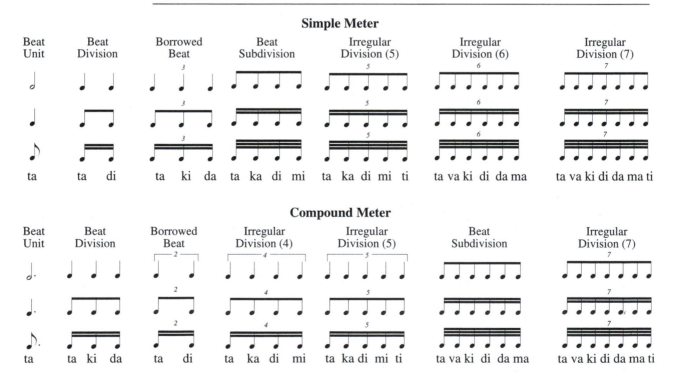

---

[3] Richard M. Hoffman, William L. Pelto, and John W. White, "Takadimi: A Beat-Oriented System of Rhythm Pedagogy," *Journal of Music Theory Pedagogy*, 10 (1996): 7–30.

Specific syllables for common rhythm patterns are shown in Chart B. The authors recommend muting the nonarticulated syllables (shown in parentheses) in complex rhythms with tied patterns and rests to improve performance accuracy.[4] The Takadimi Rhythm System can also be used with unusual meters (See Figure 4) by switching between duple division syllables (ta-di) and triple division syllables (ta-ki-da).

Figure 4. Takadimi Rhythm Syllables for Unusual Meters

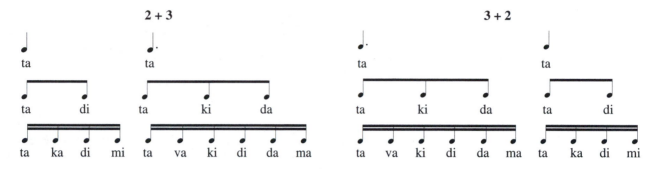

McHose and Tibbs Rhythm Syllables[5]

Developed by Irvine McHose and Ruth Tibbs for conservatory students at the Eastman School of Music, the system combines metric counting and rhythm syllables. Any note occurring on the beat is articulated with that beat's ordinal number; syllables are assigned to the division (simple meter—te; compound meter—la, li), subdivision (ta for both simple and compound meters) and borrowed division (simple meter—la, li; compound meter—te) of the beat (See Figure 5). The aural sound of the rhythm will always be associated with the same syllables, however the visual representation of the rhythm will change depending on the beat unit. Specific syllables for common rhythm patterns are shown in Chart C. Notice that the originating syllable is sustained for notes of more than one pulse or notes elongated by a tie or extension dot. No provision is made for distinguishing between usual meters and unusual meters. This system requires "the presence and formal understanding of meter before the syllables can be applied, thus limiting application in aural contexts."[6]

Figure 5. Overview of McHose and Tibbs Rhythm Syllables

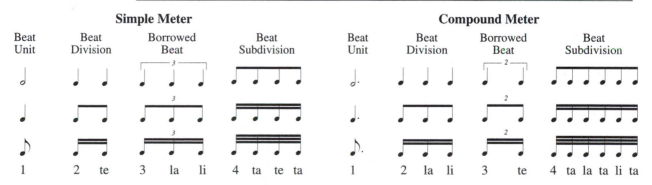

---

[4] Ibid., 19.

[5] Allen McHose and Ruth Tibbs. *Sight-Singing Manual*, 3rd ed. (New York: Appleton-Century-Crofts, 1957), 6–9.

[6] Hoffman, Pelto, and White, 11.

Kodály Rhythm Syllables

The syllables in this system are based on those devised by Hungarian composer and pedagogue Zoltán Kodály, as well as the French Galin-Paris-Cheve system. In this system, syllables are assigned to specific notational values. Notice that the aural sound of the rhythm will always be associated with the same syllables; however, the visual representation of the rhythm will change depending on the beat unit (See Figure 6). Beat function is not addressed; if it did then a macro beat followed by a micro beat would be "ta ti" not "ti ti."[7]

Figure 6: Overview of Kodály Based Syllables

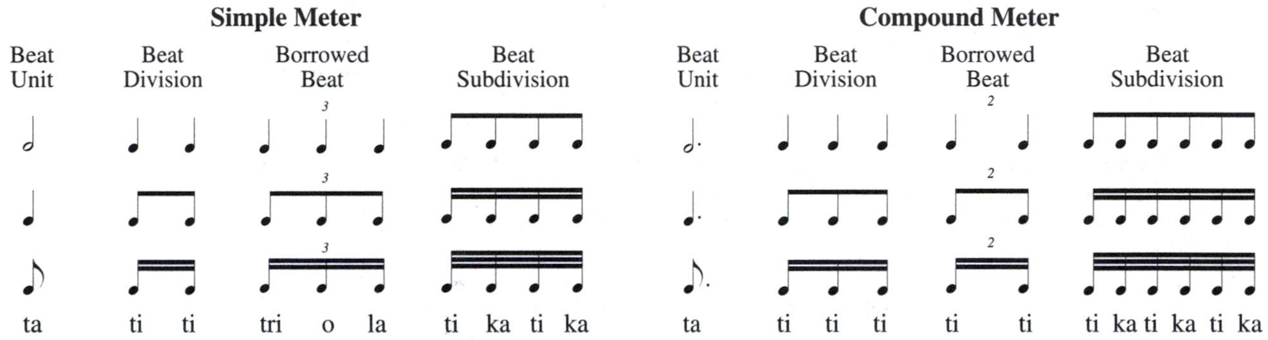

Specific syllables for common rhythm patterns are shown in Chart D. Note that the vowel sound varies for elongated notes (toh, too) and that the vowel sound is pulsed on extension dots and tied notes. As soon as skills are sufficiently developed, the originating syllable should be sustained. The system lacks a provision for distinguishing between usual meters and unusual meters.

[7] Gordon, 77.

Chart A: Gordon Rhythm Syllables (Beat Function Syllables)

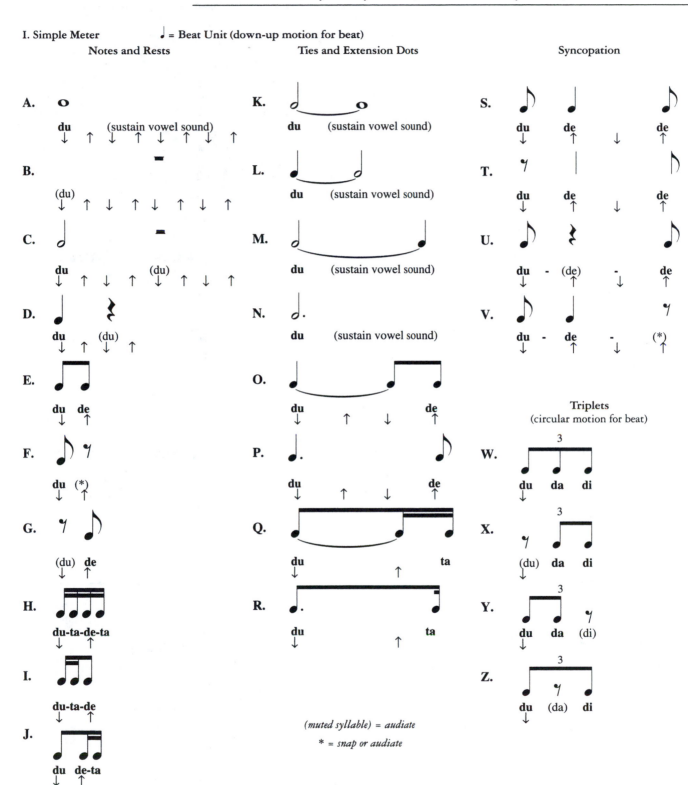

I. Simple Meter   ♩ = Beat Unit (down-up motion for beat)

Notes and Rests   Ties and Extension Dots   Syncopation

(muted syllable) = audiate

* = snap or audiate

Gordon Rhythm Syllables

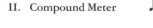

II. Compound Meter ♩. = Beat Unit   **III. Simple Meter** ♩ = Beat Unit   **IV. Simple Meter** ♪ = Beat Unit

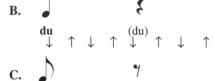
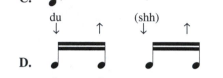
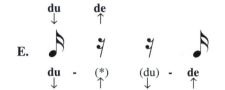

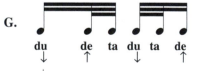
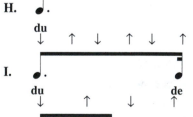
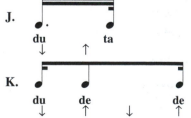
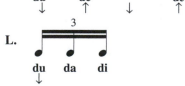

Chart B: Takadimi Rhythm Syllables (Beat Function)

I. Simple Meter ♩ = Beat Unit (down-up motion for beat)

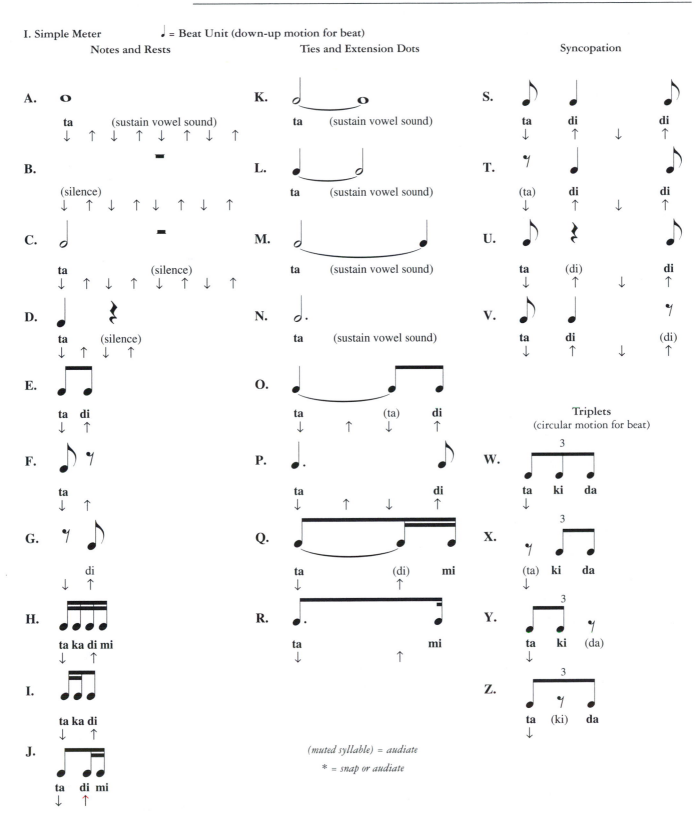

Takadimi Rhythm Syllables

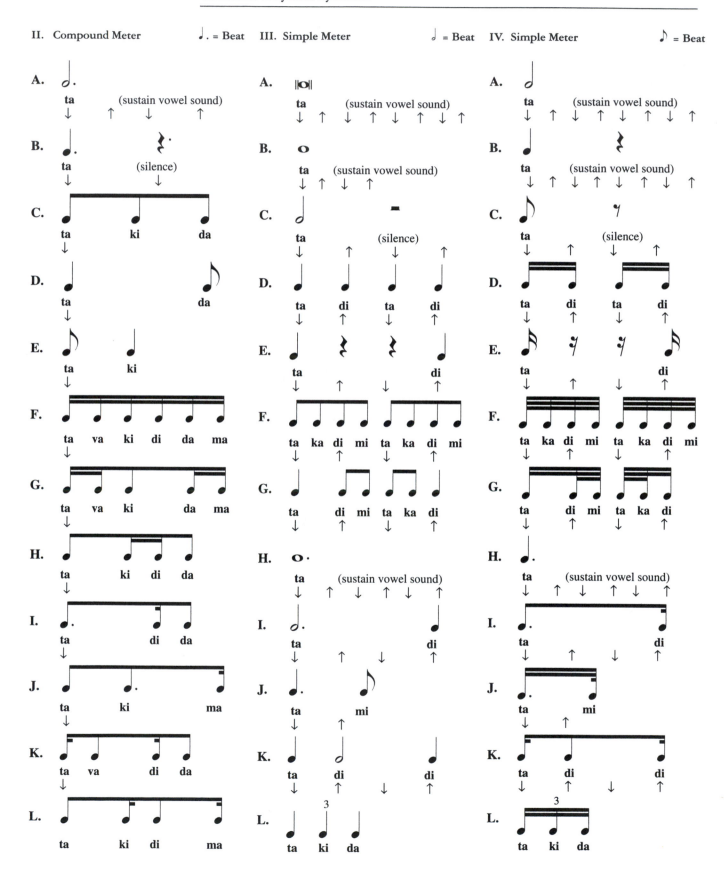

Chart C: McHose and Tibbs Rhythm Syllables (Beat Function)

I. Simple Meter   ♩ = Beat Unit (down-up motion for beat)

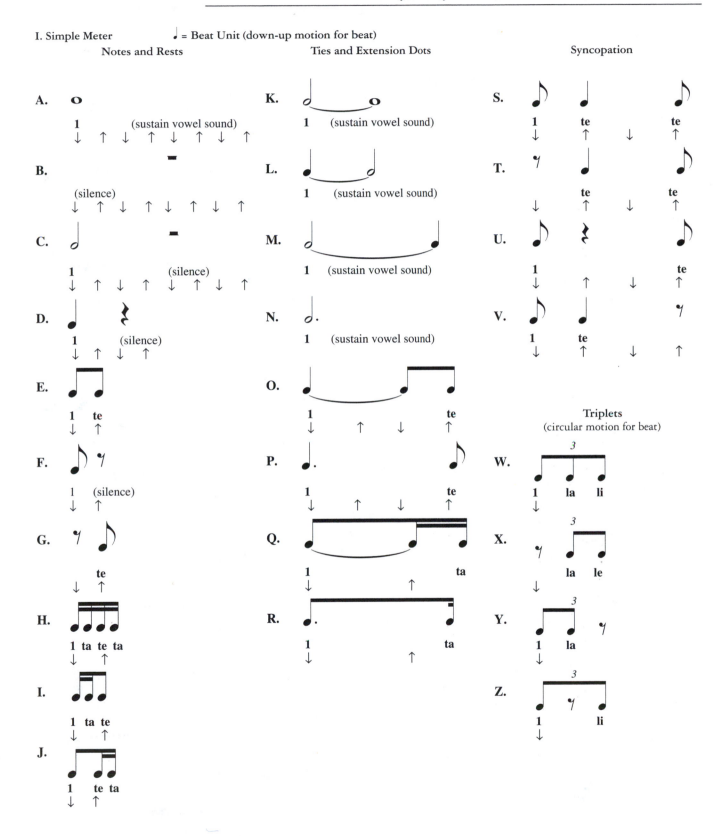

McHose and Tibbs Rhythm Syllables

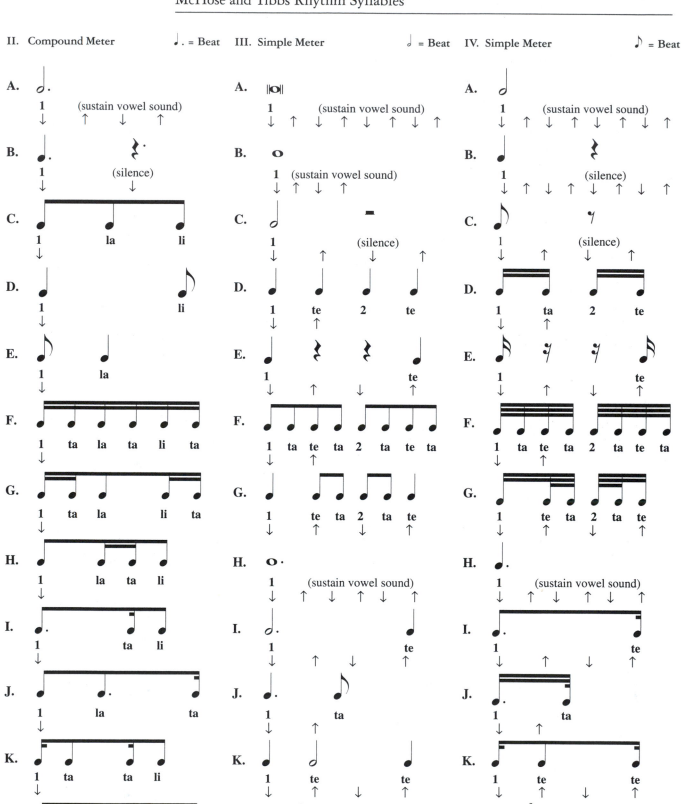

Chart D: Kodály-Based Rhythm Syllables (Time Value)

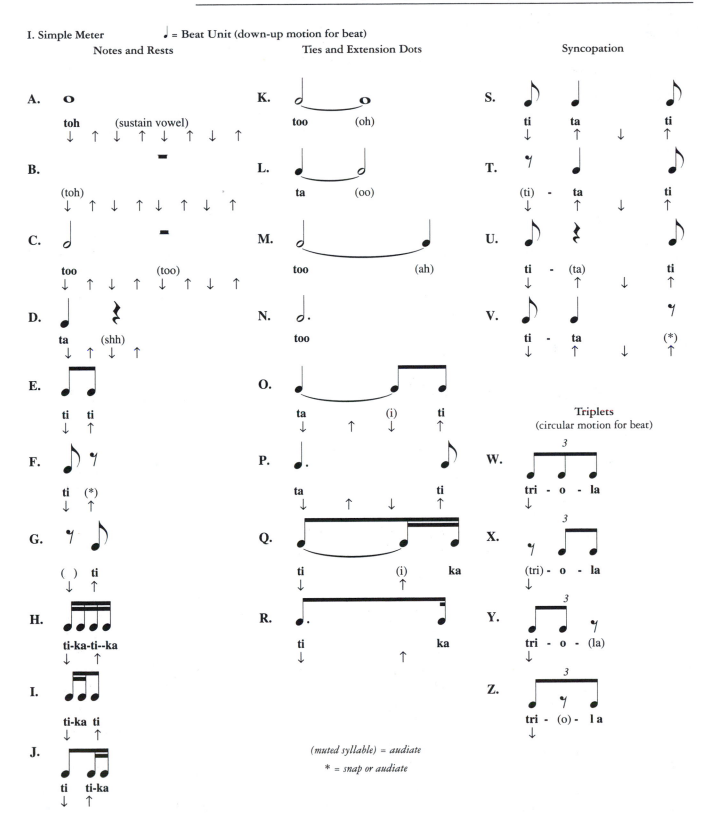

Kodály-Based Rhythm Syllables

II. Compound Meter ♩. = Beat	III. Simple Meter 𝅗𝅥 = Beat	IV. Simple Meter ♪ = Beat

A. too (sustain vowel sound)

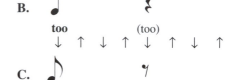

A. toh (sustain vowel sound) A. toh (sustain vowel sound)

B. ta (shh)

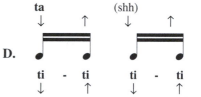

B. too B. too (too)

C. ti ti ti   C. ta (shh)   C. ta (shh)

D. ta ti   D. ti - ti   D. ti - ti ti - ti

 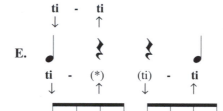

E. ti ta   E. ti - (*) (ti) - ti   E. ti - (*) (ti) - ti

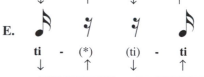

F. ti - ka - ti - ka - ti - ka   F. ti - ka - ti - ka ti - ka - ti - ka   F. ti - ka - ti - ka ti - ka - ti - ka

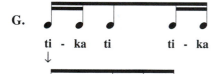  

G. ti - ka ti ti - ka   G. ti ti - ka ti - ka ti   G. ti ti - ka ti - ka ti

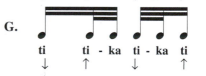 

H. ti ti - ka ti   H. toh - oh - oh -   H. too (sustain vowel sound)

I. ti (i) - ka ti   I. ta - (i) - ti   I. ta - (i) - ti

J. ti ti (i) ka   J. ti (i) ka   J. ti - (i) ka

K. ka ti ka ti   K. ti - ta - ti   K. ti - ta - ti

L. ti ka ti ka   L. tri - o - la   L. tri - o - la

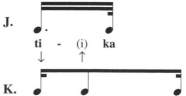 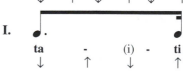  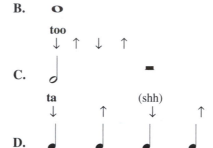

Appendix B
Tonal Reading Systems

Solmization

Solmization is a system for teaching music reading in which pitches are designated through syllables rather than letter names. The earliest system of solmization to survive into modern use is associated with Guido d'Arezzo (c. 995–1050), a Benedictine monk, choir master, and music theorist. Guidonian solmization is based on the text and tune of the eighth-century hymn "Ut queant laxis." The syllables sung to the six initial tones of the first six lines of the hymn are *ut, re, mi, fa, sol,* and *la*. Around 1600 the syllable *si* was added and *ut* was changed to do. Eventually extra syllables were added for chromatically altered notes and the syllable *ti* was substituted for *si*, so that the seven basic syllables begin with seven different consonants. The terms *solfège, tonic sol-fa,* and *fasola* all refer to this same basic system of music reading. Currently solmization is applied in two different ways, *moveable do* and *fixed do*.

The Moveable Do System

The syllables *do, re, mi, fa, so, la,* and *ti* are assigned to the degrees of the major scale. *Do* always represents the tonic or first degree of the major scale, *fa* the fourth or subdominant, *so* the fifth or dominant of the scale, and so on.

Major Scale

do   re   mi   fa   so   la   ti   do   do   ti   la   so   fa   mi   re   do

When a melody modulates, the new tonic becomes *do*. For example: A selection begins in D Major so the tonic note "D" is called *do*. A modulation changes the tonal center to A Major, therefore the tonic note "A" will now be called *do*. This method aids the study of harmony as the relationship between scale degrees is emphasized. To be successful, students must master the ascending and descending syllables. This method fosters the development of vocal tone because the syllables use pure vowels.

Altered pitches are accounted for by changing the syllables. The ascending chromatic scale is: *do, di, re, ri, mi, fa, fi, so, si, la, li, ti, do*. The descending chromatic scale is: *do, ti, te, la, le, so, se, fa, mi, me, re, ra, do*.

Chromatic Scale

do   di   re   ri   mi   fa   fi   so   si   la   li   ti   do   do   ti   te   la   le   so   se   fa   mi   me   re   ra   do

In the Moveable Do System, the minor mode can be treated in two ways:

1. Moveable *do* with *la* based minor: In this system the syllable changes to correspond to the tonality. For example: *la* is the resting tone in minor or Aeolian mode, *re* in Dorian, *mi* in Phrygian, *fa* in Lydian, *so* in Mixolydian and *ti* in Locrian. The la based minor approach

allows inexperienced singers to sing in tonalities other than major without knowledge of chromatic syllables, notation, or music theory. It is the "only tonal syllable system based on syntax."[1]

Natural Minor Scale

la   ti   do   re   mi   fa   so   la   la   so   fa   mi   re   do   ti   la

Harmonic Minor Scale

la   ti   do   re   mi   fa   si   la   la   si   fa   mi   re   do   ti   la

Melodic Minor Scale

la   ti   do   re   mi   fi   si   la   la   so   fa   mi   re   do   ti   la

2. Moveable *do* with *do*-based minor: In *do*-based minor, the resting tone is always *do*. To be successful in any tonality other than major, students must have mastered the chromatic syllables and have adequate knowledge of notation and music theory. For example: the mode will require *me*, *le*, and *te* in place of *mi*, *la*, and *ti*, respectively. Many teachers believe this method fosters an understanding of tonality relationships, chord structure, and part writing.

Natural Minor

do   re   me   fa   so   le   te   do   do   te   le   so   fa   me   re   do

Harmonic Minor

do   re   me   fa   so   le   ti   do   do   ti   le   so   fa   me   re   do

Melodic Minor

do   re   me   fa   so   la   ti   do   do   te   le   so   fa   me   re   do

[1] Eric Bluestine, *The Ways Children Learn Music*. (Chicago: GIA Publications, Inc., 1964), 92.

Numbers

The numbers 1, 2, 3, and so forth, are assigned to the degrees of the scale in the same manner as the Moveable Do System except that there is no numeral change for chromatic tones. The number method gives instant results because every student knows the ascending and descending numbers; however, skipping numbers while counting backwards often results in confusion. The method also inhibits tone production and accurate accidentals. To be successful, students must acquire thorough aural/oral knowledge of intervals.

1 2 3 4 5 6 7 1   1 7 6 5 4 3 2 1

The Fixed Do System

The syllables *do, re, mi, fa, so, la,* and *ti* are assigned to the notes C, D, E, F, G, A, and B respectively. The syllables are not changed for chromatic tones. To be successful, students must acquire a thorough aural/oral knowledge of intervals.

ti do re mi fa so la ti   ti la so fa mi re do ti

Letter Names

The letters A, B, C, D, E, F, and G are used for the appropriate pitch name. Note names altered by a sharp are pronounced: *ace, beas(t), cease, dease, eas(t), feas(t),* and *jeese.* The flats are pronounced: *us, bess, cess, des(k), es(t), fes(t),* and *jes(t).* To be successful, students must have a thorough aural/oral knowledge of intervals.

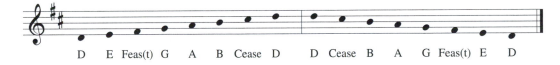

D E Feas(t) G A B Cease D   D Cease B A G Feas(t) E D

Hand Signs

Guidonian Hand

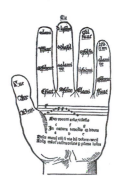

The use of hand signs as a kind of notation can be traced back to the ancient Hebrews and Egyptians. During the eleventh century, the Guidonian hand— a pedagogical device where each of the solmization syllables (*ut, re, mi, fa, sol,* and *la*) was assigned to one of the joints of the left hand, was employed to aid music reading. There is no evidence that Guido d'Arezzo invented it.

In England during the nineteenth century, Sarah Glover designed hand signs to be used in association with the *tonic solfa* system. Glover's hand signs and "moveable do" system were embraced and popularized by John Curwen (1816—1880), an English churchman and influential educator. The work of Glover and Curwen greatly influenced Zoltan Kodály (1882—1967), who integrated the use of hand signs into his methodology.

Hand signs are concrete and provide singers with a kinesthetic experience as well as being a visualization in space of the high-low pitch relationship between notes. While the hand signs can be frustrating at first, they appear to establish memory of pitch patterns more securely than if they are not used. Signs are made in front of the body using the dominant hand. The hand signs are illustrated as the person making them with his right hand sees them. Hand signs can also be employed when using numbers.

Sharps (♯)		Flats (♭)
	do'	
	ti	
li		te
	la	
si		le
	so	
fi	fa	se
	mi	
ri		me
	re	
di		ra
	do	

Tonal Ladder

Appendix C

Dictation

Dictation skills are directly related to the development of musical memory, inner hearing (audiation), and reading and writing skills. Rhythm and tonal should once again be taught separately and then combined. Initial dictations should be based on familiar 3 to 5 note tonal patterns and 3 to 4 beat rhythm patterns. Using the shorthand method outlined next can facilitate the learning process while musical memory skills are developed. The ultimate goal is to develop the student's level of proficiency to such a degree that the system is no longer needed.

Rhythm

Rhythm Procedure: Write with one hand and quietly tap the beat with the other hand. Following the down/up motion of each beat can be an aid in determining the rhythm. Isolate each beat and mark the appropriate shorthand. If the rhythm on a particular beat or two cannot be determined, continue to move forward focusing on the ensuing beats. On the second playing, readdress the missing beats.

Example:

Rhythm Shorthand

Rhythm Transcription

Rhythm Shorthand: Lines representing the beats are drawn in each measure. Notes with a duration longer than one beat are tied together for the appropriate duration; rests are represented by an upper case "R"; a triplet is represented by a three; a syncopation by an "S" and a bracket; a double subdivision of a beat by a single slash, a quadruple subdivision of a beat by a double slash, and so forth. Suggested symbols for various rhythmic patterns follow.

Simple Meters

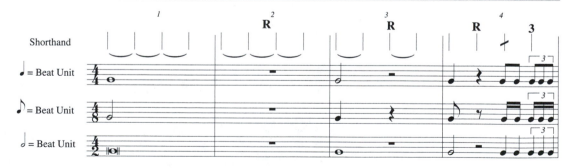

Shorthand

♩ = Beat Unit

♪ = Beat Unit

𝅗𝅥 = Beat Unit

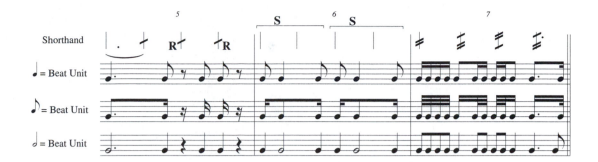

Compound Meters

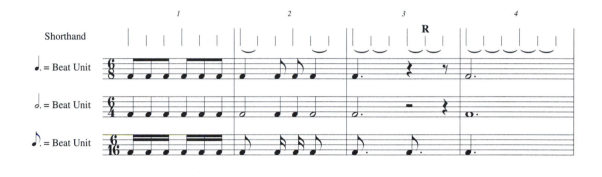

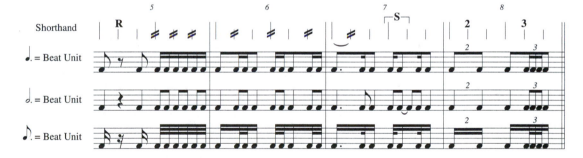

Tonal

Tonal Procedure: Write the first letter of each tonal syllable. If a particular pitch or two cannot be determined, draw a question mark and then continue to move forward focusing on the ensuing pitches. On the second playing, readdress the missing pitch(es). Translate the tonal syllables into notation by using note heads to indicate the pitches on the staff.

Melodic

Melodic Procedure: When taking melodic dictation (simultaneous tonal and rhythmic dictation), write the first letter of each tonal syllable above the beat lines and mark the appropriate rhythm shorthand on the beat lines.

Tonal Syllables

Rhythm Shorthand

Melodic Transcription

During the beginning stages of melodic dictation, it may be helpful to give the students a score with the bar lines indicated and certain notes and/or rhythms filled in.

* First playing: Focus on only the rhythm or tonal; preferably your strongest element.
* Second playing: Focus on the other element.
* Third playing: Readdress missing rhythms or pitches.
* Strive to write the tonal syllable above its corresponding beat line.

Appendix D

Conducting Patterns

Basic Patterns

One Pattern

Legato

1

Marcato

1

Two Pattern

Legato

1 2

Marcato

1 2

Three Pattern

Legato

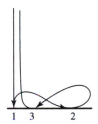

1 3 2

Marcato

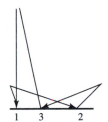

1 3 2

Four Pattern

Legato

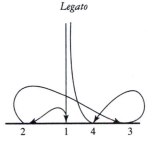

2 1 4 3

Marcato

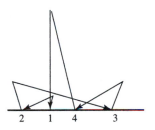

2 1 4 3

Asymmetrical Patterns

Five Pattern

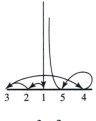

3 2 1 5 4

3 + 2

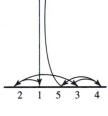

2 1 5 3 4

2 + 3

Seven Pattern

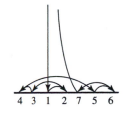

4 3 1 2 7 5 6

4 + 3 (2 + 2 + 3)

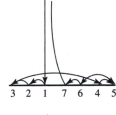

3 2 1 7 6 4 5

3 + 4 (3 + 2 + 2)

Five Pattern–Division of Beat

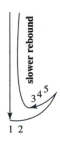

faster rebound

4 5

1 2 3

3 + 2

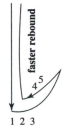

slower rebound

3 4 5

1 2

2 + 3

Seven Pattern–Division of Beat

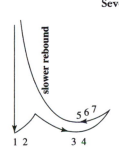

slower rebound

5 6 7

1 2   3 4

2 + 2 +3

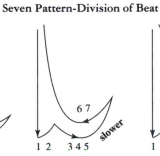

6 7

slower

1 2   3 4 5

2 + 3 + 2

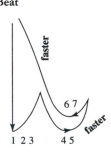

faster

6 7

faster

1 2 3   4 5

3 + 2 + 2

Appendix E

Glossary of Foreign Terms

Aber (Ger.) but
Accelerando (*accel.*) (It.) gradually faster
Adagio (It.) slower than *Andante*, faster than *Largo*.
Agitato (It.) agitate
Al (It.) to; used with other words, e.g. *al Fine* (to the end.)
Alla (It.) in the style or manner of
Allegretto (It.) slower than *Allegro*
Allegro (It.) quick tempo; cheerful
Animato (It.) animated
Andante (It.) moderate tempo
Andantino (It.) slightly faster than *Andante*
A niente (It.) to nothing, e.g. to *ppp*
A tempo (It.) return to the previous tempo

Bewegt (Ger.) agitated
Bien (Fr.) well, good
Brio (It.) vigor, spirit

Cantabile (It.) in singing style.
Coda (⊕) (It.) closing section of a composition
Commodo (It.) quiet, calm
Con (It.) with
Crescendo (*cresc.*) (It.) increasing in volume of sound

Da capo (*D.C.*) (It.) return to the beginning
Dal segno (*D.S.*) (It.) repeat from the sign
Decrescendo (*decresc.*) (It.) decreasing in volume of sound; synonymous with *diminuendo*
Diminuendo (*dim.*) (It.) decreasing in volume of sound; synonymous with decrescendo
Dolce (It.) sweetly

E, ed (It.) and
En allant (Fr.) with movement, flowing
Energico (It.) energetic
Et (Fr.) and
Expressivo (It.) expressive

Feierlich (Ger.) solemn, festive
Fine (It.) the end
Fliessand (Ger.) flowing
Forte (*f*) (It.) loud

Fortissimo (*ff*) (It.) very loud
Forza (It.) force, strength, power
Frölich (Ger.) joyous, happy

Gai (Fr.) lively, merry
Gavotte (Fr.) a French dance generally in common time, strongly accented
Gehend (Ger.) a walking pace (*Andante*)
Geschwind (Ger.) quick
Getragen (Ger.) sustained
Giacoso (It.) playful
Giusto (It.) exact, steady
Grazia (It.) grace
Grazioso (It.) graceful

Heiter (Ger.) cheerful
Hurtig (Ger.) quick, swiftly

Immer (Ger.) always
Innig (Ger.) ardent, sincerely

Kräftig (Ger.) strong, powerful, robust

Langsam (Ger.) slow
Larghetto (It.) slightly faster than *Largo*
Largo (It.) slow and broad
Lebhaft (Ger.) lively, animated
Legato (It.) smooth or connected manner
Leggiero (It.) light, delicate
Leicht (Ger.) easy, light
Lento (It.) slow, but faster than *Adagio*
Lié (Fr.) smoothly
Lüstig (Ger.) happy, gay

Ma (It.) but
Maestoso (It.) majestic, stately
Marcato (It.) marked, emphasized
Marcia (It.) march
Mässig (Ger.) moderate tempo
Meno (It.) less
Mesto (It.) sad, mournful
Mosso (It.) motion

466

Mezzo forte (*mf*) (It.) medium loud
Mezzo piano (*mp*) (It.) medium soft
Mit (Ger.) with
Moderato (It.) at a moderate speed
Molto (It.) much, lively
Moto (It.) motion
Munter (Gr.) lively

Nicht (Ger.) not
Non (It.) not

Piano (*p*) (It.) soft.
Pianissimo (*pp*) (It.) very soft
Più (It.) more
Poco (It.) little
Poco a poco (It.) little by little, gradually
Presto (It.) fast, rapid (faster than Allegro)

Rallantando (*rall.*) (It.) gradually slower
Rasch (Ger.) fast
Ritardando (*rit.*) (It.) gradually slower
Ritenuto (*riten.*) (It.) held back
Ritmico (It.) rhythmically
Rubato (It.) freely with respect to tempo
Ruhig (Ger.) quiet, calm

Scherzando (It.) playful, lively
Schnell (Ger.) fast
Semplice (It.) simple
Sempre (It.) always, continuously
Sentimento (It.) sentimental
Segno (It.) (%) Sign
Sforzando (*sfz*, *sf*) (It.) sudden strong accent
Solmization, *solfége* (Fr.), *solfeggio* (It.) system for
    teaching music reading in which pitches are
    designated by syllables rather than letter names

Spirito (It.) spirit, energy
Spiritoso (It.) with spirit, energetic
Staccato (It.) detached manner; indicated by a dot over or
    under each note.
Subito (*sub.*) (It.) suddenly

Tempo (It.) relative speed of the pulse
    Chart of Relative Tempos

Term	M.M.
Grave	40
Largo	
Larghetto	
Lento	
Adagio	60
Adagietto	
Andante	72
Andantino	
Moderato	90
Allegretto	
Allegro	120
Presto	140
Prestissimo	

Tenuto (*ten.*) (It.) sustain, held out
Troppo (It.) too, too much

Un (It. and Fr.) a
Und (Ger.) and

Vivace (It.) lively, quickly
Vivo (It.) lively, animated

Waltzer (Ger.) waltz
Wie (Ger.) as

Zu (Ger.) not

Index